Documentary in Practice

Filmmakers and Production Choices

JANE CHAPMAN

polity

First published in 2007 by Polity Press

Polity Press
65 Bridge Street
Cambridge CB2 1UR, UK

Polity Press
350 Main Street
Malden, MA 02148, USA

ISBN-10: 0-7456-3611-X
ISBN-13: 978-07456-3611-5
ISBN-10: 0-7456-3612-8 (pb)
ISBN-13: 978-07456-3612-2 (pb)

A catalogue record for this book is available from the British Library.

Typeset in 9.5 on 12 pt Utopia
by SNP Best-set Typesetter Ltd, Hong Kong
Printed and bound in Great Britain by MPG Books Ltd, Bodmin, Cornwall

For further information on Polity, visit our website: www.polity.co.uk

Contents

Detailed Contents

Information about Case Studies

This index is intended to reflect one of the several ways in which the book can be used. The diverse group of films is used comparatively and spread through the book. The reader might prefer to read the book cover to cover or to focus on a chapter at a time. For readers who want to concentrate on a certain documentary, the thematic table of contents below allows the reader to follow each case study as the production of the film progresses through the book, focusing on the main topics that each project illustrates.

William Raban: *Thames Film* (1986, DVD 2004) BFI

Jean Rouch and Edgar Morin: *Chronicle of a Summer* (1960) Pathé Contemporary Films

Dziga Vertov: *The Man with a Movie Camera* (1929) BFI

Acknowledgements

This book starts with the premise that examples of the production of documentary films merit further analysis: therefore, without the filmmakers who gave me their thoughts, time, unpublished working notes and photographs, there would be no study. During primary research I talked to many practitioners, but the contributions of Nancy Platt, William Raban, Franny Armstrong, Dermot O'Donovan, Karl Nussbaum, Celia Ellacott, Martin Clarke, Anand Patwardhan, Selana Vronti and David Palazon were outstanding.

Equally, the research on primary and secondary publications undertaken for me at Lincoln University by journalism subject librarian Paul Stainthorp continues to be extensive and far reaching. I am constantly grateful for Paul's energy, application and thoroughness, as indeed I am for the intellectual rigour and opinions of my colleagues at Lincoln, especially Brian Winston. John Tulloch, on behalf of the School of Journalism, John Simons, Dean of the Faculty of Media and Humanities, and Ann Gray, on behalf of the research committee, have all provided on-going support and essential financial assistance. Also thanks to William Raban, Franny Armstrong/Spanner Films, Nancy Platt/Christian Aid, Anand Patwardhan and Karl Nussbanm, all of whom kindly donated photographs. At LCC (University of the Arts, London) Cathy Greenhalgh provided excellent advice, and in the United States, Elliot King and my fellow members of the AJHA-AEMC responded positively to 'work in progress' at the New York conference in 2006.

The creative vision and commitment that I discuss in the pages that follow is also shared by the Polity team. Without the editorial instinct and intuitive support of John Thompson, the editorial board and Andrea Drugan, this study would never have progressed from the idea stage to what it is now. I am grateful to Andrea for her persistence and vision, and to Neil de Cort, Sarah Dancy and Clare Zon for their professionalism and application.

Last but not least, special thanks must go to my son Toby Clarke, who produces my website (which features this book: <http://www.janechapman.co.uk>), and also provided initial visual research for the cover design. Thanks, as ever, to Miles Clarke and Peter Sanderson for feedback and encouragement.

List of Illustrations

Preface
Using this study

'Practice is the criterion of truth.' (Dziga Vertov in Geduld, 1967: 105)

The ready availability of relatively cheap digital technology means that it is easier than ever to launch into the documentary field in a modest way, with small amounts of money. As more people make documentaries, have access to production, distribution and exhibition facilities, and more people watch them worldwide, the emphasis for the study of practice changes.

Documentary is so diverse, it is now almost impossible to be too prescriptive with advice, because there is always a good example that breaks the rule. Yet documentary's long and venerable history demonstrates that rules are made to be broken – even one's own rules. From this perspective, which techniques have been influential, and how does the maker achieve a particular aesthetic?

Each and every documentary is individually crafted. As a pioneer in history compilation documentaries, Emile de Antonio said: 'I've kept, by inclination, my technical command of film to a minimum, because I think there is a human idea that presupposes that shape of what's going to happen. And the technology should serve it' (Kellner & Streible, 2000: 116). Thus, *Documentary in Practice* is not a guide book, a production treatise or technical manual. It addresses key production issues by examining real life filmmaker choices and dilemmas.

Why is it that, when we all are able to start with the same basic technical equipment, then operate it, some of us will turn out a memorable film, and others will not?

This is a study of process: how documentary makers undertake and execute their projects in terms of the diverse challenges that present themselves. I identify six core themes that act as a constant throughout the various stages of the production cycle: objectivity/subjectivity, representation, reflexivity, responsibility to audience, authorial voice and ethics.

I have cast the net widely by researching documentary makers past and present and by talking to filmmakers in different parts of the world, at various stages in their careers, operating in a range of markets. I do not analyse their entire portfolios or career trajectories. I present a qualitative reconstruction, amounting to a series of journeys of discovery, taken from what they say.

The details of representation, form and the consistent unfolding of personal intent also touch on bigger truths about method, medium and process. The evidence is presented in the form of interview quotes and case studies. My main argument throughout is that this diversity of filmmaker choice implies a continuing requirement that intent, representation and form should all include an ethical dimension during the production process.

The films selected as case studies are all available for screening, and can be discussed aside from the main text, although the information for each is spread across chapters according to the stage of the production process. Alternatively, the entire study can either be read *cover to cover*, or it can be consulted *chapter by chapter*, or it can be used for specific aspects as *reference* according to the index.

1 Thinking Creatively

The argument

What is needed to make a documentary? On the practical side, the essential prerequisites appear to be minimal: some technical competence, access to subject matter and as much of a filmmaking team as may be required. In fact, more important than any of these is belief in the project, an appreciation of the choices available in form, style and approach, and of their implications in terms of audience response. This involves a process of decision making through clarifying preferences and focusing on expectations. An understanding of the options that other successful documentarians have chosen will help.

I have yet to meet a good documentary maker who is not engaged in production because he or she is committed to the genre. The starting point of the documentary maker is usually to examine an aspect of perceived reality within a selected real life location. The main unifying factor for all filmmakers who use the medium in the very many ways that are possible is the belief that making a documentary is a worthwhile thing to do. Usually, documentary makers are committed not just to the genre, but also to certain subject matter. Both are necessary. But first, the idea – from which all else stems.

Introduction: the documentary creative idea

How does the creative idea emerge? Like a seed that is transported by the wind before it settles and germinates, so documentary ideas often surface inadvertently. Then, they grow. Ideas can start off small and vague, but as they are crafted into a practical reality, they become more refined. An idea may lie dormant, or fulminating for some time, but when it does surface, there is a need to identify intention and vision from the early stages. Ideas are precisely what the documentary genre feeds on, but not all ideas translate well into the documentary medium.

The process of adaptation and translation of an idea into the documentary medium is intrinsically linked to an understanding of what can and cannot be successfully achieved. Simple ideas are often the best: ones which prompt other people to say, 'Oh yes, why I didn't think of that myself?' Such an idea appears to have always been waiting to be made into a film. It may not be a big concept, although the best documentary ideas, even microstudies of single people, events or places, present a larger truism.

Some documentary makers are able to return regularly to their chosen themes because they are not dependent on being employed by a broadcaster whose agenda may change according to the market and perceived audience appetite. From the independent filmmaker's point of view, there are strong practical arguments for staying with a subject area over the years. Anand Patwardhan, for instance, has become a subject specialist on religious fundamentalism in India. In contrast, many 'work-a-day' filmmakers (as I have been) are obliged to constantly come up with different content ideas for a story. Indeed, employment as a freelance may depend on the ideas submitted, as well as the ability to make them into a reality. Coming up with ideas becomes a way of life: as an independent producer, I was required to move agilely across a range of subject areas within educational and feature programming, to pitch ideas according to where the potential for commissions or funding seemed to offer itself.

The creative idea can emerge from a collaborative approach by more than one person. Then it can be shaped and developed up to a point where it becomes a project with resources and team involvement. The way that this happens will depend on the money that is available and who is funding it, analysed in the next chapter. Yet before a producer can submit an idea to potential funders, a range of choices will present themselves as part of a selection process.

Definitions and choices

There is little point in embarking upon a factual film simply because the funds available won't stretch to fiction. Admittedly, in production terms, there is cross-fertilization between documentary and fiction, such as character development, subjectivity and reference to off-screen space. Nevertheless, documentaries have their own agenda and deserve not to be second best.

Documentary is about reality, not a device or format conjured up by the producers for the purposes of the film, as with fiction or reality TV. The great British 'father' of social documentary, John Grierson, defined the genre as the 'creative treatment of actuality' (see Hardy, 1979: 11). What does this imply? Are we artists, or visual journalists, neither, or both? From the early days onwards, there has been an artistic and editorial conflict between the communication of truth and of perceived reality. Documentary has always ranged from actuality (what is happening right now), where the outcome is still unknown, through to re-creations and re-enactments which require much preparation and attention to detail, as of course, other films and television programmes also do. As two historians of the medium point out: 'It was Grierson that arrived at the concept of the documentary film as we think of it today: not to tell a story with actors but to deal with aspects of the real world that had some drama and perhaps importance – that we might do something about a particular situation or at least should be aware of it' (Ellis & McLane, 2005: ix).

The purpose of documentary can also provide some help with definitions: documentary production first became a 'movement' in Britain during the 1930s. Ever since that time, the genre has often been understood as a vehicle for social comment, even social change: 'The documentary is not a step to fiction film but a step to freedom. Commercial fiction film is only real estate . . . Maximise rents for a space called a seat' (Emile de Antonio in Rosenthal & Corner, 2005: 166). Sometimes there are also other very good reasons to choose documentary over fiction. Quite simply, as the great ethnographic filmmaker Jean Rouch stated: 'there is a truth that the fiction film cannot capture and that is the authenticity of the real, the lived' (Jacobs, 1979: 437).

A documentary idea needs to be grown within the context of an identifiable genre that has its own voice, content and style. Thus the ability to decide on a way forward requires an appreciation of the nature of documentary genre. Some discussion of definitions permits a greater appreciation of the scope of expression that is available, even though every project is different. What are documentary's distinctive characteristics? This has been the subject of much discourse, past and present. According to Ellis & McLane (2005: 2), these fall into five categories: subjects, purpose (viewpoints or approach), forms, production methods and techniques and the sorts of experience that audiences are offered. When planning a project, all of these factors need to be considered.

1 Subjects: these tend to be specific and factual, usually about a matter that will be of interest to the public, even if the documentary deals with private lives. Places, people, events are all real, even if they happened a long time ago.
2 Purpose of the film: this will be to make others aware of the subject, to inform the audience, to influence them towards a specific viewpoint, even sometimes to take specific action.
3 Form: this is based on actuality so it can have value as historical evidence and record. The form is determined by subject, purpose and approach: 'Documentary makers limit themselves to extracting and arranging from what already exists rather than making up content. They may recreate what they have observed but they do not create totally out of the imagination as creators of stories can do' (ibid.).
4 Production methods and techniques: these always involve shooting on location, not the construction of an imaginary studio set for filming. The extent to which sounds and images are manipulated is usually defined by the need to make them closer to the actual, rather than for arbitrary creation of mood or atmosphere.
5 Audience experience: audience response usually centres on the wider communication message rather than the detail of how it is expressed. Therefore, the audience responds generally to the subject matter (which instructs in some way), rather than to the individual filmmaker, even though an aesthetic experience is offered.

Every documentary is different because it is individually crafted. The diversity and multiplicity of approaches within the range of factual films has prompted a number of attempts at categorization, plus an inevitable debate as to whether this is either feasible or desirable given documentary's fluidity. Nichols (1991; 2001: 99), for instance, divides the genre into expository, observational, interactive, performative and reflexive modes. Categories such as these are considered further in chapter 3 from the practical standpoint of the inevitable aesthetic choices in documentary production.

Finding an idea

Creative people are constantly looking for a new perspective for on-going themes: it is the lifeblood of the documentary trade. The presenter of the BBC 1 documentary series *Europe by Design* that my company, Chapman Clarke Films, produced, when talking about how he operated creatively, explained to me as his producer: 'My mind is like a saucepan of mixed vegetable soup. When it begins to boil, certain vegetables come up to the surface first – those are the ideas that I go with first.' It doesn't sound very scientific, but there are other ways of analysing the process!

What many documentary ideas lack at the beginning is a sense of the visual. Viewers can read a caption or part of a document on screen, but they must also watch an image. It will be the image that captivates them, so it is better to think visually right from the beginning. A symbiotic fusion between words and pictures is one of the potential hallmarks of documentary production. Some people develop visual images of the edited final product in their heads, others envisage a strong sense of message and the content needed to achieve it: both are valid. Filmmaker William Raban (see case study on p. 8) believes that one should: 'always try to see what the screen experience is going to be – not the cut film' (author interview, 2005).

How a documentary maker sees a subject extends to considerations of place as well as people. Both routes usually require a feel for narrative. A powerful narrative thread can make the concept unforgettable. Incidents, events (historical or present), characters, landscapes, objects and physical interactions rather than monologues all provide good documentary material, but they all need a story. The creative process of documentary making can make an apparently small, pedestrian or local idea into a memorable film. More generally, challenging subjects such as discrimination, legal disputes, failings of an institution, can all be demonstrated using the documentary format, but the format requires that you *show*, not tell. Admittedly, the audience can listen to an interview that relates the story, or a narrator, but some documentary projects may not require mediation.

If you can't see it, you can't shoot it! This is not to say that the subject is impossible, rather that the documentary maker's particular choice of content, form or representation may not seem viable. For example, Dermot O'Donovan, a freelance television director whom I interviewed, pitched an idea for a regional television contract. How he intended to make the project changed completely during the early stages. The idea for the documentary, *Last Among Equals*, came through a personal contact. 'I was approached by a senior executive from the Leonard Cheshire charity about making a profile film about the founder himself, who had been a famous Second World War Royal Air Force hero' (author interview, 2005). After the War, Group Captain Cheshire, who married charity leader Sue Ryder, opened a series of residential homes for severely disabled young people, arguing that such people had their own specific needs for care. The approach from this important non-profit making organization led Dermot to discover, unexpectedly, something in their archive which interested him.

After a two-day search through their records, 'I discovered that the founder had made his own film in about 1960 called *Let Me Live* on the subject of the Leonard Cheshire home near Penzance, Cornwall.' Dermot was fascinated by this archive film. What had started as a tip-off for a life-profile drama documentary, with all the concomitant funding problems that accompany such larger budget projects, had now changed as a result of research. The find also provided Dermot with a local angle and hence a market for the new idea. He considered the potential and decided to develop it as a documentary for the regional television station. 'I therefore pitched the idea to Carlton Television for a documentary on attitudes to disabilities, using the Leonard Cheshire film and history as a strand but with my own filming locally, at Penzance' (ibid.).

Exclusivity of story can be important and timing can be a factor if funding or broadcasters need convincing. Yet a documentary should not simply repeat news coverage, it has to provide a more in-depth understanding, or inside view of something that an audience would not obtain from the news. Commissioning editors have other criteria as well, and these are dealt with in the next chapter. Appreciation of what these are likely to be tends to exert a form of prior self-editing on documentary makers who pitch for the broadcast market. Documentary makers who go for the art-house and independent circuits do not experience such constraints.

Sometimes the unpredictable happens, or a documentary maker hits upon a story by chance. The idea may be suggested by somebody else: I once came across an offbeat idea for one television feature documentary when I met some other producers at the Cannes television market. They, in turn, had come across a short paragraph in a building-trade journal that had prompted their curiosity. From those few lines of print, a 52-minute film eventually emerged, but it was very different from the small suggestion that we had started with.

Not every 'lead' will bear fruit. On many occasions I have started to find out more about the topic, explored the possibilities further, then found that the idea is not tenable – for a range of different reasons. Funding may not be possible, market research may reveal that somebody else made exactly the film that you intended only recently, or the theme, when examined more closely, turns out to be insufficiently visual, or unsuitable for the documentary genre. The chances of hitting a 'cul-de-sac' when researching a story are quite high; in fact most research tends to involve a change of direction or some lateral thinking, when the documentary producer ends up turning to a related field. Thus, not every research effort leads to a good story: there may be a dead end. Some subjects may simply not appear capable of translation into documentary reality, which is a visual medium.

Franny Armstrong and Anand Patwardhan are both activist filmmakers, one from the UK, one from India. Both made a documentary about the same on-going story, but reached their idea via different routes. At this conceptual stage, the main differences between the two prospective films in terms of approach and potential audience fall into the insider/outsider category. Further differences are analysed in subsequent chapters

Franny Armstrong: *Drowned Out*

Franny Armstrong is an 'up and coming' activist filmmaker who started her filmmaking career with videos for the Vegan Society. Previously she had an online company and has since directed *McLibel* and other documentaries as an independent filmmaker with her company Spanner Films. Armstrong's films have a political motivation. 'I hate the word "activist", because most so-called "activist" films are awful. But I am one because I want to tell important stories so that people who watch them will change their views' (author interview, 2005).

Her film was re-edited into a shorter version for screening by PBS in the United States and renamed as *The Damned* (2003). It deals with the same environmental protest theme as Anand Patwardhan's documentary, so comparisons of technique and approach can be made between the two. Both filmmakers start from the same viewpoint or editorial stance in that their intent is to make an activist film in support of the indigenous protesters: but the way each filmmaker does it is different. This comparison between approaches continues throughout the production trajectory.

Franny Armstrong first hit on the same on-going story, prompted by an article that she read in Britain's *Guardian* newspaper: 'I had been intending to spend the solar eclipse of 1999 staring at the Cornish sky through plastic glasses. But over a shoulder on a crowded train one morning I came across an article in the *Guardian* newspaper entitled "Villagers in Shadow of Dam Await the End of the World" '(26 August 2002). It reported that villagers in India were refusing to evacuate their houses for the building of a further stage of the dam. They were prepared to drown by staying in place. With non-

Anand Patwardhan with Simantini Dhuru: *A Narmada Diary*

Anand Patwardhan has been making 'engaged' documentary films since he was a student in the USA in the 1970s, and is often billed as India's answer to Michael Moore. His strength 'derives from his perseverance, compassion, and extraordinary insight into the human condition' (Goldsmith, 2003, ch. 10: 14). Anand's filmmaker intent derives from a belief in supporting people who are oppressed and the less well off: this dictates the choice of subject to be filmed. In the case of *A Narmada Diary*, as one writer says, 'Joining hands with others in India who are deeply involved in the struggles for a just society and for communal and ecological harmony, Anand Patwardhan gives his private views a most public face' (Sharma, 2002: 284).

A Narmada Diary was made over a five-year period in the first half of the 1990s with camerawork by Simantini Dhuru, whose sister is an activist in the Narmada Bachao Andolan (the Save Narmada Movement or NBA). The film catalogues the struggle of the NBA, the campaign that still today spearheads indigenous protest against the mega-dam construction in India's Narmada Valley. At that time, construction of the Sardar Sarovar hydroelectric dam threatened to drown over 37,000 hectares of fertile land, the homes and the lifestyle of the 'Adivasis' (indigenous people), who have lived there for centuries.

'I discovered early the joys of mixing my "art" with the desire to speak out about issues I was involved with. In the beginning, I saw filmmaking more in utilitarian terms, as a means towards an end, as a pamphlet that would be more exciting than the usual fare and would overcome the shackles of illiteracy. In time, I was seduced by the medium itself and began to take more interest and pay

violent protests and a determination to drown rather than to leave their homes and land, the people of the Narmada have become symbols of a global struggle against an unjust form of development that is displacing between 150,000 and 250,000 people.

Armstrong immediately decided that she should film the water rising and the threat to their survival. Within six days, she was over in India filming. Coming from abroad, she aimed to capture a particular episode in the on-going struggle in order to raise the awareness of audiences outside India about the Narmada Dams controversy.

more attention to the craft of filmmaking and the ways of storytelling. But I don't think my original motivation ever left me' (Maclay, 2004). The pamphlet approach that Anand refers to is very much in evidence in *A Narmada Diary*. The project started with an informal archiving of various events.

Patwardhan already had inside access and aimed to follow the organization leading the protests, the NBA, over a protracted period, in order to make a documentary record that would serve to raise consciousness and the organization's profile within his own country.

Representing a subject

How do we choose to express an idea visually? Diversity of genre means that it is almost impossible these days to be formulaic, because filmmaker options and the order of doing things will vary according to the nature of the project. As Nichols puts it: 'How should we represent the lives of social and historical others in film form is a question to which no single set of answers has prevailed, be the form narrative or non-narrative, documentary or fiction . . . how (documentarists) choose to undertake the act of representing themselves and others remains open to extraordinary variation' (Grant & Sloniowski, 1998: 12–13).

Documentary usually aims to reveal human behaviour in some way, but this can be more challenging than it sounds. Jean Rouch (see case study later in this chapter) provided an example that demonstrates the need for an approach towards representation, not simply a recording: 'I think to make a film is to tell a story . . . That is, you have something to say. I go in the subway, I look at it and I note that the subway is dirty and that the people are bored – that's not a film. I go on the subway and I say to myself, "These people are bored, why? What's happening, what are they doing here? Why do they accept it? Why don't they smash the subway? Why do they sit here going over the same route every day?" At that moment you can make a film' (Levin, 1971: 140–1). That is, you have devised a method of representation of a problem, with an angle.

The starting point for an idea can be personal: a drive for representation that builds on, or corrects, the memory of one's own prior experiences. Influences on the filmmaker and their consequential subject interests, are critical. Content itself can also be very personal: a factor that links closely to the maker's intent. There is usually an interaction between personal outlook, background influence and the concept. For example, producer R. J. Cutler developed the concept for *American High* as a docusoap television series at a time when he was approaching his own twentieth-year high school reunion: 'I felt alienated from the current generation of high school students coming of age at the turn of the century, and felt that this would be one way of reconnecting' (Rosenthal & Corner, 2005: 330).

I once produced a BBC 2 five-part series entitled *Showreel*: the commission involved running an annual competition for amateur filmmakers, then compiling clips from the final 50 shortlisted potential winners into a series of 40-minute television programmes, intercut with short documentary features about professional filmmaking and how it is done, with an award ceremony as the final programme. One of the successful films was a very personal documentary, made by a filmmaker of mixed Afro-Caucasian origin, who reconstructed a 1970s childhood memory of wanting to be white. There was one central, haunting scene with no commentary or dialogue, that was repeated several times. The young girl was trying to remove her black skin with bleach. The images spoke for themselves. They were constructed selectively and creatively, for as one writer puts it: 'if you want to make good, believable, useful documentaries . . . you have to get over the idea that you can suck reality into a camera and blow it back at your audience' (Hampe, 1997: 33). Capturing actuality should not be confused with capturing reality. The latter will only be reassembled as fragments of what has been filtered by the eyes and ears of the crew and limited by the available technology.

William Raban: *Thames Film*

Raban has firm roots in a specific category of filmmaking (experimental landscape), which helps to define his choice of theme. With this project, two factors were important from the start: timing, and the visual concept, or way of treating the subject.

William Raban is a leading experimental filmmaker and one of the main protagonists of the landscape film tendency. He believes that: 'making films is about showing people things, not telling them how to interpret the world' (Luxonline, 2005). When, during the 1980s, Raban first went out in his boat, which was moored on the River Thames at Greenwich, he was struck by the different view of the city from the river. He studied the river for two years, observing the logic of the plan and layout of the city from the water. This prompted his desire to make a film about the river. He calls his work a 'labour of love', stressing that there is no money in his sort of work. As yet he had no funding, but he already had a purpose: 'I wanted to show the presence of the river in the city – London's biggest open space – and to reveal the tides and the arterial route that connects the city to the open sea' (Raban, 1998: 16).

Timing was precise. This fearful force, this subliminal spirit of nature that in the past had acted as a spine for so much human energy, was about to undergo a huge, ambitious makeover with the planned Docklands redevelopment. The remnants of past glory still lay buried amongst the decaying brown dereliction of the waterfront wharfs and warehouses. Raban discovered traces of the old river trades. 'My main interest was to work with these images before they disappeared', he says (author interview, 2005). Since then, the landscape of the Thames has changed considerably, so *Thames Film* is now a classic historical archive in its own right. In this documentary record, 'Modernity is put on trial' by a study of the sites and meanings that 'time has inscribed into them' (Buckell, 2005: 50).

Immediately Raban was able to visualize a treatment for his idea. The entire film would be shot from his boat. He wrote: 'I see a way of dealing with visual and aural images . . . all shots of the water will be moving. The movement of the boat will render smooth tracking shots over expanses of land and water possible. The river's flow will lend form and consistency. My method will be to spend a period gathering images onto film, probably shooting on both colour and black and white. This will be the basis of the visual track. The assembly of the sound will happen after the shooting' (memo to Marion, 2 January 1984).

Raban quotes Thomas Aquinas as his starting point: 'Art imitates Nature not through mere appearances, but in her manner of operation' (Raban, 1998: 14). The creative roots of William's approach can be traced – literally – back to trees, or more precisely, to a time when he wrapped some tree trunks in a canvas soaked with organic dyes. He would then revisit it, adding washes of coloured dye until he finally removing the canvas, discovering that the influence of weather and natural decay had left what has been called a 'material piece of time' (Peter Gidal in Luxonline, 2005). Raban considers that the 'Tree Print Series' worked like photographic time exposure: that was the point of departure for a series of experimental time-lapse films of different landscapes. His concepts for films have shown a continuous fascination with landscape and seascape for over 20 years, returning to the same subjects years later: 'Not only does he never use his medium in a matter-of-fact way, he is also able to keep looking differently at the same thing' (Zuilhof, 2001: 299). In his production strategies, Raban simultaneously addresses film as a process in two, linked ways: to observe the location and to reflect on film.

In an attempt to identify some of the main ways in which documentary represents reality, Corner (1996) defines four different uses of image, and three of sound. On the image side, he defines the first two as forms of observationalism: reactive and proactive. 'Reactive' involves minimum intervention, an indirect method of 'fly on the wall' which makes the audience into witnesses who need to work hard at interpretation in order to extrapolate significance. 'Scopic mobility' can be limited to the visualization of process. Documentary is dependent instead on the strength of the event being filmed, and there is a risk that coherence, and also the interest of the audience, will be lost. Therefore the initial selection of subject matter for filming is crucial. As an example, television channels have been inundated with docusoaps. According to one writer, between 1999 and 2001 there were 65 docusoaps on the major British channels (where the format originated), mostly about people in a particular line of business or walk of life (Rosenthal & Corner, 2005: 174). Essentially, a film crew follows their everyday ups and downs in the hope that some entertaining material may emerge. As an extension of observational documentary, they are easy to make and, despite the high shooting ratio, still far cheaper to produce than drama. The selection of topics often leans towards 'the pleasingly exotic, amusing or bizarre, while the viewing position is often established as one of wry detachment and the "shock of the real" brought reductively close to a form of commodity consumption' (Rosenthal & Corner, 2005: 5).

'Proactive' observationalism allows for greater management of movement, space and, more generally, what is to be filmed. This can mean more directorial choice in how something is depicted and the function that sequences fulfil within the larger film. Observation is still there, but it serves a purpose, and time may be compressed overall, with greater use of narrative and depictive controls. Rouch and Morin's *Chronicle of a Summer*, analysed later in this chapter, fits this category.

'Evidential mode 3', as Corner calls it, is an illustrative one used frequently in current affairs, where visualization is subordinated to verbal discourses supporting a hypothesis or argument. The choice of style or 'mode' for a project can lend weight to the claims of the filmmaker, illustrated by the fact that a traditional current affairs approach will immediately encourage the viewer to consider the issue under discussion. Nancy Platt's *Venkatamma's Story* fits this example (see case studies in later chapters).

Corner's fourth mode, 'Associative', means that visualization is usually involved in creating second-order meanings as a visual exposition or evaluation for symbolic, aesthetic or referential purposes. *Thanatos and Eros* (see case study below) as an art-house film, is an example. With this sort of approach, aestheticism does not necessarily help informational requirements.

In terms of speech, Corner identifies three choices for the filmmaker:

1 Overheard exchange: the apparent reason for conversation arises from what is being filmed, although the level of 'objectification' within the overall visualization will vary, as will the performance and self-consciousness of the people being filmed.
2 Testimony: interviews, variously obtained and used. Levels of apparent truth/objectivity or of subjectivity/partiality can be reached by visual and sound editing and by juxtaposition. Use of interview material as voice-over can refocalize visual portrayal, encouraging viewer empathy.
3 Voice-over and presenter address ('piece to camera' or PTC): narration can be used to bridge shots and is useful where abstract, propositional matters need explaining and where disparate visuals require linkage. It is possible to use subjective exposition with a number of different speakers, or those at the opposite ends of the spectrum, to achieve objectification and distance through a more formal 'voice of God'.

Trying to be objective/subjective?

'Whenever you point a camera, you make a statement. Whenever you cut a piece of film, you make a statement. I'm not interested in objectivity' (Emile de Antonio in Kellner & Streible, 2000: 214). Each individual cinematic eye will see differently: unlike apparently objective news reporting, documentary requires a strong expression of personal theme. How can the documentary maker convey a personal understanding or opinion of the content and people filmed if there is an obligation towards objectivity? The idea that this is a desirable goal is relatively recent, emerging from television journalism with its aim of presenting both sides of a story.

In our everyday lives, we tend to alternate between assessment of the subjective (based on personal feelings, something we are doing at a given moment, for instance) with the objective (not influenced by personal feelings, such as aspects that we cannot influence or control, but that are always there). Similarly, documentary can be both subjective and objective. A personalized strategy, such as the photo-collage technique of art-house director Karl Nussbaum, goes beyond documentary to push at the boundaries of accepted wisdom concerning subjectivity and authorial voice.

Karl Nussbaum: *Thanatos and Eros: The Birth of the Holy Freak*

Nussbaum's personal approach is what makes his work idiosyncratic, but it goes beyond standard definitions of documentary. He did not want to rely 100 per cent on standard non-fictional techniques.

Nussbaum, the son of a Holocaust survivor, has been making films for over 18 years, screening them at European and American film festivals and museums. In the late 1980s he was a founder member of Film Crash, a New York-based film collective. He has a fellowship at the MacDowell Colony and a residency at the Virginia Center for the Creative Arts (VCCA), as well as working as a freelance promo director for MTV2. He specializes in a photo-collage method that is integrated with both documentary and fictional technique.

Karl Nussbaum's motivation and authorial voice is blatantly personal. One day his 7-year-old son, who was born with a slightly malformed hand, came to him and asked, 'Does strange sex produce strange babies?' Then he turned to his German grandfather, who is a Holocaust survivor, and asked him, 'Where was our Savior during the Holocaust?' Then the child began to relate his story about the Holy Freak. Karl then decided to examine 'what a child learns about love in the house of a Holocaust survivor and the bizarre savior myth he creates for comfort'. 'I never know where a film will lead me as I make it, but it gives me something to hold on to and a way to go forward. Everyone has to have something to believe in, in order to go on.' As the project began to evolve, he decided to make 'an eccentric, personal travelogue of my return to the country that killed my family and of my struggle to understand what love really can and can't do'. The result is controversial: 'Nussbaum may be a navel-gazing narcissist, but he can get away with it, so potent are his near mad, always candid ruminations' (Susan Alper, in review of the 8th Annual Montreal Jewish Film Festival, 2003).

Some people argue that the search for objectivity is not only mission impossible, but also two-faced. British director Peter Watkins has good reason to believe this, as his famous BBC drama documentary was banned from television screens for 20 years: 'If I could wage full-time war, I'd wage it on such words as "objectivity" and "propaganda". I mean *The War Game* has been shot down for being pro-paganda, and this by the BBC, which has transmitted pro-government, pro-nuclear-weapons films.' Watkins sees this as an example of Western society's confusion over perceptions of reality (MacDonald, 1992: 411).

It can be argued that the documentary maker has an obligation *not* to be objective: we are interpreters of the world rather than objective recorders of reality. Activist documentary makers such as Patwardhan or Armstrong argue that they are advocates for a specific social or political standpoint. *Cinéma vérité* and direct cinema, for instance, can be interpreted as a reaction to the so-called 'objective' television documentary, whereas a diary approach will endeavour to establish truth via a more personal record with an individual perception which is also likely to be more subjective. If the filmmaker cannot be truly objective, this is not to say that he or she cannot search for 'truth' as perceived. Awareness of this quest emerges throughout the production process in a number of different ways, according to the nature of the project.

Inserting an authorial voice

It is often said that filmmaking should be about showing, not telling. In this case, how does one input an authorial voice? The way that the filmmaker permits the audience to formulate an opinion, based on his or her own judgement, is crucial – especially when it involves a political assessment. The activity of documentary production tends to imply a critical relationship by the maker towards aspects of social life. As a project grows, the version of reality that is being portrayed will prompt an interrogation of values and editorial decisions involving a range of authorial attitudes. Filmmakers have to consider how challenging the film is likely to be in its criticisms of others, of society, of accepted world views and of morality.

Authorial voice is firstly about original intent. The original concept will dictate the documentary material that is chosen, structured, fashioned and packaged for presentation. The filmmaker selects a technique or number of different techniques that will act as a vehicle for authorial voice. Each one brings certain advantages and disadvantages, for no single technique provides the panacea when it comes to documentary expression. For instance, the value of the traditional 'expository' approach (voice-over commentary with illustrative shots) is that the frame of reference is not questioned, but taken for granted in a way that enables the producer to get on with the content with considerable economy and speed of analysis, succinctly making points. In current affairs, this technique is often essential in order to analyse the issue quickly. This is done 'partly by eliminating reference to the process by which knowledge is produced, organized, and regulated so that it, too, is subject to the historical and ideological processes of which the film speaks' (Nichols, 1991: 35). Although a questioning viewer may wonder about the production process – where the fact and figures were obtained, for instance – this is subordinated in favour of the message which needs to be delivered.

Conversely, use of an observational or reflexive style (see below) does not mean that there is no authorial voice. Quite the reverse, it is simply expressed differently, perhaps more obliquely, in an indirect way. If an observational project is to rise above the mundane and trivial, then audiences must be able to draw some more general thoughts from the details of the particular subject or storyline. Rabiger refers to this as a 'balance between tracts of autonomous, unfolding realism on the one hand and signs and portents that signal us to look beyond the literal on the other' (2004: 92). That signposting amounts to a form of authorial voice.

The way that authorial voice is conveyed almost anonymously, in a compilation historical film without a narrator or any presenter or filmmaker on screen, does not necessarily mean that no strings are being pulled. They are simply being pulled in a different and usually more complex fashion. Such a strategy foregrounds ideas before director personality.

Emile de Antonio: *In the Year of the Pig*

This was the first film to place American involvement in Vietnam into an historical perspective and, simultaneously, to challenge it. How did de Antonio start to insert his authorial voice?

'*In the Year of the Pig* was a film that was generated by anger at our war. All of my work together is an attempt to deal with the history of the United States in the days of the Cold War' (Jackson, 2004). De Antonio was a pioneer in using specially conducted interviews, together with archive without any narrator, for passionate historical compilation documentaries. He wanted to make a film that 'was not a lecture, not a scream' (Kellner & Streible, 2000: 99).

De Antonio 'marshals documentation to express a point of view' (Weiss, 1974: 29), strongly at variance with that of the American government. Yet he uses hard factual evidence, 'My films are made with documents, whether I film the document or whether the document exists. The structure, the technique, everything else is invented' (Kellner & Streible, 2000: 112). The filmmaker does not speak to us directly, 'A young American sees the film, and he doesn't hear de Antonio talking to him, but he too can reach a conclusion on the subject of the war' (Emile de Antonio in Ciment & Cohn, 1970: 29, author's translation). Nor does de Antonio always accept the word of his witnesses. Furthermore, he always constructs a piece that provides a broad understanding of an issue, as well as a juxtaposition or counterpoint of participants.

One of his other famous films about the McCarthyite trials, *Point of Order*, was the first political film that did not have that intrusive, narrative voice. 'It came out of the material itself. The very idea of *cinéma vérité* is repugnant to me. It is as if the filmmaker owned truth of some kind. I have never felt that I owned truth. I tried to be as truthful as I can but I know I am a man of deep-seated prejudices and many assumptions about the nature of society which colour all my thinking and feeling and the work that I do' (Jackson, 2004).

> I confront our history on my own terms. Brecht said that only boots can be made to measure. He was right . . . I approach all my work from a consciously left view point . . . as the old Hollywood saying has it, 'If you have a message, use Western Union.' Well, all my films have messages, but I don't want to send them by Western Union . . . For me, film is tug, pull, conflict, process. (Rosenthal & Corner, 2005: 108, 153, 166)

De Antonio had been thinking for some time that the media, with all their coverage, never explained background context, or why the carnage of war was happening, so he wanted to do 'an intellectual and historical overview . . . going back to World War II and just before . . . Then two academics came and said, "We have seen your other films, we think you should make a film about Vietnam", and it all suddenly went "click"' (Rosenthal, 1978: 10).

> The documentary film artist lives in opposition . . . My films come from the life and times of my country. Our government provides us with subjects daily: General Plague; thermonuclear war . . . declaration of war on the poor at home, and on the Third World everywhere. Let PBS and the networks sell news. Let the documentarians' world be full of surprises. (Rosenthal & Corner, 2005: 163)

Taking reflexivity into account

Reflexivity is about the way that a documentary appears to audiences to be made, by demonstrating on screen that the filmmaker is interacting with participants and the production process. For instance, in *Roger and Me*, the storyline revolves around a research process which in many films would amount to no more than a behind-the-scenes pre-production effort with telephone calls, negotiation and arrangements. Viewers would only see the end result: the person or event that is filmed. However, Moore is acknowledging his own process (but not that of his team) in front of the camera.

Reflexivity is a three-way process: producer–process–product. Documentarians ask the audience to see their genre for what it is – a construct – by putting their research on film, by showing the audience what they found and how they did it. 'To be *reflexive* is not only to be self-aware, but to be sufficiently self-aware to know what aspects of self are necessary to reveal so that an audience is able to understand both the process employed and the resultant product and to know that the revelation itself is purposive, intentional, and not merely narcissistic or accidentally revealing' (Rosenthal & Corner, 2005: 35).

Should audiences be made aware of the troubles that a filmmaker goes through to produce a film? Should aspects of the production be featured in the finished film in order to reflect process as well as product? If so, what should this involve? Such questions are not merely theoretical: many ethnographic artists argue that there is an inevitability connected to our use of reflexivity as, 'a means whereby we can instruct our audiences to understand the process of producing statements about the world. "We study man, that is, we reflect on ourselves studying others, because we must, because man in civilization is the problem"'(Diamond in ibid.: 47).

The presence of the camera, and where the documentary maker chooses to take it, can present surprising complexities. Ways of being reflexive emerge as this study progresses. Some documentary makers feel that such elements emerge almost naturally and organically during production. However, not all documentary makers choose to be reflexive. The expositionary approach, mentioned above, is usually not reflexive, although there are always examples that challenge the general rule. Occasionally in current affairs and investigative films, audiences are made aware of process by references in commentary such as 'We asked for an interview with the management of the company, but they refused.' There are degrees of reflexivity, and a film that contains one such reference, but no others, would be at a low level.

It is possible to argue that decisions on methods and amount of reflexivity only serve to provide additional complications for the filmmaker. Indeed, awareness of it, and ability to exploit it successfully, is easily confused with self-reference and self-consciousness. Reflexivity is no panacea: '(it) does not provide the unassailable assurance of the filmmaker's morality or sincerity that some viewers might hope for' (Barbash & Taylor, 1997: 32). A filmmaker can be reflexive without being overtly personal. With documentary, there is a need to identify intention and vision from the early stages because the original concept will dictate the documentary material that is chosen, structured, fashioned and packaged for presentation. To achieve a good balance of reflexivity is to introduce an additional texture to the film that may otherwise be lacking. However, the balance can be upset. A first-time filmmaker whom I interviewed, David Palazon, wanted to make a film that would 'empower' the people that were to be featured in the film, by creating a democracy of production. This meant that the participants would set the pace. It would be their film. Such a strategy amounts to a gamble with creative vision, especially if the production team move dangerously near to a total abandonment of authorship and power. By comparison, the experiments of the great Vertov, and later of Rouch, showed that the filmmaker was still very much in control.

Dziga Vertov: *The Man with a Movie Camera*

Dziga Vertov was one of the most experimental and imaginative documentary practitioners – yet he saw his role as a journalistic one of reportage. Vertov's analysis of the post-production process is presented in chapter 5.

With his 'Kino-eye' movement the Russian filmmaker invented a new and lasting vocabulary for documentary and prepared the ground for *cinéma vérité* some 40 years later, as espoused by Rouch in France. For this film, he envisaged, 'a dashing survey of visual events deciphered by the movie-camera, fragments of actual energy (as against theatrical energy), with their intervals condensed into a cumulative whole by the great mastery of an editing technique' (Michelson, 1984: 87).

Vertov's 'Kino-eye' method was a new way of seeing things with the camera, which redefined the production process and radically revised aesthetic canons and priorities. He defined it thus: 'not merely some so-called artistic trend (left or right). Kino-eye is an ever-growing movement for influence through facts as opposed to influence through fiction, no matter how strong the imprint of fiction. Kino-eye is the documentary cinematic decoding of both the visible world and that which is invisible to the naked eye' (ibid.).

For Vertov, the 'Kino-eye' is in the realm of 'that which the naked eye does not see', but this is not a question of news footage, with its so-called 'objectivity', or at least detachment. Vertov's starting point, he maintained, was the 'utilisation of the camera as a cinema eye – more perfect than a human eye for purposes of research into the chaos of visual phenomena filling the universe' (Geduld, 1967: 92).

For Vertov, the great discoverer, and Rouch, the great ethnographer, the ordinary eye sees untruth, but the *cinema eye*, helped by specific cinematic methods, can see truth. For Vertov, reflexivity reflected a *process* rather than a revelation of self, one which was distinct from previous fictional traditions. This meant making the audience aware of creative, methodological and technical considerations that would serve to raise consciousness of film form as dialectical materialism.

Jean Rouch and Edgar Morin: *Chronicle of a Summer*

Jean Rouch was inspired by Vertov's work to introduce a 'reflexivity' of process into his project.

Rouch was a pioneer professional ethnographer, as well as making the first descent of the Niger by dugout canoe in 1946–7. He made over 60 films in Africa and also ventured into fiction projects, but *Chronicle of a Summer* (made with sociologist Edgar Morin) was the film that launched *cinéma vérité* and technically it provided a milestone because it represented the first trouble-free use of an efficient and portable synchronous sound system for filming. In *Chronicle of a Summer*, Rouch turns to 'this strange tribe living in Paris' in an attempt to discover how they feel about their lives in the summer of 1960. From a starting point of a simple question, 'are you happy?', the project became moving, unique and stylistically significant to the history of documentary, because of the way it probes spiritual and emotional reality in its use of non-fiction techniques. I return to Rouch and Morin's technique of blurring the boundaries between technicians, actors, subject and filmmakers in future chapters.

How should we find our ideas? 'I think that our duty as film-makers is to make films bearing witness to violence. These films ought to stimulate something, ought to be the stimulant to let people reflect on their situation: Does the family still exist? Is money worth something? Things of this kind. Scandalous films must be made' (Levin, 1971: 145).

What was the background to the project? 'We thought that the Algerian War was going to end . . . and Edgar Morin and I wanted to make a film that would bear witness to a very important period in French life. That was the point of departure' (ibid.: 143).

Rouch and Morin saw their film as a journey in which they admit to being travellers, in order to reflect the emotional reality of a participant, which counterbalanced the so-called objectivity of the outsider. Thus they believed in a subjective commitment in order to rise above the level of mere reportage. Morin said: 'Jean and I were in agreement on one point. That it was necessary to make a film with total authenticity, true as a documentary but having the content of a fiction film, the inner life of the people' (Jacobs, 1979: 443). In order to make a documentary that was emotionally committed and aesthetically relevant, as filmmakers they had to identify with the subject by admitting their own subjectivity and involvement. As Rouch said: 'I don't think it's possible to be a witness to the things happening around you and at the same time not take a stand. I think one must take a stand' (Levin, 1971: 142).

> I look on the human sciences as poetic sciences in which there is no objectivity. And I see film as being not objective, and *cinéma vérité* as a cinema of lies that depends on the art of telling yourself lies . . . I'm one of the people responsible for this phrase (*cinéma vérité*) and it's really in homage to Dziga Vertov, who completely invented the kind of film we do today . . . I agree with him – that the camera eye is more perspicacious and more accurate than the human eye. The camera eye has an infallible memory, and the film-maker's eye is a multiple one, divided. (ibid.: 134–5).

Rouch was more concerned than Vertov with the personal as it relates to research and the effects of filming research: 'I've tried to show that civilizations which have been considered primitive or have been despised until now did have something to say and that they knew things that we had to learn. That's what I learned in Africa – and I learned a lot more than I taught. That's very, very important' (ibid.: 144–5).

Considering audiences

Media products are always made for a particular audience, but what obligations does the documentary maker have to the audience? As with a book, a viewing experience will represent a process of interaction between reader and text; the way that this works depends on the prior assumptions and outlook that an individual brings to the experience of viewing. Every documentary tends to flag up its premise quite early on, and makes it obvious how it is intends communicating with its audience. The approach may involve expanding the viewer's assumptions, or sharing with them a baffling or complex issue, unravelling a mystery of some sort, or engaging their emotions. The unfolding of knowledge may involve giving both sides, or only engaging with one side of an issue, but in depth.

How important is the relationship between filmmaker intent and audience and how far does it vary according to exhibition outlet? A current affairs film, for example, that requires 'balance', will probably aim to give equal weight to both sides, in order to inform the audience. An 'observational' documentary will approach the audience in a different way, presenting a topic in all its complexity and leaving the audience to reach their own conclusions.

Considerations of audience are connected to the issue of how the film will be exhibited and funded, dealt with in the next chapter. This in turn will influence content. The audience is dependent on where the money is coming from, so the approach to a television audience is different to art house or cinema. Allowing for the fact that every film is unique and that each has its own 'problematics', how soon should one start to consider the audience? Right from the front, according to William Raban: by which he means the front of the film. He believes that the director should give an early signal to the audience for them to understand the basis on which the image is being constructed (author interview, 2005).

More generally, the maker needs to be able to justify the documentary that is in his or her head in terms of what the audience will get out of it. Why should they sit and watch it? Whether viewer interpretations align with prescribed producer intentions or not, different people can nevertheless arrive at a variety of different meanings, even within the limitations of a documentary. This process has been called '*audience jouissance*' by French theorist Roland Barthes (O'Sullivan et al., 1994: 152). Hence, considerations about influence on the audience form part of a documentary maker's preliminary analysis about intent. The filmmaker needs to consider how the audience will 'read' or construe the various visual devices that they are confronted with.

Connie Field: *The Life and Times of Rosie the Riveter*

Filmmakers need both a subject and a way of presenting it that takes audience into account. Connie Field hit upon the subject of women workers during the Second World War in the US; she evolved ways of treating the content that supported her filmmaker intent. There is a necessary triangulation between producer aim, subject and treatment.

The idea was to document the experiences of women who were recruited en masse by crude propaganda into the workforce for the Second World War home front effort. Field's preliminary considerations were influenced by her agitprop background, which led her to aim to make the film accessible to the widest possible audience (Johnston, 1981: 21).

> I wanted to make a film about an area of history that seemed hidden . . . There were these thousands of women doing jobs which had been seen as traditionally male, and then when they had been pushed out of them, it's as though the whole phenomenon was forgotten . . . I was concerned with the way that women were represented, and how media and social ideas changed as economic necessity changed . . . so many of the issues then relate directly to today. (Williamson, 1981: 45)

> I (also) ask myself, is the subject something that will help people understand the social conditions under which they live in a way that can help them change those conditions? Also, will the subject lend itself to film so that the impact of information can be both emotional and dramatic? I also consider how the film can be used as an organizing tool and whether there are active groups which will actually use it. (Rosenthal & Corner, 2005: 164)

Field's intention was to represent interviewees as central characters, who remember, reflect and define the content, rather than acting as illustrative examples of some other agenda. Field had a clear guiding philosophy right from the outset: 'I feel very strongly that interview documentaries can be extremely powerful if people are revealed in such a way that you can care and feel for them and can receive their stories as drama' (ibid.: 157).

The title for the film came from a contemporary pop song. Use of archive propaganda as comparison provided a contrapuntal central theme. As she points out, '*Rosie* was made as a documentary because the story could not have been told as a fiction film. One of the main concepts was myth versus reality . . . Therefore, the documentary form, which allows for the juxtaposition of real experiences as told by the women themselves with the actual newsreels of the day, creates a stronger impact' (ibid.: 165–6).

For many committed journalists and filmmakers, visual trickery should not obscure message. The ideal that they strive to achieve through their work is that the content or theme should be scrutinized within the public sphere and can serve to amplify debate. When people watch a factual or documentary film, they expect (often subconsciously) to open up to new experiences that will be mind expanding or knowledge enhancing. This process has been defined as, 'a pleasure in knowing, that marks out a distinctive form of social engagement' (Nichols, 1991: 178). During the course of engagement, people strive (again subconsciously) to position their own situations in life within the world's bigger order.

Emphasis is now on audience participation and diversity, which means that filmmakers have to consider how to build various mechanisms into their creative strategies that will mitigate against the inherent passivity of the medium and enhance an audience's ability to create individual meaning. During the 1980s, a research exercise was carried out whereby various groups from a range of educational, professional and social backgrounds watched a series of documentaries on nuclear power; the response in terms of pro- or anti-nuclear perspectives was very different according to the affiliations of the groups. In other words, audiences contribute a 'framework of understanding' with prior views (Corner et al., 1990). Even the most personal of subject matters is likely to open consciousness of a possible wider issue, and the mark of the production team underwrites the audience experience. 'There is always a guiding hand which nudges us towards taking a particular view of (these) events. Like pleasure, knowledge is not always innocent' (Kilborn & Izod, 1997: 233).

Anand Patwardhan: *In the Name of God*

With this choice of subject, Patwardhan communicates a serious and dangerous issue to audiences.

Over a career spanning three decades, Patwardhan has used a discerning eye for recording events and their larger significance. *In the Name of God* deals with the very current subject of religious fundamentalism as it relates to the Hindu–Muslim clash, and the political threat to the survival of secularism. 'New projects begin only when events and ideas begin to oppress me too much' (Goldsmith, 2003, ch. 10: 11). Patwardhan's responsibility towards the audience is to empower people, to make 'the unheard voices heard' by recording things that are actually happening, that are not being represented in the mainstream media. Audience interaction is all important.

Jacket design for Anand Patwardhan: *In the Name of God*

> It comes in small ways, from individuals who speak out at screenings, from letters from viewers, from essays written by school and college kids, from a movie star who decided to become an activist, from a fundamentalist who questioned his own belief system, from an usher at a posh club where the film was screened who bicycled for miles to track me down and get a Hindi version of the film. The list, fortunately, is very long and has always saved me from sinking into doubt and despair, no matter how hard the circumstances. Even the fact that the insights that are offered challenge existing presumptions and views has led fundamentalists to try to suppress my work, proved to me that they found the work threatening, i.e. effective. (Maclay, 2004)

Patwardhan collects material on the same theme over a long period before he decides how to fashion it. He explains: 'I must first be moved to feel strongly about certain issues to make a film' (Gangar & Yardi, 1993: 23). He then holds a mirror to the psyche of his country as he selects subject matter from India's political crises that reflect issues of polarization, representative voice and class. 'I think what I'm doing is basically saying: "Here's a liberal humanist who's inviting other people" – I believe other people are the same if only they would recognize it, and so – "come and see it this way". What I choose to film are moments of terrible, irrational, inhuman behavior which don't make sense to anybody, once they happen to look at it in that perspective. So I'm just inviting people to look at it in that perspective.' (Akomfrah, interview in *Pix*). Patwardhan wants to move his audiences 'emotionally to fight injustice and the violence that exists'; hence his support for the movement to protect civil rights and secularism (Gangar & Yardi, 1993: 21).

> The main thing I have been obsessed with is the rise of fundamentalism, fundamentalist violence. If it was harmless, I would ignore it. But in India everyone can see the kind of hatred that's resulted in increased levels of mindless violence against those whom the people who are killing don't even know; anonymous murders for a cause, which make no sense, not even for the people who are doing it. (Akomfrah, interview in *Pix*)

In the case of *In the Name of God*, with more than 80 per cent of Indians being Hindu, Patwardhan sees the rise of fundamentalism within this faith as a growing danger: 'when a majority becomes fundamentalist, genocide can happen . . . Religious fundamentalism is more politics than religion . . . violence begins when religion is used for political power' (ibid.).

The particular stage of the conflict which Patwardhan documents in *In the Name of God* was prompted by a specific event with crucial timing. Hindu fundamentalists decided to march on the mosque at Ayodhya – a sacred site in North India – and demolish it. This event was the 'peg', although the theme was by no means new. A nobleman of Babur's court built the Babri Mosque in 1528. From the 1850s onward, various Hindus have tried to lay claim to the site, identifying it as the birthplace of Lord Ram. Patwardhan now had an opportunity with his film to examine the forces that play havoc in the name of religion, in particular the fact that most Hindus and Muslims living around Ayodhya had co-existed peacefully for years. This fact enabled him to offer an argument that opportunistic Hindu nationalist leaders were appropriating the conflict and deliberately aggravating it when the situation turned incendiary in 1992.

Patwardhan decided that the story was to be played out in the run up to the destruction in December 1992. The devastating physical expression of events, caused by the inflamed psyche of the Hindu fundamentalists, enabled him to raise wider issues about religious intolerance, the politicization of fundamentalism and the threat that it poses to secularism.

The 'guiding hand' that nudges the audience along in documentary is not confined to political authorship. Documentary usage in a range of different situations will influence assumptions on content, and the 'guiding hand' will exist in every project where intent and message have been given prior consideration – as indeed, they must. The way that these are linked to the perceived responsibility towards an audience is especially well focused and carefully defined in non-broadcast 'corporate' documentaries and is examined in subsequent chapters. These can be projects made specifically for a whole range of organizations, including the non-profit making sector.

Assessing the ethical implications

We need to recognize in advance the obligations that filmmakers have to the people being filmed and, separately, to the audience. What is required is an awareness of how our actions will influence the people with whom we are working, and an awareness of the implications of our decisions in terms of how audiences will read the end result.

Michael Moore: *Roger and Me*

What was Moore's starting point and how significant was his chosen approach in terms of setting the pace for later ethical issues in production, and subsequent legal problems? Would the alternative styles that he rejected have been less controversial?

This film was directed, produced and written by Moore, although he had no prior film production experience, working previously as a print journalist, including editor of the *Flint Voice*. He started from the premise that he didn't want to make a worthy social study, 'another "Dying Steel-town" documentary' of his home town, but 'wanted to tell a somewhat offbeat, funny story about what the richest company in the world has done to its hometown' (Michael Moore in Cohan & Crowdus, 1990: 27).

In his quest to present a narrative that was both comic and critical, Moore already had a very clear position on how to represent the misfortunes of Flint. Responsibility for the quality of life of its workforce lay with the management of General Motors (GM). Therefore the choice for Moore was how to represent a series of actions taken by the leadership of the company – represented by General Motors Chairman Roger Smith. Michael Moore's intent was to take issue humorously with corporate and governmental justifications for social and political actions. He decided to use a combination of features, which have led to the project being described as 'anti-corporate polemic, comedy, autobiographical essay, exercise in "amateurism" and ongoing saga of investigative reporting' (Corner, 1996: 156).

The implications of the methods and form that Moore adopted, in particular the phenomenon of the director as 'star' will be explored later. As we follow the production process, 'we might also question at what cost its popular success has been achieved' (Cohan & Crowdus, 1990: 30).

Documentary production involves contrasting influences that stretch our desire to be ethical. If we are to capture actuality, we need to be true to the subject as perceived and to the people depicted, but artistic aesthetics confuses the morals, to the extent that journalistic codes of ethics cannot be easily applied to documentary. These days the public's right to know as a justification for intrusion of privacy is a defence on ever shifting sands, which is under constant challenge.

How can the traditional journalistic obligation to be objective, fair and honest survive when, in the case of documentary, the camera cannot simply deliver an unmediated reproduction of the truth? Even with observational documentary, which aims to minimalize the filmmaker interventions, camera presence can still have an effect, and filmmakers can be accused of voyeurism.

The technologically produced image represents a construction and an interpretative act that is underlined by culture, ideology and point of view, even if not deliberately acknowledged. Yet talk of 'fakery' can falsely presuppose that under normal circumstances, the camera never lies. Already I have alluded to a number of projects that extend our understanding of what can or cannot be accomplished. There are no easy answers at any stage of the production process. Production requires mediation, but how much is ethical?

Those filmmakers who decide to challenge the parameters of the documentary genre also raise a wider question. Exactly how distinct can the maker be, without being too contrived? There are directors such as Trinh T. Minh-ha, who actively set out to do just this. For audiences, this can provide a troubling experience which raises a number of questions concerning production methodology. How important are the informational sources? Does the visual artistry divert or enhance the messages? Do viewers feel duped by the realization that reality is under fire? Is this documentary? The fact that we are dealing in relative concepts further confuses the issue.

Trinh T. Minh-ha: *Surname Viet, Given Name Nam*

This project presented issues of depiction of reality, documentary authenticity and the relevance of mediation. Where should documentary makers draw the line when it comes to experimentation?

'I am always working at the borderlines of several shifting categories, stretching out to the limits of things' (Mayne, 1990: 6). Trinh wanted to examine questions of identity, popular memory and difference between various cultures. As her vehicle, she used interviews with women now living in the United States about previous experiences during the war in Vietnam which were not their own. They re-enacted reminiscences of other Vietnamese women, as researched and written down in French by another author, then translated. Trinh found the book entitled *Vietnam: un people, des voix* by Mai Thu Van (Pierre Horay, Paris, 1983), which consisted of a series of interviews, in a French bookstore.

Trinh managed to make a film about Vietnam without filming there. Instead she decided that we should question our face value acceptance of what she calls 'the politics of interview', the nature of language, and the complex experiences of people from other cultures. For Trinh, reflexivity is characterized by an experimental approach which involves 'making visible what remains invisible (ideologically, cinematically) . . . It cannot be separated from the material, whether one chooses to call this material documentary or fiction' (Minh-ha, 1992: 183).

Selection of title has a specific symbolism for Trinh, representing a fusion of personal with political. The title comes from recent socialist tradition: 'When a man encounters a woman, feels drawn to her, and wants to flirt with her, he teasingly asks "young woman, are you married yet"? If the answer is negative, instead of saying no, she will reciprocate, "Yes, his surname is Viet and his given name is Nam" ' (Mayne, 1990: 7). 'To unravel the "name" of Vietnam in the context of translation is to confront the much debated politics of identity. For translation . . . implies questions of language, power, and meaning, or more precisely in this film, of women's resistance vis-à-vis the socio-symbolic contract – as mothers, wives, prostitutes, nurses, doctors, state employees, official cadres, heroines of the revolution' (MacDonald, 1992: 377).

Conclusion: the most important requirements for a documentary project

There are several starting points: an idea with potential that merits further investigation, an understanding of the many choices that will be available as a project evolves, and enthusiasm. Documentary makers become involved in a subject and a project in considerable detail over a fairly long time, so commitment is important and perseverance is everything. Documentary production involves a form of crafting that can be slow, even with digital technology, so enthusiasm should extend not simply to the selected theme, but also to the genre itself and the importance of the medium. De Antonio spent 15 months non-stop, seven days a week, on the production of *In the Year of the Pig*. In the present digital age, it would have taken just as long.

The last word on importance of the genre goes to Anand Patwardhan:

> Who would believe that Hitler's death camps existed if we did not have the actual footage? Who would believe that Hindu mobs poured petrol on small children in Gudjarat and set them alight? Who would believe that in the 70s Ronald Reagan's advisor Brezhinsky, addressing Muslim children in Pakistan, preached the gospel of 'Jehad' (Islamic Holy War)? And if not for the documentary, instead of images of Gandhi, would we not have to suffice with those of Ben Kingsley? (Goldsmith, 2003, ch.10: 15)

Summary

When developing an idea for documentary, the nature of this visual medium needs to be taken into account. An appreciation of how documentary is defined is essential in order to assess the full range of choices and which are likely to be most appropriate for the project under consideration. Motivation to communicate a subject to a wider public, interesting content and creativity are all more important than simple mastery of technology. Documentaries are each individually crafted, and this process can be lengthy, so persistence and commitment are necessary. Filmmakers always think ahead to the next stage of the process – fundraising, budgeting and pre-production research are the next steps.

2 Fundraising and Budgeting

The argument

The best documentaries tend to be made by people who feel that they have a mission, a burning passion, to tell a particular story. However, the ultimate question is 'who will fund the production and the marketing?'. There are two basic schools of thought on financial issues for documentary: the 'just do it, let it evolve, play it by ear' philosophy that allows the project to grow as you progress, and the methodical, strategic approach that allows for a more ambitious end product because funding has been procured – hopefully, from somebody else. This second tactic, most obviously manifest in broadcast television and corporate-sponsored commissions, involves flexibility and compromise over original intentions. There are also combinations of the two schools of thought.

Introduction

The process of raising money has its own benefits as a means of 'honing' the project, of meeting people and making contacts. Documentaries attract funding through a surprisingly eclectic number of routes, ranging from self-financing and private contributors through to business sponsorship, corporations, government and non-governmental organizations (NGOs – regional, national and supranational), foundations and television channels or stations.

This chapter examines strategies for the presentation of potential creative content for documentary makers looking to procure funding through a variety of sources. Information is analysed from the standpoint of impact on producer intent, and how the 'modus operandi' for fundraising influences creative factors. The central aspect of any bid has to be the content proposal, or treatment. Although a completed film may differ considerably from intentions written on paper for funding purposes, nevertheless the opportunity to plan an approach itself constitutes a form of film directing. Good directors use paper first. The requirement to visualize the future film in great detail will help to clarify the narrative structure, and increase the chances of shooting the right material at the right time. For grant funding, preliminary research needs to be detailed if the filmmaker is to really feel on top of the content.

A 'Do It Yourself' (DIY) formula can range from individual donations through deficit funding or loan strategy, to the grant-aided route. Each of these options can end up with the producers later trying to recoup expenditure through television, cinema and/or DVD and other forms of aftersales. If the aim of a documentary project is to reach as many audiences as possible, as effectively as possible, which is usually what financiers want, then it is important to think strategically from the start in order to create opportunities for them to participate in the effort. Distribution strategy is analysed further in the final chapter.

The various assault courses that documentary producers go through to procure money provide a real test of commitment, for the fundraising path can be a long, frustrating and arduous process, which may well be fraught with disappointments. More positively, it serves to focus thinking about content and style, involving lateral thinking whereby, on occasions, individuals invent whole new models for funding and distribution. As with the creative side of documentary production, there is no one single formula that works: there are many, and these are diverse.

Begging and borrowing – individual donations

The plus point with donations is that there are usually no conditions attached such as ownership of rights, profit shares or repayment. However, it is worth remembering that, if time equals money, any method of operating can be relatively costly. It sounds easy: hire a camera through a community arts centre, use the visual editing software that comes bundled into most computers, burn a DVD at a copy or camera shop. Yet choosing to go 'low budget' on a film does not necessarily mean less commitment, quicker or easier production.

Although camcorders and lightweight video mean fewer people are needed for filming, documentary is still labour intensive. The advent of digital technology has not reduced the time needed to make a well researched product: patience, dedication and money are still needed whatever equipment you use. Good documentary making is painstaking, even for the technologically skilled operator. A first-time filmmaker whom I interviewed, Selana Vronti, tried to go it alone with no budget. 'I don't know if you can work like this for ever. It is very tiring and the quality level of your work may fall. Filmmaking is based on teamwork. I don't like doing everything by myself. Also the audience has seen so many good things; they can quickly distinguish bad movies' (author interview, 2005). Nevertheless, some styles of production, such as the video diary style, lend themselves to low-budget operation, and in some ways the intimate approach compensates for technical deficiencies.

Producers sometimes persuade facility houses and organizations with post-production equipment to give discounts during 'down time' (when the machinery is not normally being used). In addition, the list of other attempts to beg or borrow is virtually endless. It can include restaurants, hotels, video stores or film archives. Filmmaker Barbara Kopple used photocopying and collating facilities in banks for her fundraising paperwork, even if they were unable to donate hard cash! (Kopple & Perry, 1980: 305). Asking local businesses for help in kind with goods and services is an acknowledged tactic; there are specialists and agencies that offer a service in raising corporate money.

For my Chapman Clarke Films co-production with Britain's ITV (Carlton Television), entitled *Forever England*, which involved filming over a two-year period at intervals in Japan, ANA (Air Nippon Airways) provided us with flights for filming, in return for a 'with thanks' end credit. In broadcast television examples of self-financing sponsorship are usually limited to top up in kind, such as this example. ANA had no creative influence and did not request any.

It is claimed that statistically, most documentaries get the majority of their money from individuals (Carole Dean in Search & McCarthy, 2005: 166). In the United States, house parties are also a recognized form of fundraising. Specific communities who have an interest in the subject matter can be targeted. According to one business advisor for independents, this sort of success entails, 'a high degree of initiative, cheek, contacts and luck on the part of the producer, but it does happen more frequently than most sensible people might think possible' (Viljoen, 1997: 143, 146).

Emile de Antonio: *In the Year of the Pig*

> It's the boring responsibility of filmmakers to raise money. I myself don't want to ask the foundations and the government for money. I don't want to be judged by those assholes. I prefer to do my 'bear act' . . . put on my bearskin and perform for people, tell them how wonderful it's going to be, and how brilliant I am. Then they write checks. (Kellner & Streible, 2000: 122)

Emile de Antonio's films were always funded by private individuals, 'rich liberals'.

> One of the things I like is raising money under certain conditions. For *In The Year of the Pig* I decided I would raise money from many people instead of just five or six. I knew this woman who was unhappy and middle-aged and her husband was about to leave her and she had a lot of money and I said to her, 'Let's have a party once a week and we'll invite everybody from fashion models to millionaires and I'll come in and make a pitch for the film on Vietnam and you give them shrimp and a drink.' She said, 'Wonderful idea' . . . I didn't know these people, but it was easy. I got money from Paul Newman, Steve Allen, Robert Ryan, a Rockefeller young woman, a whole host of people who were very angry about the war in Vietnam and two of the greatest fashion models in the world. I think the units were $600 each and the lowest anybody wrote was $1,200 and the most was $100,000. (Jackson, 2004)

'I've a moderately good record of making my own high-handed rules, which is that I pay people back but they get no profit, because I figure they have more money than they need anyway. But they're entitled to be paid back, and they get a tax benefit' (Rosenthal & Corner, 2005: 107). However, according to Marc N. Weiss, who worked for de Antonio on four films, 'all of his films have been on important subjects and have made money for their investors' (Weiss, 1974: 29). *In the Year of the Pig* was nominated for an Academy Award; every de Antonio film has been shown at important film festivals.

Certainly, most private investors like to have a tax incentive as a concession for their decision (whereby they can obtain tax relief on investment), although not all countries allow this. Furthermore, the percentage return that a producer can offer investors is difficult to calculate and to guarantee. The usual requirements that equity financiers make, for instance, for an 'end date' by which they expect to recoup the investment, is also virtually impossible to guarantee. No surprise, therefore that film production is considered high risk, but more glamorous and exciting than regular stocks and shares as a destination for funds that are surplus to the immediate requirements of investors.

Producers tend to ask for modest individual investments – say, £500 per person. If donations are larger than this, there is a risk that if participants have always been used to profit as a bottom line, this basic instinct could re-emerge when the initial infatuation with creativity has worn off. The answer is to select people who believe in the importance of the issue.

Both of these filmmakers found ways of making their documentaries without a television commission or grant-aided funding.

Franny Armstrong: *Drowned Out*

Franny Armstrong and her colleagues have financial backing from private individuals. Their aim is to keep control of the project without having to procure industry money, which they feel is likely to lead to unacceptable compromises. Previously Armstrong had an online business with a partner, and about £10,000 of her own money from that venture went into *Drowned Out*. This route is one that many famous documentary makers have taken. Frederick Wiseman, for instance, used his own credit cards to fund aspects of the production of the groundbreaking *Titicut Follies* (Rosenthal, 1971: 67). In addition, Armstrong had some support from a few other individuals, who were fans of her previous film, *McLibel*. This is an approach that she has been able to build on.

Drowned Out cost £35,000, of which £20,000 went on post-production. Armstrong already had a camera. Living costs whilst shooting in India were minimal, because the 40 or so protesters on the site that she was filming lived off communal food donated by farmers further up the river. They moved around mostly by boats, which the NBA protest movement had purchased with the help of Arundhati Roy's Booker prize-money donation. Nobody working on the Spanner Films production got paid for the project, although the production team, including the editor and musicians, all have percentage 'points' for profit share according to their contribution. The editor's is 4 to 6 per cent. Luckily, reversioning was feasible for *Drowned*

Anand Patwardhan with Simantini Dhuru: *A Narmada Diary*

'I can't be motivated by purely commercial interest. I can't make advertising films for that matter, or make a film just for the sake of making money to make another film. So far I have been lucky to eventually find ways to make the kind of films that I want to make' (Gangar & Yardi, 1993: 25). For Patwardhan, the challenge is therefore how to find enough money to continue the work on projects with a fairly long trajectory.

> If the filmmakers of today are willing to go the route I went, they would make a film even if they did not have money. That's what I've always done. I don't think about the money first. I borrowed money, equipment . . . kept shooting . . . I think if you're really involved you find ways of raising the necessary amounts of money. As long as you're not seeing the film as a source of livelihood, primarily. (Kripalani, 1998: 174)

At first, Patwardhan was dependent on other people for the shooting, but then, partly for reasons of economy, he began to shoot and edit more himself. 'My films were unplanned and shot over a very long time, making it expensive (by now I had started paying salaries!) and difficult to tie down a camera person' (Goldsmith, 2003, ch. 10: 11). 'I mostly work with a tiny crew of people who have worked with me for many years – usually close friends. Payment comes in at some point, but the film comes first, and has to be made with whatever is in the bank. When the film recovers its costs, further money is recycled into the next film' (ibid.).

Out, funded by PBS, who acquired a shorter version and entitled it *The Damned*. The American public broadcaster's money covered extra filming for an update.

Most of Patwardhan's funding has come from small donations.

Patwardhan makes a point of stressing that he has never taken grant funding from abroad, even for his sales and distribution organization, Samvaad, which functions as a library for other organizations' community films, as well as his own. The reason that Patwardhan will not take money from abroad is that his films are often critical of the state: 'I don't want to be accused of being funded from the "outside"' (Goldsmith, 2003, ch. 10: 11). Therefore he does not look for funding and doesn't write proposals. Instead, he tries to sell his completed films to broadcast television as acquisitions. He admits, 'The only actual hard cash I've been able to raise (in advance) was from Channel 4 – sales or pre-sales . . . I raise small amounts of money by selling films after they are made and I put it back into the next project.' (Akomfrah, interview in *Pix*). He also makes video/DVD sales in between television screenings.

Deficit funding via banks: a personal experience

For many years, Martin Clarke and myself, as television freelancers, had been used to only working on part of the production process; I was a researcher and he was a film editor. Although television production has always been a team game, nevertheless, the urge to do almost everything ourselves in order to keep control of a project was strong. When we decided to launch as a production company, we went to our local bank manager, who requested our CVs/résumés. When he saw the extensive film and television industry credits, he took advice from the manager of the Wardour St branch in London's Soho, where many independent cinema producers had their accounts. They responded with the official line of mainstream bankers: film finance is considered speculative, so they are only prepared to cash-flow a production on the basis of funding contracts. Therefore, all we could expect was an overdraft facility with which to launch our careers as independent producers, going it alone. However, as Martin and I discovered when we casually gave a copy of our résumés to Barclays Bank, even a small production team with good industry experience has the effect of creating investor confidence. As we had already advanced £10,000 of our own money, and had a house with which to stand guarantee, for the moment, the bank supported us with an overdraft. It did not last forever.

The project that we launched grew organically from a seed of an idea to make a short travelogue about little-known parts of Normandy that could eventually be distributed within the holiday industry. At this stage the potential market was only a vague aim. The documentary short continued to grow until it became a television feature series entitled *Feeling for France*, that was transmitted in many different countries worldwide, with an American distributor seeking PBS sponsorship for us. I acted as reporter/producer and Martin acted as director, sound recordist and editor. For the shooting we hired a camera operator. In postproduction, Martin could handle most things technically, I wrote the commentary and voiced it, but we still needed equipment hire, stock and processing, archive film, stills, transfers and dubbing.

The good news was that we were never required to prepare a proposal or a budgetary document, because we were effectively doing the project for ourselves. Nobody dictated content, therefore one further advantage was being able to escape from the treadmill of constant proposal submissions. Those halcyon days of modest and naive business start-up, with only a business plan to write in order to obtain a bank overdraft, and no requirement to explain creative subject matter, were a far cry from the rigorous project management systems imposed on us in later years by the procedures of broadcast commissions. The onus was now on us to recoup the investment with sponsorship or aftersales. We discovered that it is preferable to have the bedrock of an important financial investment from an end-user.

Grant-aided funding: analysing the landscape

Funding a documentary requires not simply an element of luck, but also patience and preparation. These days it is unusual to obtain total funding from one grant foundation. Luckily there are lots of them, including endowments for the arts, foundations and grant councils. The producer can tailor the amount requested to the proportions given out by individual organizations. Research into the field is critical in order to assess not only who to approach, but also how much to ask for. Such organizations attach importance to the *topic* for the documentary, not simply to the presumed appetite of the market for it, which is television's criterion. This means that subjects that have not yet reached mainstream public awareness can be launched in the marketplace, allowing the producer to anticipate audience reaction rather than following it by succumbing to the influence of yet another existing television hit.

The good thing about grant money from foundations, which tend to divide up into national (federal), regional (state) and private funding bodies, is that there are usually no conditions on content, so the filmmaker retains creative control, as long as the documentary is within the range of what was described in the proposal. For some filmmakers, this free hand is essential: *Roger and Me*, for instance, received grant-aided funding from Michigan Council for the Arts – and their support represented a very brave decision as Moore was a first-time filmmaker. First-time filmmaker David Palazon, whom I interviewed, succeeded in obtaining grant aid of £5,000 for *El Documento* from a local community business fund, not specifically aimed at filmmakers, called 'UnLtd' in London. In the US, it is usually local organizations that will fund less experienced filmmakers. With grants, you don't have to repay the money, and unlike investment finance, there are fewer conditions attached.

Traditionally, grants have been appropriate for non-commercial projects that would not otherwise get made, but as the public sector in many parts of the world needs to be shown to be profitable, or at least, not to have wasted money, attitudes are changing. The traditional categorization of commercial and non-commercial is no longer so clear cut: educational and public service-type films can all find a market, even if their profit is not enormous.

Most countries have an arts council with a role to propagate culture, which can include documentary as an art form. Sometimes arts councils, unlike most other foundations, will take distribution rights as a condition of funding. Private- and government-funded foundations in the US tend not to take rights, although broadcasters and ITVS/PBS-funded organizations will do so. Grant-funding bodies place an emphasis on the full lifespan of the film, from research through to eventual promotion and distribution, not just the end product. After all, funding organizations want their projects to be viewed by as many people as possible.

The world of production finance often appears to be a merry-go-round of chicken and egg demands, with one investor not wanting to commit until there is proof that another, or several players from the trade, are also on board. For instance, with lottery funding in various countries, the producer may be required to provide proof of existing funding from other recognized sources and will probably have to supply a budget and schedule. There are sometimes limits to the percentage of the total budget that such organizations will contribute – typically, it can vary from 10 per cent to 50 per cent.

Filmmakers need to become well informed about the organization, especially why, how and by whom it was created. I recently attended a presentation by the person in charge of grant aid for a private foundation. She devoted a substantial amount of time to explaining the heritage which underwrites current policy. The values of the founder are likely to be carried through to this day. The charters of foundations usually provide a mission statement; details of projects already funded give an indication of the kind of work that is supported. For instance the Paul Robeson Fund wants politically progressive, grass roots, activist projects (Barbash & Taylor, 1997: 295).

Certain categories of documentary, such as critical, investigative or political films, are often underrepresented. Yet this in itself may be a shortfall that organizations will want to address in the future: it is worth investigating any possible forthcoming change in emphasis or policy. 'It is the politically and personally challenging analyses of recent historical and current events that are hard to explain across cultures. These are the documentaries that create the most controversy' (Ellis & McLane 2005: 330).

The grant-aided sector has become seriously underfunded, especially in the United States and politically 'engaged' documentary has suffered what amounts to a 'kulturkampf' (Zimmerman, 2000). *Rosie the Riveter*, for instance, was funded by the National Endowment for the Humanities, but soon after it came out, director Connie Field stated that funding for the political documentary was under threat: 'The only way is to pick up dribs and drabs everywhere – that's one of the reasons why "Rosie" took over four years' (Johnston, 1981: 21). Elements of the 'documentary economy' have a notable influence on what gets made and is screened, and this in turn affects documentary's terms of engagement with the audience.

However, there is still interest in serious and committed projects in some countries, although styles of approach have changed. Sometimes it is possible to approach the same organization for production funding following development funding. As the field is so competitive, a good trailer is important, although in the United States, major funders receive huge numbers of trailers and tend only to watch the early part. Another aspect requiring research relates to the fact that in the US there are only a handful of foundations who fund either US-generated projects filming abroad, or foreign-generated films shooting in the US.

Outside the US, Canada has a strong documentary tradition, backed by government funding, and is active within the international field of co-production. Producers sometimes pitch in with their projects for co-productions during presentations organized at a large number of annual documentary pitching events such as Hot Docs and the Toronto Documentary Forum. The number of conferences on offer increases every year, and now includes events for specialist producers of history, science and wildlife documentaries.

The European Union has traditionally supported financial partnerships in an attempt to encourage documentary production as an expression of cultural identity, and similar approaches have existed in other countries, such as Canada, where the maintenance of cultural diversity is also treasured. Policy initiatives to support documentary often face a dual and potentially conflicting imperative: to achieve business success whilst preserving national or regional identity. The potential for a strong European media production industry is certainly supported by the numbers; a survey of documentary programming carried out as early as 1993 indicated that 20,000 hours had been produced and transmitted, but that 10,000 companies were competing for this business (Kilborn & Izod, 1997: 178).

In some parts of the world, national, regional and even continent-wide funding bodies (such as the EU) have policies on language and specific cultural requirements for their territories which can involve residential qualification, employment of local personnel and/or facilities. The sums available may not be very substantial, as usually, funding is intended to come from a variety of sources. The amounts given to those who qualify and are successful with their bids are aimed at projects that express tastes and interests for local consumption, which means being seen to meet the needs of the regional or national market. In Germany, for instance, there has traditionally been a variety of federal and regional funds, but these are best accessed by national producers and tend to involve the use of German creative talent. Therefore a proportion of either the filming, or the post-production work, has to be carried out in the region supporting the finance scheme. The aim is to stimulate the local production base for employment and growth of the indigenous media industry. Many regional funds require that you live in the area.

Writing funding applications, proposals and treatments

Karl Nussbaum: *Thanatos and Eros: The Birth of the Holy Freak*

Nussbaum was willing to work with other people in another country to obtain funding. His experiences demonstrate the persistence, and also the hardship, that is involved.

Karl Nussbaum was on a trip to Hamburg, Germany when a friend in the KurzFilm Agency told him that the Cultural Board of Hamburg was looking for international artists to sponsor. He promptly began to compose a proposal for the grant.

> I basically thought of what I would want to shoot in Germany that I couldn't shoot in Brooklyn. I had been mulling over images and ideas for a while, but writing the proposal started to pull it together for me. It made me think, 'what does Europe, as a concept, mean to me?' There are stereotypes that Americans have: Europe as a romantic place to fall in love on vacation or honeymoon in, a place where all the old monster movies happened and a giant graveyard where wars had taken place. I wrote the proposal in twenty minutes – two pages – and turned it in. I promptly forgot about it. I have spent months writing proposals to large grant operations and Jewish groups, only to be rejected.
>
> Four months later I heard that I had received the grant and to come over for 2 months to live in a beautiful atelier, receive $1,000 a month and begin shooting. After my two months, along with my friend and associate producer, Ute Holli, we had organized about 3 days of shooting with a crew and cast. But I didn't have the money to get the film out of the lab. Someone encouraged me to apply for film funding from the city's film funding agency, Hamburg Filmforderung. I filled out the forms and prepared a budget with another German film friend. Then they told me they would only give me money if I had a German co-producer. My friend Ute had introduced me to a well-known producer in Hamburg. I went to him with my proposal and my earlier film. He read it and said he would work with me right there. We got the grant (about $28,000 US) and began work.
>
> It was a very difficult film to make and we ran out of money. Later, my co-producer, Peter Stockhaus, got another grant from the Westphalia FilmForderung for post-production and promotion use. My Director of Production, Claus Bosch dos Santos, pulled in all kinds of favors from equipment houses and studios so we could make the film on the cheap. My post-production supervisor and technical chief, Matthias Neumann, also became a co-producer, pulling in deals, equipment and favors to finish the film. I spent a total of 6 years working on it and had to put my own money into it, including a remix in America. I also pulled in favors from friends at MTV and cut a deal with a friend at a sound house and at another dubbing facility. All told, I believe we spent $40,000 for a 60 minute film.
>
> Ultimately, making a low budget, independent art film is extremely hard – having to organize and persuade hundreds of strangers to help you make your crazy film. At the end of the project I would find myself sleeping on the floor of the editing studio and living off of bananas and peanut butter just to finish the film. I worked moving furniture during the day to be able to pay for tape stock and would stay all night in the studio and ride my bicycle back in the middle of the night, through the freezing snow just to keep editing. I was poor and desperate, but I got the film done. (author interview, 2005)

Extracts from written presentation of Thanatos and Eros *for fundraising:*

A 30 minute, 35mm, experimental documentary, made of collaged bits of 35mm, 16mm, and super-8 film, slides, Hi-8 and digital video; fragments of old movie dialog, recorded phone conversations, original music, metaphoric scientific and religious stories, and autobiographic voice over. The film begins with a sync-sound scene, followed by several silent narrative vignettes that dissolve into abstract images of the character's thoughts and unspeakable feelings. Visually, these sections are a densely layered series of painterly images dissolving over simple film loops, with pieces of documentary video footage woven in.

> The film concerns itself with how the second generation unconsciously inherits the emotions of the Holocaust survivor; how the dreams and lost goals of the dead relatives have been placed on the first born child after the Shoah. What a child learns about love relationships in a house of ghosts and contradictions. What kind of myths the children . . . create to understand the strange emotional environment they're growing up in.
>
> The Holocaust is a real horror story and as the narrator, I go from a child viewing the Holocaust as an artificial monster movie, to living in Germany as an adult, documenting today's reality and its people; from searching for romantic love as salvation to eventually finding self reliance and peace through friendships and healing a family. I am working with personal stories and visual diaries to make an overwhelming experience personal, and to bring those feelings to a younger audience.
>
> Nussbaum also wrote a synopsis, a section on style and technique and a section entitled 'background and genre reference'.

The key creative components in documentary planning are the proposal and treatment: both are generally sales documents to obtain funding. 'I hate writing proposals', Franny Armstrong admitted to me (author interview, 2005). However, the documentary writer usually has to write something. Generally, with promotional material it is useful to have ready a one-sentence summary of the project, aimed at attracting attention, as well as a more detailed written presentation. The proposal approximates to the sort of one-liner that television listings magazines carry; the treatment can come in various degrees of detail. What Hollywood calls 'high' and 'low' concepts always require a 'USP' – unique selling point – and simple categorization makes life easier for people who need a quick take on the essence.

Obviously, the information supplied by the funding organization needs to be studied carefully. Application forms will have sections for the proposal or summary, treatment, budget and schedule. They require information concerning how the money will be spent, distribution plans and examples of previous work, although they will probably only view a few minutes of it. Grant proposals can become detailed – *Rosie the Riveter* extended to 40 pages – but this is mostly work that will have to be done anyway sooner or later.

Lateral thinkers need to consider ways that their concept can be angled to fit a particular funding opportunity. To be successful, an applicant has to construct a robust argument about the importance of the project and why it should be made. In addition, some thought needs to be given to the considerations and agenda of the people providing the money – what do they want to get out of it? Even the best documentary makers have received lots of rejections; in a competitive field this is par for the course. Feedback from the sponsor about ways in which the project could be improved, or suggestions about other organizations to contact, is useful. Obviously, the process of writing-up a subject, rewriting it to fit various funding criteria, and filling in applications, is a time-consuming job in itself, which requires persistence as well as the ability to convince others that they need to support the project. The shelf life of the idea must be long enough to survive a protracted timescale. A short sell-by date for a documentary project makes it commercially untenable.

The sort of proposals required by US federal grant funds, for example, effectively demand all the same elements that would appear in a treatment. The two words 'proposal' and 'treatment' can have different meanings in different contexts, which can be confusing. With grant applications, the word 'proposal' is used to mean a fully costed and detailed offer of a project, which will include key players in the production team and also a descriptive, creative document, outlining how the documentary will come across to the audience, which elsewhere would be referred to as a 'treatment'. Both proposal and treatment need to address filmmaker intent.

A well-written proposal, indicating the filmmaker's lines of enquiry, will convey efficiency, professionalism and imagination, all of which are required in a competitive environment. Furthermore, the act of writing ideas down in order to share them with other people can provide a way of testing and improving their viability. Funders need to be convinced about how the documentary producer will make the project interesting. They will also want to be assured that detailed thought has been devoted to selecting the right examples, naming the right people and choosing the appropriate locations and examples to be filmed. Points such as how to use participants, methods of visual illustration, different sorts of sounds, archive film, or possible reconstruction will all need to be addressed. With the latter, actors can be expensive. Is there a performance or demonstration to film? Are graphics needed for presentation?

William Raban: *Thames Film*

Raban's proposal was written in an inspirational way.

The filmmaker applied to Britain's Arts Council for funding to support the production of *Thames Film*. He submitted a 20-page document as his proposal for a 26-minute documentary, all original shooting, with no archive footage, although this changed later. He is very skilful at articulating accurately and fluently in writing what he intends to illustrate through his sound and pictures using the medium of film.

In the document Raban lists all the research and angles that he has investigated and uses key phrases that indicate the thoroughness and rigour of his thinking, such as,

> The river fills from the sea to a height of seven metres. The water is endlessly travelling, making as much as twenty miles in one six hour tide. The direction and rate of flow of the tide can be incorporated to move the camera, lending rhythm, speed and duration to the visual scan. Extraordinarily, the Thames flood tide is stronger than the ebb, so this might suggest an overall movement away from the sea converging on the centre. (Raban, proposal to the Arts Council, 1984)

Raban received approximately £5,000 from the Arts Council. He shot three-quarters of the film, then applied for more by producing a promotional leaflet about the project and showing some of the rushes. He successfully procured a further £4,000. Knowledge of industry structures and independent filmmakers' circles helped his efforts to obtain funding. 'My earlier involvement in the London Film Cooperative made me realize how important exhibition and distribution are as part of the production equation' (author interview, 2005). In these pre-Internet days he had also established a bulletin called *Filmmakers' Europe*, that listed all the principal venues in Europe and North America where filmmakers could exhibit their work and exchange information.

Industrial and corporate commissions: usage and treatments

Traditionally, the skills of filmmakers have always been used by organizations with a message to communicate, and some of the best documentaries have been public-service films full of creativity and subtlety, giving scope to the filmmaker's inventiveness. Budget finance is allocated when the project is decided upon, then production companies are engaged to make the idea into a reality, according to a brief from the sponsors. The sponsor will want to ensure that the corporate message, or at least the organization's culture, is not infringed.

Sponsored or industrial films are a fast growing employment area for filmmakers, who cover areas such as recruitment and training, teaching and advising, demonstrating a product or promoting a service, building an image and raising funds (Rosenthal, 1996: 260). For instance, the classic Second World War government information or documentary 'orientation' series *Why We Fight* (1942–5), supervised by Frank Capra, was designed to give American recruits to the armed forces a clear understanding of the rationale for their participation in the Second World War.

Although industrial films use the same techniques as other documentaries – location filming, real people, commentary and natural sound – a corporate video is seldom intended to be completely stand alone. The circumstances in which it will be viewed and used will underwrite the entire production process: so, for instance, a film for an exhibition stand with a passing clientele, or a museum video that complements other installations, can still be documentary, but may well have a different style or structure to a film that is shown to a captive audience in a classroom, where the follow-up activities will be highly prescriptive. Videos in training situations usually act as a springboard for further audience activities or discussion.

The perceived needs of an audience, which need to be considered when writing a treatment or proposal, are well illustrated by the example of a corporate training film for a big hotel chain that I once made. The company had establishments throughout Great Britain, all differing in architectural style and age. The management decided to go to considerable trouble in order to standardize interior decor by categorizing all of the hotels into four broad groups. Hotels in each group were all to have the same interior design – right down to identical wallpaper, paintwork and furniture, allowing for rationalization in purchasing policy and maintenance. Previously, individual managers had been free to select decor according to their own individual taste. Understandably, they valued their independence and liked to do things their own way. Our job as filmmakers was to persuade them that standardization was acceptable. The audience for the video therefore consisted of every hotel manager in the country, brought together for a conference. The audience needed to walk away afterwards feeling enthusiastic for the changes afoot. 'You cannot receive an industrial film passively. If you do, it's a failure' (Rosenthal, 1996: 259).

Whereas the documentation necessary for grant applications tends to be lengthy, sponsors generally like proposals to be short. At the same time, the treatment of the idea has to provide enough originality of approach to prevent these very same people from saying that the concept is old hat. Ideally, as with any other documentary pitch, the main idea that the viewer should be left with, should be capable of communication within a single sentence.

Jane Chapman: *It's Your Choice*

Formulating a corporate pitch

This project, which won 'Best Careers Information Film' at the New York International Film Festival, was pitched as 'real people in real life situations', the essence of documentary. By asking lots of questions of the sponsor, as the writer I also became the salesperson, with a mission to find the main arguments to support the client's message, and incorporate them in to the script. This does not mean that one can't be imaginative or unorthodox. The creativity comes in finding ways to do this, which will depend on audience and usage. *It's Your Choice* came with a booklet, for use by careers teachers to screen to 16-year-olds after they had taken their national exams and were facing a decision about what to do next. The brief stated that the aim was 'to encourage pupils to think positively about their future and to seek more information and advice'.

In the film we had to present a range of career options: either to leave school for work or further training, to stay on to improve their exam results with retakes, to start a further vocational or training qualification (e.g. BTEC), or to take the next level of academic qualifications ('A' levels) and to go on from there to university. Analysis of the needs of a specific sector of the educational market prompted the decision to make the film. The approach was to present unbiased information to these young people about the available choices, reflected in the title *It's Your Choice*. Clearly the film would need a form and style of representation with which young people could empathize.

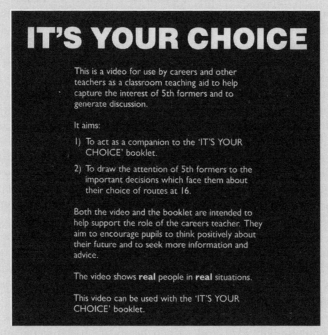

Aspects of the proposal for *It's Your Choice* became a feature in subsequent marketing

Treatment: It's Your Choice

Introduction: a 20-minute informational film entitled *It's Your Choice*, to be used by careers teachers in schools.

1   Aim: to outline the post-16-years educational/training choices that are available to young people.
2   Background: in the UK too many young people are leaving school at 16, when they could gain further qualifications or education and/or training. Youth unemployment is a problem in certain parts of the country, and access to better information about the range of alternatives to the 'dole' is needed.
3   Focus: equal weight is given to four alternative options, without any attempt to favour one over the others. The viewer is provided with coverage of each option, and can then make up their own mind.
4   Style/format: the film progresses through each choice, one at a time, represented in each case by a young person, whom the camera follows, telling their own story. As we enter into the educational worlds of the key characters, the style will be young and informal, in line with the audience profile.
5   Technique: narration will be kept to a minimum in order to allow the participants to tell their own stories. Their narrative is about how they arrived at the path that they are now on educationally. A young female narrator's voice will only be used briefly, to top and tail the film. The pace will be quite fast and lively as the camera follows them, supplemented by modern music and informational moving captions.
6   Viewpoint: there will be no value judgements on the quality of options so that each choice is given even treatment. This way we aim to avoid preferences, leaving the viewer to decide, therefore making no suggestion of social and/or educational hierarchy. This editorial approach is audience empowering, as the title of the film suggests.

Although our company was successful in winning the competitive tender, the challenges that were to emerge in translating the above proposal into an effective documentary short film raised issues of balance and representation in addition to certain stylistic requirements in order to cater for the intended audience.

Reimbursing through sales or 'acquisitions' and distribution funding

Even for smaller budgets with a more limited market, a specialist distributor will probably still be needed. If this is a condition of funding, or if the documentary maker wants to plan ahead for future revenue from the film, then such factors have to be considered in advance of filming. An understanding of distribution is also an essential part of any study of markets. Distribution considerations are based on the issue of rights, which in turn are likely to be linked to funding strategies and the conditions imposed by financiers, who could specify owner-ship of the right to exploit the product.

Whereas a commission to make a film means that the funder can call the tune, with a completed production, it is different. Then access to broadcasters means dealing with a different set of people – 'buyers', who are more approachable, from my experience, and won't dictate content or style, because they can only make a decision based on the completed product in front of them. Most documentary producers who retain the distribution rights will try to recoup production expenditure through aftersales, which is dealt with in the final chapter.

Therefore the main advantage of the acquisition/sales route, which we also took with our first Chapman Clarke Films series *Feeling for France* (mentioned earlier in this chapter), is that the filmmakers have more freedom to make the project as they want to do it. The plus point is the exposure of the film if it is broadcast, which in this case included television stations in Britain, the US, the Middle East and elsewhere. Nearly all the case studies in this book were made for independent distribution, but were later sold as acquisitions to television internationally. The disadvantage is that licence fees from selling a documentary are not high, so sales to television acquisition departments will probably only just cover money already spent, especially if interest rates for debts are taken into account and the sales happen over a protracted period.

If a documentary maker finds their own funding, he or she is in a stronger position to retain the rights and hence more control. For many producers, the ability to raise finance so that a project gets made is now as important a creative skill as making the product itself. Distributors have given me the following pieces of advice concerning artistic considerations about style, which will influence the whole production thereafter.

1   Decide in advance on a particular length, style and format that is fairly universal: for instance, a one-hour length (actually about 52 to 54 minutes, allowing for promos and advertising breaks).
2   Films with voice-over narration rather than sequences with lip sync dialogue are easier to sell to foreign-language markets, as another version can be made by simply changing the voice-over track, whilst the tracks for music and sound effects (M and E) can remain the same.
3   Conversely, lip sync such as presenter pieces to camera, involves either dubbing or subtitles, which adds to expense.
4   Finally, the subject must have a shelf life and not date too soon (unless it is current affairs) to enable maximum sales to be achieved. This can take two years or more. The increase in international distribution has created business opportunities for DVDs, which can offer an extension of shelf life within established political, educational and cultural networks.

If a project suits an existing programme strand, some television stations may commit to a 'pre-sales agreement' whereby they advance money at an early stage in order to buy into the production so that they can screen it later. Similarly, a distributor can secure rights for the future product by agreeing an 'advance against distribution', that is, up-front money that will be deducted later from back-end sales. However, a project has to be very 'hot', or a filmmaker's reputation exceedingly high, to benefit from such early support.

Cinema challenges

Many art-house cinema or film club audiences will be better informed and more motivated towards viewing than an easily distracted TV channel zapper. The overcrowded, competitive broadcast marketplace reduces the potential impact of individual documentaries, whereas a smaller theatric audience may consist of a 'special interest' community group or campaign; this kind of audience will also be politically aware and committed, with a greater appreciation of technique, filmmaker intention and style than most other audiences. Discussion after the screening can then have a real influence on the thinking of the filmmaker for the future.

Thus, a cinema audience can appreciate a documentary with a slower pace because they are less likely to leave their seats and walk out! Also the big screen and Dolby 'surround sound' allow the audience to become fully immersed in the filmic experience. However, some argue that, more positively, the recent enthusiasm of US cinema audiences for documentary 'lies in the fact that commercial television so embraced "reality" shows like MTV's *Real World*, *Survivor*, *Big Brother* and on downward to *Extreme Makeover*, that a ready-made audience accepted the conventions of Michael Moore and other first person documentarians as ordinary entertainment' (Ellis & McLane, 2005: 333).

Although Moore achieved a major distribution deal for *Roger and Me* with Warner Brothers, who paid more than $3 million as an advance against worldwide rights (Cohan & Crowdus, 1990: 25), most independent cinema documentaries have struggled. It is the success stories that have led to discussion of documentary's cinema renaissance. Certainly, audiences expect to pay to see something that is not available on television, and they will need to feel that the film is a unique cinema-going 'event', which can be talked about later. Therefore, despite some remarkable success stories, theatric distribution remains a difficult nut to crack. In production and budgetary terms, cinema release needs to be planned for; shooting for a feature documentary will probably be on high definition video (HDV) or 35 mm film with digital editing. Lighting will need to be greater and quality will be a prime consideration for the big screen. A separate distributor may be required for specialist 'theatric' distribution as opposed to television sales, in which case the producer should separate out the rights for discrete negotiations.

Analysing the broadcast scene

'The greatest gift to the United States would be the complete destruction of television in its present state' (Emile de Antonio in 1983; in Kellner & Streible, 2000: 125). In the past, some observers have seen a stark polarization between two main choices for the documentary maker. The first involves creativity for those who go it alone, eventually projecting themselves, as de Antonio did (although his films were shown on European television), within the film festival and theatric market with screenings at venues such as art-house cinemas and film clubs. The second involves compromise and loss of artistic individuality for those who choose to sell their souls in advance to the commercialism of broadcasters for a commission, the gateway to millions of viewers.

This received wisdom contains more than a grain of truth: the realities of professional life for producers who depend on commissions to earn a wage are sometimes grim. The evidence presented in this chapter suggests that documentary makers in the broadcast and corporate sectors, who work on a commissioning basis, all face a requirement to be particularly well focused on scheduling, budgets and perception of audience. The hallmark of working for a contract is the need for creative compromise in order to survive. Flexibility is the name of the game, in the face of institutional constraints and severe competition.

Sometimes there is convergence between the two camps, when grant-funded films sell as a finished product to television, for instance. Despite this discernible crossover, the political economy of the television industry has always impacted on the way that documentary is made for each sector. Television techniques are all-pervasive, also influencing documentary production styles in the non-broadcast industrial sector. This is illustrated by factual television's drive towards entertainment, which has also influenced documentary in an on-going process of crossover. Generally, there has been a reduction in funding for work entailing serious or investigative research, although the latter is now easier from a practical standpoint due to micro equipment, such as hidden cameras. 'This [reduction in funding for serious work] has partly followed from narrowing strategies of commissioning, scheduling and/or distribution, which are themselves the consequence of the increased use of the "market" rather than the "public" frame for thinking about audio-visual production' (Rosenthal & Corner, 2005: 2). In the case of television, the development of the medium has been critical. Audience use of recording (DVD and video) and of channel hopping makes life more difficult for broadcast schedulers. The latter means that attention must be given to the nature and length of every shot if audience boredom is to be avoided. This 'soundbite' culture has an inhibiting influence on documentary production.

In terms of what this means for potential commissions, there is a requirement to adapt to the terms of the television 'package', which consists of channel, slot and target audience as well as method of presentation for the pitch. Multichannel broadcasting – a more relatively recent phenomenon outside the United States – has challenged the Reithian (the all-powerful Reith was the first Director General of the BBC) concept of the general audience, and in the process led to changes in scheduling and commissioning policies. Although there are now specialist factual channels, they often rely on bought-in products and only pay small acquisition fees. 'Narrowcasting', or the provision of programming for a smaller and smaller segment of the public audience, has meant more special-interest outlets, but also severe competition. This comes at the expense of 'a reduced degree of editorial freedom and a loss of communicative confidence in the address to a specific audience' (Rosenthal & Corner, 2005: 4).

There is also a content element that poses a dilemma. In television, if either the producer or the broadcaster (or both) want revenue from international sales, then the inclination is to target as many sectors of the market as possible in order to maximize sales income. As far as the filmmaker who wants to operate within this market is concerned, the challenge is therefore, 'to produce documentaries that are identifiably rooted in a particular time and place and at the same time have the capacity to speak to a much wider audience' (Kilborn & Izod, 1997: 179).

The temptation is for the producer to avoid risk by opting for a subject that is inoffensive and will attract a wide audience. Sometimes cultural specificity can be sacrificed at the altar of universal blandness. As filmmaker Peter Watkins said: 'The point that I keep trying to hammer home these days is not only that the ideas on TV are conservative, but that the *form* with which they're presented . . . diffuses them' (MacDonald, 1992: 411). Therefore, worldwide, in broadcast television, assumptions about audiences inform scheduling decisions as well as promotion of programmes. Market research with its profiling and targeting is translated by decision makers into future actions that influence direction and funding. This process is common practice in advertising and commercial television, but public-service broadcasters are equally sensitive to such considerations (Chapman, 2005: 437–45). Documentary is not immune.

As an independent producer, I once attended a meeting where the local commercial broadcaster briefed aspiring programme suppliers before they submitted ideas for a commission by telling them the details of a recent market survey of afternoon viewers. Revelations such as female consumer attitudes towards gymnasium usage, supermarket shopping and newspaper readership were supposed to inform our creative formulation of new projects that were to be pitched competitively for certain broadcast slots. Such factors can surface every day in a producer's negotiations with broadcasters who request certain approaches. They also influence the budget available and the perceived audience that a producer is expected to target.

Traditionally, the female and daytime television audience has been associated with 'soft' subjects. Often appearing in the form of reality television, these have proven their ability to withstand competition from mainstream entertainment shows on other channels. 'It sometimes seems that every boundary of documentary ethics has been crossed by reality TV' (Ellis & McLane, 2005: 333). Also, the tendency is to trawl the programming of other channels in a quest for successful models – then to clone them.

Where decisions about style and approach are concerned, it is worth bearing in mind that today's audiences are 'documentary savvy' and sophisticated in their appreciation, and that this can be a positive. For instance, it is possible to use irony in voice-over which represents shared understanding by both maker and audience, although what works in one country does not necessarily work in another. Comedy works on shared mutual recognition, which leads to audience appreciation and amusement. For our one-hour television documentary *Forever England*, the Carlton Television commissioning editor suggested that as reporter, my commentary should be in an ironic style, 'a female version of Clive James'. Although British and Australian audiences are accustomed to his observational wit, he is not well known in the United States.

What all television fiction – and non-fiction – series have in common is that they have been subject to a rigorous process of technical and editorial compromise in order to fit the bill. Therefore producing a film commissioned by a broadcaster effectively means making a tailor-made product. From the broadcaster's point of view, the cost of generating their own products is always going to be more than the price of buying in ready-made programmes. The advantage of commissioning their own films is that they can be made with a house style, made to measure and cater for the needs of the perceived audience. Those producers who choose to work for television have to accept many prescriptions, procedural rules, intervention and a high level of accountability. Hence the intricate procedures to ensure creative and economic control that reinforce the old adage, 'he who pays the piper calls the tune'. Producers are subject to intense scrutiny of budgets, production schedules and – more controversially – potential advertiser as well as consumer appeal.

In a climate where broadcasters play safe on ratings, documentaries which entail extensive preliminary research, or where the final outcome of the entire filming exercise may be uncertain, are also less likely to be commissioned (Kilborn & Izod, 1997: 185). There are, of course, content implications here: social concerns, for instance, will probably be presented in an accessible format, rather than an investigative form. Commissioners by and large seek to marry creative innovations to broad audience appeal, preferably with international sales potential and/or possibilities of 'secondary' exploitation such as DVD, website and digital streaming. If a broadcaster or other funding organization finances a project 100 per cent, they will probably claim the right to sales – at least for a limited period of three years. Broadcasters, cognizant of the need for brand identity to win viewers, have created 'strands' for factual programming, that is, on-going series with a clear identity in terms of the house style, length and category of film that are transmitted; Britain's *Cutting Edge* and *Panorama* are veteran examples, as is the PBS series *Nova*. Franny Armstrong repackaged *Drowned Out* for the PBS strand *Wideangle*.

From time to time broadcasters such as PBS in the United States announce a new series title, or theme, and invite producers to pitch in for grants to make individual films; competition is huge. The Corporation for Public Broadcasting looks at proposals. The Independent Television Service (ITVS) funds promotion and production of independent programmes for public broadcasting markets, with an annual call for proposals, as well as for some specific series. ITVS have a fund for non-US producers aiming at PBS, whereby they will manage programmes to completion, distribute, promote and engage communities through outreach and education (Search & McCarthy, 2005: 12). Documentary makers may well succeed in fitting a particular story to a suitable outlet, but usually adjustments will be required.

Jumping hurdles for a television commission

There tend to be two hurdles to jump: firstly to persuade a producer or production company, if the documentary maker is not already part of one, to pitch a project for a production contract: Whether or not a production company takes on a particular project will depend on their assessment of whether or not they can successfully raise the funding to make it. This in turn depends on contacts, workload, track record, development portfolio and their general assessment of the likelihood of success given the openings within the market that are available to them. Secondly, to persuade the commissioning editor to fund the project.

This becomes an enormously difficult game of Russian roulette because of competition from others pitching in, and the unpredictability of the decision makers. The level of compromise at the documentary development stage will vary according to filmmaker outlook, aspirations, financial situation, and also certain practical considerations such as how near or far away he or she is from concluding a firm arrangement, or 'closing the deal'.

What broadcasters require is track record, and without it potential producers and independent production companies find it almost impossible to obtain access to a commissioner. In this scenario, the aspiring documentary maker without much experience, who approaches a production company with an idea, needs to find out more about the potential relationship. They need to be absolutely clear about the role they will have if the project is commissioned, the financial benefits that will accrue and what will happen if the project is *not* commissioned, in terms of the ownership of the idea reverting back to the originator. Communication about timing and intentions is crucial.

The documentary maker who works for television is forced into an awareness that individual films are only part of a bigger audience-winning package which is compiled by the schedulers. A further strategy adopted by broadcasters to combat channel hopping and pre-timed video/DVD recording is to attract the public's attention for a whole evening or daytime session of viewing: so documentarists need to avoid thinking about their film in isolation. The same applies in distribution, where trading between broadcasters and distributors is often conducted by 'bulk buying'. The whole process of trying to obtain a commission is therefore challenging and frustrating. Television commissioning editors are not the easiest of people to deal with: 'they have the whole world chasing after them, they have something that everybody wants, so they can also exercise the control that goes with it', as filmmaker Nancy Platt told me (author interview, 2005). Longer-running series can offer the producer more financial security in his or her struggle for survival of the fittest.

> Documentary splits into separate camps: at one extreme are the big production houses. These groups are compelled to seek economies of scale and are pulled towards series production, where overheads can be spread across more screen hours, but where the film maker's individuality is inevitably submerged. At the opposite end of the spectrum is the small producer who thinks in terms of individual artistic production. (Chanan, 1993: 40)

Commissioners have their own procedural requirements for proposals – after all, if they are going to spend a lot of money, they will expect the project to be well crafted, and delivered on time, to budget. For broadcaster commissions, the producer needs to provide an outline which gives the subject and the way it is to be approached, plus suggested length, possible slot, and details of the track record of the proposed producer. The filmmaker always has to be ready to answer follow-up queries, such as a request for further information on content, and must be aware of what further work is necessary. Decision makers like to be able to envisage the completed film in their heads before committing money – and a good treatment which details filmic style will allow them to do so. The proposal and treatment are sales documents, used to obtain a commission.

In the United States, the success of such a pitch meeting carries a lot of weight for gaining a commission. Therefore American producers spend time preparing for this crucial face-to-face encounter. As too many people are competing for the attention of commissioners, who are busy people, they tend to react by giving individuals only a short time. With one brief shot, it is necessary to grab their butterfly attention using a few well chosen sentences: elaboration may come later. 'I believe the pitch is the foundation of your film. You need a 20 second pitch, a one minute pitch and a two minute pitch depending on who you're talking to. People make decisions on you in less than 60 seconds, so that old adage "Gone in 60 Seconds" can work against documentary filmmakers who are not succinct' (Carole Dean, in Search & McCarthy, 2005: 166).

Just because one editor may reject a project does not necessarily mean that it is no good; it just may not fit the style of the department, or series. The timing may be wrong, or there may be other behind the scenes considerations that the documentary maker cannot influence. For 14 years as an independent producer, I spent a large amount of my time developing ideas to pitch to British broad-casters: only about 1 in 10, or sometimes 1 in 20, was accepted. The independent producer or the freelancer have to bounce back and try again, maybe elsewhere, if they are to pay the rent or employ other people! It was a commissioning editor himself who pointed out to me, after I had casually presented him with a 'back of the envelope' sketch of an idea: 'Jane, do you realize that these days, attention-seeking promotion and slick presentations have become the industry norm? Some companies have entire departments that spend their whole time devising ideas to present in a glossy format to us.' The competitive environment within television programming has led documentarists and others to spend time working on their skills and techniques for pitching to commis-sioning editors.

The harsh reality of brutal competition within broadcast commissioning has also led to painful self-editing, as freelancer Dermot O'Donovan explains:

> For every ten bright ideas I have in the bath, or hear in conversation in the pub, only one stands up to scrutiny in the cold light of day and makes the 'ideas' list. For every ten on the list, initial research into resources, audiences etc. indicates that only one is worth serious investment in time and energy to work up and submit to a particular broadcaster at a particular time. For every ten submitted proposals, only one survives the trials of focus groups, available transmission slots and finance, and is commissioned in the end. So, the relationship between 'Eureka!' and transmission is 1 : 1000!! Maybe if I took cold baths instead? (author interview, 2005)

Nevertheless, commissioning editors are buyers who want to buy. They don't want to reject everything. Serious players in the market tend to research what commissioners want and try to provide it. They know the person's name, spell it correctly and find out more about them. Their background research includes some information about their slot and why it is the best place for a specific project. They check channel websites, attend open days and industry confer-ences. Above all, they watch the commissioner's programmes and the documen-taries that act as competition to the commissioner.

Apart from the general issue of level of compromise that a producer is willing to accept with a broadcast commission, the potential success of a commission is often influenced by factors of timing in a more pressurized way than that faced by a self-financed film. Sometimes it will not be possible to cover certain events as planned because the broadcaster's timing may well mean that the event is over before the contract is signed. In the past, for a 25-minute regional documentary, I have been given only two weeks for research, a one-week shoot and ten days for post-production, because the broadcaster needed to move quickly, and because the budget was modest.

A further issue with the question of timing arises with the delay for a response to the pitch. Although most broadcasters will have a policy on replying – or at least acknowledging proposals within a certain timeframe – they also tend to have their own procedural milestones and schedules at various points in the year. So, if the producer misses the boat in one year, he or she has to wait another year for the relevant dates to come around. Commissioners' budgets are also committed over a year-long period. Of course, current affairs documentary slots have special commissioning procedures that are faster and more reactive; in this case, decision making has to be quicker – but timing is still the essence.

When selecting the documentary subject, timing can become a double-edged sword. On the one hand it can provide a good excuse to revisit a topic or event 'ten years on' or on, say, the fiftieth anniversary; on the other hand the documentary maker is locked in to a timeframe by the forthcoming event. On many occasions I have been made to realize that the forward planning of commissioning editors is not the same as my timing for development. Then I have been faced with the decision either to take the idea elsewhere or to wait and meet the agenda of the broadcaster who seems the most appropriate for that particular theme. Changes in timing can necessitate alterations to content.

Copyright and stealing of ideas

Frequently commissioning editors receive a number of proposals on the same subject, which may have been prompted by news coverage. Very few ideas are truly original. Therefore, if a theme is repeatedly in the news – like terrorism, for instance – lots of people are often thinking about angles on the same issue at the same time. After all, subject matter for documentaries is based on reality, which by definition is already in the public domain. Almost every writer claims to be a victim of an idea being copied, or 'stolen', but the practice is not illegal and is not covered by copyright law.

In general copyright only exists when a work has been recorded, in writing or on tape (or other formats). Although some people lodge a copy of their treatment or script with a bank or lawyer, the only effect this has is to register the date that the work is in circulation. In the United States proposals and treatments can be registered with the US Copyright Registration Office at the Library of Congress in Washington. In the United Kingdom, if the producer is a member of PACT, they have a script registration service. But this will not prove infringement of copyright by a similar idea. There is no intrinsic or commercial value in undeveloped ideas. If copyright only exists in a completed work or one that has already been produced in some tangible form, how can it be defined? 'Copyright is ownership of property – intellectual property – and only the owner of the property is entitled to copy it, issue copies to the public, perform, show or play it in public, broadcast it or adapt it' (Viljoen, 1997: 7). An idea is less likely to be stolen if the proposal contains as many specific details, thoughts about style and original plans as possible. These act as identifying examples of the producer's creative input, hence ownership. The terms of contracts for projects where the producer has developed the content sufficiently to qualify for copyright or other legal protection differ from the terms stipulated in a situation where a broadcaster, for instance, has suggested the content to a producer.

Even formats which are treated like well developed ideas have no legal copyright. On one occasion my company received development funding from Britain's Channel 4 for a documentary series with a 'format', which I called *Housebusters*. The concept involved people uncovering the hidden history and stories attached to their homes. Unfortunately the broadcaster requested that I go for co-production with various regional commercial (ITV) channels so that the series would cover different parts of the country, but achieving agreement (and therefore money) was difficult and time-consuming. The following year the BBC brought out a long-running series with a similar, but not identical, concept. On this occasion, I had never even talked to the BBC. We did not take any legal action. Of course, the number of potential permutations on any one subject is enormous. If there are any differences in the finished product, nothing can be done, and there have been a number of court cases that proved this to be the case. Before considering a proposal, most stations in the United States ask producers to sign an agreement acknowledging that they will have no redress if something is made similar to their idea. Letters of acknowledgement by broadcasters on receipt of a proposal in the UK also carry a 'health warning' about their having no liability to the producer, but there is a chance that such a disclaimer could be disproved in court, if there was proof that the broadcaster had infringed copyright.

When a producer wishes to incorporate resources such as photos, illustrations or video found on the Internet into the eventual film, he or she must obtain the original material from the copyright owner and clear the rights before the final documentary can be distributed and exhibited. Problems can arise when the source has been copied or used on several different sites, and they may well claim that it is copyright free, but unless the authors created the material themselves, they may well not have permission to use it. Official sites are more likely to be reputable in this respect (Emm, 2002: 29, 148).

Sometimes a producer may want to adapt an existing literary or artistic work for the cinema or television, in which case he or she must make a specific agreement – usually for the copyright of the treatment to be assigned. During the course of production this preliminary document will be expanded by other copyright materials (recordings, etc.) to such an extent that it would not be practical to separate any copyright in the original treatment. The completed documentary will, of course, have ownership of copyright attached to it. If the producer is able to secure any material for a documentary with underlying rights or the participation of an important artist or presenter, then these become elements that make the project much safer legally.

Formulating a budgetary plan

Grant applications and also broadcast commissions tend to require full, detailed budgets. Broadcasters and sometimes other grant-aided financiers have their own extensive budgetary forms that producers are obliged to fill in. The budget needs to be as accurate as possible; miscalculations can lead to anxiety, even financial ruin, unrealistic expectations, practical difficulties in achieving what was intended, and disappointment.

Budgets serve to clarify the filmmaker's precise creative intentions when it comes to translating an idea into the reality of production. Serious money is at stake, and it would be irresponsible for funders to part with it without a rigorous procedure for applications. The worst possible outcome after all that work is that the application will be turned down, but the process of putting it together will have resulted in a sharp learning curve and tested the maker's commitment and ability to communicate the project. That is worthwhile project development. A budget plan, or at least a review of all likely costs, entails a full understanding of the production process and an awareness of the cost – in time and money – of film crews, special effects, graphics and editing. I am not giving specific average costs for individual elements such as film crews, as these vary from country to country and are often negotiable as an all-inclusive 'package' that includes labour and equipment.

1   Crews are usually budgeted per day. For an essay-style film, with original filming that is to be accompanied by voice-over and interviews, one day of filming can render up to five minutes of finished product, therefore a five-day shoot will be minimum allocation for a half-hour documentary. However, this is only a rule of thumb used for television budgeting.
2   Editors are usually costed per week, with a minimum period for off-line of two to three weeks for a 'standard' half-hour television documentary, with additional time for online, transfers, post-production dubbing and voice recording. Graphics are calculated as an all-in price for the job, according to how long it will take.
3   Writers are usually paid about 3 per cent of the budget, and directors about 12 per cent. With narrators, it will depend how famous they are. All of this tends to be open to negotiation, although the unions and guilds have price guidelines for minimum rates, which act as the benchmarks for broadcaster minimum rates.

It is advisable to complete all the deals – including royalty payments – before pre-production starts. Broadcasters will often encourage producers to negotiate 'buy-outs' with creative artists in order to avoid royalties and repeat fees. Individual prices can soon date, whereas the approach to formulating a budget is more generic.

The following elements need to be considered:

- research: travel, hotels, general expenses;
- shooting: crew, production manager;
- equipment: camera gear, lights, microphones, extras;
- location expenses during filming: travel, accommodation, food, vehicle hire;
- stock: tapes, discs, dubs;
- post-production costs: editor, equipment hire and room, other assistant staff, transfers for library and archive material, graphics such as titles, subtitles, credits, music transfers, recording studios;
- general admin costs: transcripts, translations, insurance, royalty payments, advertising, publicity, couriers, telephone/fax/e-mail, office rental;
- personnel: director, producer, writer, narrator, researcher, general assistants;
- company profit: contingencies.

Most of these elements will be necessary in some form or other, even if they aren't recognized as costs, because the producer doubles up on several different jobs, or works from home, or because there is free access to some sort of equipment. Identifying the above costs is the simple part of budgeting; measuring them in terms of how long they will be needed is more difficult. A prior awareness of possible pitfalls during production will demonstrate filmmaker competence, such as being able to identify that a particular requirement merits extra coverage in the budget because of a specific creative demand.

In terms of how choice of techniques influence a budget: real people doing things (as opposed to dramatic reconstructions) give more authenticity, credibility and are cheaper than actors. Graphics and animation for statistics and information are a useful tool, but require detailed costing. This in turn is only possible when creative content can be translated into a specific brief for those people involved in the production. An 'essay' format is simpler and quicker to make because it requires fewer filming days than a *cinéma vérité* approach, where you choose to capture a 'day in the life' of a number of key characters over a longer period. The latter will entail more filming days and a much higher shooting ratio than the former, as case studies reveal.

The budget, or lack of one, can influence both small and large issues; these can reoccur later, or sometimes be omnipresent throughout the production. Examples to bear in mind at the writing stage include:

1   Choice of locations. Travelling long distances between places not only takes time, but costs money. It will be more cost effective if the various places where shooting is planned are within easy reach of each location; it will be even cheaper it there is only one location – but then the content may not be so interesting.
2   Actors. Dialogue (synchronized sound) is slow to film and costs more than extras or walk-ons without speaking parts. Dramatizations can also incur cost with sets, props, extra lighting and crew, costumes and make-up. For documentaries it is best to keep the stylizations simple; any reconstructions should be modest at this stage.

3   Famous-name presenters can also be expensive. Budgetary constraints tend
    to mean that the number of filming days allocated to a television commission
    will be limited. The amount that presenters are paid usually means that they
    are only hired for part of that period; sometimes their contract will be limited
    to only a few days, or in the case of a one-off documentary, one day only.
    Therefore the presenter must be given a specific and restricted role that has
    to be planned in advance.
4   Special props. This may be equipment because of the nature of the shoot (e.g.
    aerial views by helicopter), special vehicles, location catering, computer
    graphics.
5   Complex editing. This could be for a number of reasons, such as a range of
    different archive sources in different formats for an historical subject, or the
    existence of a large amount of previously-shot footage to be integrated with
    new actuality.

If it is possible to negotiate the contract (because it is not a standard one), staged
payments will help filmmaker cash flow. A lawyer can advise, but media lawyers
are expensive. What a media lawyer usually will not be able to anticipate are
specific problems within the production process that influence the budget. The
prospects of a budgetary problem occurring which will challenge some aspect
of the creative approach are very high, and not confined to any one style of
production.

With television commissions, the budget usually comes later, after the editorial people have decided to go with a particular proposal/treatment. The budget
forms are used as the basis for negotiation with 'cost controllers', who work for
the broadcaster, with a brief to scrutinize producer budgetary calculations.
Broadcasters have their own systems for costing that involve figures for different
categories of documentary and how long they will take, given the style, locations
and length. Unfortunately, these calculations tend to remain fairly secret. In the
lucky event of development funding becoming available, there are a number of
elements that it can cover: rights payments, researcher fees and producer trips
for research, 'recess' for location, casting if actors are to be used, legal costs,
preparation of a full budget and schedule, office and administrative overheads
and a small amount of out-of-pocket expenses. Most organizations that fund
development take charge of the copyright of all the development materials until
full production starts, at which time rights are renegotiated in good faith. This
practice was first devised as a form of insurance against producers disappearing
with the development money!

From the creative point of view the impact on production process and method
is more important than the actual budgetary numbers, which can soon become
outdated. There are always content and stylistic implications caused by budgetary factors. For instance, in chapter 1, a television freelancer, Dermot O'Donovan,
recounts how he abandoned a plan for a drama documentary format in favour
of a more mainstream documentary style, as a result of discovering some old
footage that he could use. This find turned out to have budgetary implications
for him. The archive film was donated free of charge to the production by the
organization who were the subject of the film. This was obviously a financial

advantage to the broadcaster, Carlton Television, who funded the project, but as Dermot explains 'for me it meant budgetary cuts as lots of archive film would be used, with fewer shooting days' (author interview, 2005).

Conclusions

To a certain extent the choice of financial strategy depends on the nature of the project, the outlook and ambitions of the filmmaker for a project. Whatever the strategy, there are several common factors: first, time is money; second, expenditure needs to be reflected as far as possible in the quality of the final product. Meals for the producer won't show up on screen, but money spent on an experienced picture editor will; third, financial and creative factors are intrinsically connected, and difficult to separate out. Last, but not least, committed filmmakers are not deterred by lack of funding; if you have to make a film, you will find ways of doing it.

Arguably there is a need to question television's relationship to documentary, especially as it is not the only avenue for funding. 'We need to be brutally realistic about what television can do for documentaries these days. We need to remember that documentary filmmaking existed before television came along and we should wonder why we decided that this was the only place to make and show documentaries' (Search & McCarthy, 2005: 4). Despite the popularity of documentary, in the television context it is difficult not to agree with former television executive Leslie Woodhead, when he wrote in 2001 for the website <http://www. Docos.com> 'In a time when even the most public-spirited broadcasters seem frozen in the headlights of ratings and profits, the space for documentary to explore difficult issues in faraway places shrinks every year.' Generally, in the commissioning process, the scales are not even – commissioners always have the upper hand. I can remember being particularly amused by the acerbic truth of a cartoon that PACT once published in their in-house journal. It was a copy of an old lithograph, depicting a medieval knight on horseback who was visiting a village. At his feet are serfs kneeling in supplication, as his vassals. A caption had been added below the picture, 'A commissioning editor visits producers'.

The documentary maker who is also a 'jobbing' independent producer or freelancer has to be flexible. In essence, the compromises and the focus that are required for success with both television and corporate commissions represent a shared experience for all the producers who choose these particular employment routes. For corporate films, it is possible to use the same creative skills and innovation that can be employed in other sorts of documentary, but producers need to consider whether they can agree with the message of the sponsor. A 'jobbing' documentary maker is likely to make films a lot more frequently if they are successful, but they also have to live with their consciences when making adjustments in order to obtain funding. Audiences in broadcast are large and the stakes in this competitive field are high. Compromise is likely to be the bottom line – but will it become a Faustian pact with the devil?

Summary

Decisions about funding are inescapable because time equals money and outside help in some form will probably be required. It is desirable to have a strategy, and there are various models to choose from. The grant-aided route allows support for unconventional and artistic forms, but the filmmaker may have to comply with the rules of the funder. Television and corporate commissions are for experienced practitioners, but inexperienced people can find a production company to work with. Budgetary factors influence every aspect of the production process.

3 Researching and Planning

The argument

In pre-production, the development of the project evolves from the general to the particular as content is broken down into component parts and reinterpreted into a tangible filmic form. The process of translating documentary vision into reality demands the ability to think visually. With this perspective, the documentary maker clarifies intended methods of representation and plans for content. The essence of pre-production planning is filmmaker choice, with a consequential impact on the emerging film. Some decisions arise because research has hit a cul-de-sac elsewhere, some are forced on the filmmaker by time factors or other practical considerations. The web that documentary makers can start to weave during pre-production is a complex one. The case studies demonstrate how much effort good documentary makers put into research. However, there is something to be said for also retaining an element of surprise during filming – not everything can be pre-planned.

Introduction: planning and scripting at various levels

During pre-production the filmmaker focuses on four specific but interrelated and overlapping aspects of practical research, which all contribute to the direction of the project. These comprise: further subject information, selection of people and/or places to film and archive sources, focus on aesthetic form and schedule for the collection of material (shoot). The level of importance of each aspect varies at different points in the pre-production trajectory, as the subject matter evolves and any practical problems arise.

Although the order in which these elements of research proceed will vary according to individual approach and the nature of the project, every filmmaker inevitably converts conceptual vision into specific examples, such as locations, sequences, interviewees, other visual evidence and ways of shooting. Decision making operates at a number of different levels during pre-production: at the macro level of strategic options on the overall form of the piece and at the micro level in the ways that individual aspects are selected because they fulfil filmmaker intent for representation, or because pieces of research information provide an argument for the content. Some types of documentary require more preparation than others. The nature of 'scripting', for instance, depends on the structure of the film, and should be interpreted flexibly in the case of documentary. There are varying definitions of what may constitute a form of script, depending on the style of project (Kochberg, 2002: 21–2). Three different potential requirements emerge.

Firstly, there is the project that can be pre-scripted (and sometimes story-boarded) in some detail because prediction is possible. The film may be based on interpretation of an existing text, such as a poem, or diary. A classic example from the documentary canon is *Night Mail*, where the W. H. Auden poem inspired both the rhythm and the imagery. Raban's *Thames Film* is another example.

Secondly, there are many documentaries where linear development is used for 'real time' presentation which is logical and straightforward. My first ever expository-style series, *Feeling for France*, fits into this category: the filming schedule and the recording of actuality on the day represented a form of scripting, constituting the all-important content. Here, quality of shooting is critical. Nancy Platt's *Venkatamma's Story* provides an illustration.

Thirdly, there are documentaries, often issue-based, where the structure is defined by the interpretation of the filmmaker in post-production, and a huge amount of footage may have been obtained. Here the actuality is used as raw material for subjective interpretation by creative decision making (itself a form of scripting) in the edit suite. An example would be Frederick Wiseman's *Titicut Follies*, where meaning is conveyed by the choice and juxtaposition of sound and image (Grant & Sloniowski, 1998: 238–53). Anand Patwardhan's and Michael Moore's films follow this style.

However, it is not always possible to accurately apply the differentiation supplied above. I prefer to analyse the reasoning behind certain forms of advance planning, rather than to try and fit projects into a prior definition. Whatever the strategy, factual content requires thorough research, for this underwrites form in all cases. Here there should be no short cuts; the filmmaker needs to conquer the relevant information, whatever the style of the film.

It is also worth bearing in mind that even with documentaries which appear to rely on the importance of the moment, there are decisions to be made in pre-production. For instance, if one selects a *cinéma vérité* approach, how does one capture the sense of immediacy, yet avoid the film becoming trivial or boring? In *Chronicle of a Summer*, Rouch and Morin used the pre-production process to select participants and to seek their active cooperation for activities to be filmed. They spent time in advance overtly arranging and 'obviously handling the form of the film' (Jacobs, 1979: 440). Even Craig Gilbert, with the observational marathon *An American Family* (see case study later in this chapter), used the pre-production period to negotiate specific ground rules for filming with the participants.

Researching in detail and adapting the treatment

Covering the ground with research helps to facilitate editorial decisions that will be required later in the production process. The more one knows about a subject, the quicker it can be to gauge the best way forward; this is the strongest argument in support of doing lots of informational research. Knowledge increases choice, for any one subject area can provide innumerable specific examples as material for filming. Special interest groups can help the filmmaker in a variety of ways ranging from hard informational primary research through to contacts, advice and suggestions for filming, including interviewees and locations, archives and picture collections. They may even know which competitor films on the same subject have already been made. In short, background research informs editorial judgement, which a documentary maker who is a subject specialist will find easier. In turn, this knowledge is required for the shaping of content, itself a major form of decision making. The filmmaker may not be a subject specialist at the beginning of research, but the process of finding out information and choosing people to appear, or people to advise on content from behind the camera, makes one an expert by the end of the production process.

With documentary, both primary and secondary research are usually required. Secondary or background information collected from published sources may not be 100 per cent accurate, so facts need to be checked for accuracy. This provides the maker with a safety net against potential criticism and complaints. Published information is only as good as the work that goes into it, so documentary researchers tend to interrogate it, maybe reject some of it, or build on elements that they accept. Not all the background information on the subject will be used, but it is still necessary to collect and study it in order to feel on top of the subject, to appreciate the bigger picture, and to evaluate the nature of other previously published material. An assessment of what has been published in the past will help to determine what should be said in the future. Hence documentary makers tend to collect large files of cuttings, articles and print-outs on their chosen subject.

If there is a written treatment or proposal, then this document needs to be transformed into a reality. The treatment document may be rewritten until it consists of only what will be seen and heard on screen, with a series of paragraphs, one for each sequence. It should eventually be capable of division into two columns as a 'shooting script': one for pictures, one for words. This process is all about thinking visually. If you can't see it, you can't film it. Primary research, in the form of content that relates to people and places to film, often begins with the development of one main character or situation, then branches out from there. Filmmakers tend to think in sequences – that is, action in one location, one point of time, or material which is brought together for one topic within the bigger theme of the film.

Emile de Antonio: *In the Year of the Pig*

The thoroughness and inventiveness of this filmmaker's research is reflected in the finished product. His sources were eclectic and his methods of planning unconventional.

'Many who do compilation documentaries today come from an anti-intellectual generation, or have no historical sense, and they're motivated primarily by flashy images or simple prejudices, when what they should be looking for are historical resonances that are filmic . . . I think you've got to do a hell of a lot of homework' (Rosenthal & Corner, 2005: 153, 94).

   The first thing de Antonio did was to spend three to four months reading over 200 books (in English and French), magazines and newspapers on Vietnam, as a means of finding out how to approach the images. He did not visit Vietnam: 'It's unnecessary. Because not only art, but also facts are in the mind. Just think of all the millions of reporters who go to Vietnam who are idiots, who see nothing' (Kellner & Streible, 2000: 216). As he acquired a substantial knowledge of the subject, he drew up what he called a 'chaotic draft' of the project. This involved using a big marker pen to write key words such as 'Dien Bien Phu, May 8th 1954' on the walls of his office, which he had lined with huge sheets of corrugated paper. He also wrote up ideas such as 'torture' and 'inhumanity' and pasted up pictures next to them. Later he pasted transcripts of sections of interviews in strategic places on the wall.

> I went to Europe and got French footage. The (Vietnamese) NLF headquarters was in Czechoslovakia in Prague. I went to Prague and got their footage. I went to East Germany. The East Germans have the greatest film archive of all and I got whatever I wanted from them. I was at Leipzig in the East German Film Festival . . . and I met a Vietnamese colonel who said, 'We've heard about what you're doing and we hope it succeeds. Can I help you in any way?' I said, 'Well, do you have any footage?' He said, 'Oh we have a nice film that we have here and I'll give it to you. It's called *The Life of Ho Chi Minh*.' There were some good shots in the film from that. (Jackson, 2004)

He was also the first Westerner to obtain this official Vietnamese film of the leader who was to emerge as the hero of *In the Year of the Pig*.

The filmmaker's requests for archive from the US government and NBC were turned down, and he also had difficulties with American news agency archive providers: They asked me what was the position that the film was taking and I replied. 'That's not your business, you're only selling it.' 'You'll have nothing.' 'Okay, I'll tell the press that.' I knew that the press would talk about it. And so they said, 'Very well, you can have what you want' (Ciment & Cohn, 1970: 31, author's translation).

In all, de Antonio ploughed through hours and hours of archive film, covering 30 to 35 years of history. The fact that he had approached some unpredictable sources meant that he was the only person who had located much of the footage (Eisenschitz and Narboni, 1969: 48, author's translation). He met with Russians and people from Hanoi in Paris, all of whom donated footage. He obtained access to the French army's film library, which holds the most important collection of Vietnam footage in existence, dating back to 1902, including rare footage taken by a French sergeant called Schöndorffer that nobody had ever viewed, 'absolutely brilliant . . . a fascination for the ways things work and the life of the war' (Ciment & Cohn, 1970: 31, author's translation).

De Antonio selected footage 'that illustrated the point of view that I had already' (ibid.: 29, author's translation). 'There is something absolutely grotesque to me in the shots of General Clark and LeMay . . . With their obvious anti-Asian prejudices they sound like the most idiotic guys you have ever met in your life. The hand, the mind trembles at the thought of idiots like these controlling the kind of power that they controlled' (Weiss, 1974: 32). He relishes the exclusive 1930s footage of:

> these absolutely arrogant Frenchmen in their colonial hats and white suits being pulled in rickshaws by the Vietnamese. They arrive in front of a café where there is a tall Moroccan with a fez – the scene encapsulates the whole French colonial empire – and when the Vietnamese put their hands out for payment, the Moroccan sends them away like trash. To me, that said everything you could say about colonialism without ever saying the word. If anything shows the primacy of the image over the word, what the image can reveal, it's the image of those rickshaws. (Rosenthal & Corner, 2005: 96)

For interviews, de Antonio wanted to use testimonial voices over archive pictures: 'the expert isn't shown at random. His location is carefully planned in the film, just as a comic strip or something that would be laid out in a collage.' De Antonio sees his films as 'classical collages' in which the selection and placing of interviewees is strategic (Weiss, 1974: 31). This is explained by the order in which he approached the production process. Interviews, like 'pick-up shots', are decided upon during post-production. The supervising editor had already assembled a rough cut of the archive film, into which interviews could be then be slotted. De Antonio had a list of people that he wanted to approach (conservative establishment figures, 'liberal experts', major French academics and historians), and a good idea of what to ask them, 'although with these sort of interviews, you know, you can't control how they develop – which is a good thing, of course' (Eisenschitz & Narboni, 1969: 48, author's translation).

'It's too easy to use a communist or somebody who shares my point of view', so de Antonio selected eminent scholars like Professor Paul Mus. 'He had parachuted into Vietnam and negotiated with Ho Chi Minh on behalf of General de Gaulle. He is the man who said: 'When the history of the twentieth century is written, Ho Chi Minh will be known as its greatest patriot' (Kellner & Streible, 2000: 217).

Investigative research is particularly labour intensive, requiring not only tenacity and persistence, but also an eye for detail. Dermot O'Donovan, whom I interviewed, made an investigative documentary for British regional television, entitled *Fakes and Pharoahs*, about the illegal trade in fake antiquities between Egypt and other countries.

First and foremost, he had to try to establish the truth about what happened and the legal situation:

> I followed intricate lines of enquiry and discovered more and more about the shady world of antiquities. At every turn there was another contributor, greedy for money and willing to dish the dirt and claiming that all the others were liars and rogues! Central was an eagerness to dish the dirt on the Egyptian government, but without saying so too directly. It was challenging to both find people and to persuade them to be interviewed and to feature in the film. Most were cagey about being chased by various agents, at the same time insisting that only *they* knew the full story. In the end, I was convinced that *I* was the only one who knew all the facts! (author interview, 2005)

Clearly, in the interests not simply of accuracy, but also of avoiding litigation and the wrath of his employers, O'Donovan had to make a big effort to ensure that he was correct.

Considering authorial voice and objectivity

Decisions are made in pre-production that set the pace for the rest of the production. One crucial question involves who is going to communicate information content, and how it will be done. This includes issues such as the level of personalization that is preferred and whether interviews will form part of the film's text, offering options for other people to act as transmitters of editorial content. If a number of different strategies are adopted for the transmission of authorial voice, then the balance between the elements will also become an issue: how many sync sequences, testimonies, how much voice-over commentary, if any?

There are documentaries in which the expression of authorial voice is complex, and also subtle. There are others where it is overt and heavy-handed, ironic, rhetorical or didactic. Each of these elements has its own merits, and disadvantages, and authorial voice can include aspects of filmmaker strategy such as using the project to excite audience emotions. A good documentary viewing experience can change the way people *feel* about the issue, as well as presenting them with the information about it.

Anand Patwardhan: *In the Name of God*

As the filmmaker never appears on screen, how does he introduce an authorial voice?

Patwardhan's approach to his personalized investigative essay form involved advance research that enabled him to select various events to attend with his camera, shooting the actuality of events as they unfolded. He would ask people key questions on the spot, and select activities to capture that demonstrated the situation which he wanted to describe, but Patwardhan resisted the idea of a preconceived plan to control what is filmed and how it is portrayed. Nevertheless, he was able to reveal information that hitherto had been largely ignored.

Sequences were to consist of live footage of scenes and events combined with extensive interviews with people at the location from different sections of society with varying interests. Interviews were to play a leading part in the structure of the documentary because they could demonstrate the political coercion and illegal financial dealings of the Hindu nationalist Vishwa Hindu Parishad (VHP) party.

People and places are by no means an arbitrary cross-section; Patwardhan's selection of sequences is underwritten by a strong editorial judgement based on a contextual understanding of the bigger significance to the events in the temple-mosque story which he planned to film:

> secularism is under siege . . . by far the biggest danger to the secular fabric comes from those who are appealing to the 80 per cent Hindu majority to redefine India as a Hindu nation. They argue that Hindus have been patient for too long and the time for non-violence is over. They describe Mahatma Gandhi as a traitor to his religion because he allowed muslims to form Pakistan. (Chatterjee, 1997: 32)

How Patwardhan chooses to demonstrate the institutionalized manifestations of Hindu fundamentalism is crucial. He planned to shoot their public campaigning, demonstrating how the Bharatiya Janata Party (BJP) assault on the Indian media (with distribution of video and audio cassettes and control of parts of the film industry) has become an integral part of the

Choices concerning aspects of authorial voice will inevitably reflect the producer's values and beliefs concerning what should be shown, or not shown. Is the maker going to present views that he or she does not agree with, or leave them out altogether? Will the latter course of action lead to accusations of bias? Documentary filmmakers such as de Antonio give a platform to ideas and people that they disagree with, subscribing to the 'give them enough rope' philosophy. As he said, 'Honesty and objectivity are not the same thing. Nor are they even closely related . . . Documentary is not only polemic, but it is often a quest for revelation, a quest for the truth' (Weiss, 1974: 35).

How the evidence is presented can vary. It may evolve through the filming of a situation as it unfolds, or it may be presented as a short example, in a way that selectively extrapolates reality. The former approach will help to build audience trust, whereas the latter may make viewers feel that they are being manipulatively led into a selective argument and trapped by the expression of that particular filmmaker's prejudice. Authorial voice can also cover attitudinal aspects, such as respect for institutions and people in power (or lack of it), the way that conflict and aggression are represented, how gender is depicted and what set of people are seen to be proactive in the film, as opposed to being seen as victims.

Focusing on the elements of representation

How to represent the ideas that are being developed is the central concern during pre-production. How to build a narrative is a challenge for pre-production as well as for post-production – editors can only work with what is available – and supply of material is first decided upon during pre-production. Standard definitions of structure dictate that the story, as a form of narrative, should have aspects of conflict and elements of suspense involving strong characters, some exposition of information and context and a climax of opposing elements, ending in a resolution of tensions. Obviously these are not always as clear cut in documentary (which is dependent on real life constraints) as in fiction, where the writer has a relatively free hand with technique. Very often it is the framework provided by the form, such as a video diary, that influences the way forward and prevents the film from drifting too far from the original concept. Selection of form does not need to be absolute; levels of mix and match are feasible, but the film must retain a consistency and flow.

Some filmmakers agonize about the title and the beginning of the film, for both of these convey signposts and signals to the viewer. The title can encapsulate the film's philosophy, such as in our corporate film *It's Your Choice* (i.e. we're not going to impose any choice on you or be prescriptive – you the viewer have to make your own mind up). The effort and planning that sometimes goes into an opening shot is well illustrated by a television history series that I once researched, entitled *The Manufactured Landscape*, looking at the impact of the Industrial Revolution in Britain. One of the episodes dealt with the nineteenth-century transport revolution. The director had a vision for the opening shots: he wanted to show then and now; the horse and cart compared to motorway madness today; muddy, narrow lanes before canals, roads and the invention of the railways changed the landscape.

The idea was to visually portray 200 years' worth of change in just two shots during the opening of the film. We decided the best available motorway shot was 'Spaghetti Junction' in the Birmingham area. I couldn't find the correct position to achieve the ideal image in one shot only. We could have used library film, but we wanted to create our own, and in the end employed an expensive location manager from the area to take the crew off the road onto private land in order to obtain just one important shot that only lasted five seconds. The director achieved his vision, even if it was costly. Location research is a skill within its own right, but the role of a location in terms of the way that a documentary maker uses it will vary.

William Raban: *Thames Film*

The ways that Raban chose to represent the history of the river are varied but always filmic and consistent.

The central theme of time was to be expressed in *Thames Film* as part visual poem to the river, part historical document. 'Just as the images for the film have to be gathered, so the background material has to be researched.' Raban's first reflections on his chosen subject were primarily visual, but his 'way of looking also tackles themes that have led many to utter great words' (Zuilhof, 2001: 299). His research into the historical and economic development of the river led him to the conclusion that his film needed to capture the 'interpenetration of the natural and the fabricated'. This led to an obsessive fascination with maps and charts of the Thames. 'I realize that this is because the topography of subject is most crucial. The river is the penetration of one element by another. They are equally interdependent upon each other for the river's existence' (memo to Marion, 2 January 1984). A study of the conditions and topography of a river is actually a study of time and change, for any river has its own pace in nature. 'I want to make a film that is an observation of the River Thames. It will be a landscape film, a documentary film and a film about a journey. The images and sounds will be drawn from the river, viewing the river itself, its banks and the traffic on its waters' (Raban, proposal to the Arts Council, 1984).

From Raban's hitherto unpublished working notes of how he approached the development of this film, it is clear that he saw it as a three-way process: the collection of images, the recording of sound and the researching of background sources. The last of these three provided a 'Eureka' for him – a philosophical inspiration that became his guiding light. He came across a single phrase in one line of poetry from T. S. Eliot's *Four Quartets*, which was to steer his thinking in a specific direction. It was simply a few words that preyed on his mind. The river is described as a 'strong brown god'.

The poem refers to the Mississippi river, but was written in London, overlooking the Thames from the poet's house on the embankment at Chelsea, now commemorated by a blue heritage plaque on the outside of the building. The metaphor of 'Old Father Thames' as an awesome dark source is also referenced in the writings of William Blake's *Jerusalem* and Joseph Conrad's *Heart of Darkness*. Just as Conrad's river is an arterial route to imperial trade and the concomitant human exploitation, so the concept of darkness here refers to the role of the river as the centre of London's trade and former colonial power, hence oppression. The poem provided the impulse, the prompt that was to clarify Raban's intentions during pre-production: 'The landscape is intensely rich, encompassing scenery of land, water and sky that is a-historic and timeless insofar as it is now as it always has been. This archetypal picture is offset by an immediate contemporary view: derelict, decayed and broken, yet still functioning, it evokes an image of the aftermath of industrialization' (Raban, proposal to the Arts Council, 1984).

The unexpected discovery of archive sources during research added a completely new dimension. Frequently archive is discussed as picture image rather than sound, but Raban realized that the inspirational Eliot poem was most authentic if the text was read by the poet himself, and he tracked down the original recording of T. S. Eliot reading it at Britain's

National Sound Archive. The recording was poor quality, but it had an authenticity value. The author's educated voice seemed 'very precise and measured – he's an engineer with words'. The next step was to obtain permission to use it from the author's widow, who was 'very generous' (author interview, 2005). Raban made no attempt to remove any of the scratches.

Raban came across the Port of London Authority (PLA) archive two months into filming, 'It was serendipitous', for this archive provided a range and assortment of material that could now supplement actuality from the boat. At that time there was no public access to the collection, and its contents lay hidden in a waterfront warehouse. The curator gave Raban total access to the uncatalogued archives, which included documentary classics such as *Waters of Time* by Basil Wright and other old films and paintings. Since then the archives have been published on DVD as the PLA Collection, distributed by the Museum of London which also holds screenings of them. Raban didn't like the soundtracks of old films, but he opted to 'frame them' authentically as clips that provided their own voice-over. The range of documents and books contained in the archive was also to provide content that could be read or quoted from in the voice-over. There was now an opportunity to weave layers of old footage, photographs, maps, drawings and sketches with his own present-day film.

Amongst the boxes of old parchment archives, there was a volume from 1787 by a travel writer called Thomas Pennant, who described the same 66-mile journey that William was filming. In a way this was to act as his script, which transformed *Thames Film* from mere actuality capturing the point of view of the river itself, to a structured 60-mile journey, using Pennant's words and following his eighteenth-century route. This archival piece turned out to be a pivotal find because it provided the key edit points that made the structure into a reflective essay on time and change: 'time regulated by the effects of tide, daylight and seasonal change' (*Thames Film*, 1986). From an original plan to study and capture the river Thames in all its complexions according to weather and time of day and season, the project had now developed into an historical study.

As Raban transcribed the illustrated handwritten account, he studied it and reflected upon Pennant's assertions, finding that he disagreed with many of them. Attitudes had changed.

> His view of the landscape, both city and river, was largely materialistic, tending to dwell upon the 'rewards of industry'. This generally held ideal of the age was what had spearheaded the Industrial Revolution, whereas today, such optimism based on the belief in limitless progress has disappeared. For the contemporary traveller this derelict landscape is resonant with echoes of past activity. It is a landscape that poses many questions, and despite its silence and melancholy aspect, it enthrals the curious with all its possibilities. (Raban, progress report)

Having reflected on the differences in attitude that in turn were connected with differences in the physical manifestation of the landscape, Raban wrestled with a means of creating a dialogue between old and new in the soundtrack. He thought of using two voices, a young one that would relate his own feelings about the river, and an older, 'perhaps wiser' voice for Pennant. There could be a conversation between the two. The problem, in terms of retaining the authenticity of Pennant's views, was how to handle the abundance of eighteenth-century prose, which is far more verbose than today's literary communication. He therefore rejected the idea as being too complicated. Later he discovered Hogarth's 'Peregrinations' which is also an account of a journey down the Thames, but made at an earlier time. Thus by the time that Raban submitted a progress report in order to obtain further funding, he had a rich collection of original sources which consisted of numerous English, Dutch and French charts of the estuary from the sixteenth to the nineteenth centuries, Joseph Conrad's *Heart of Darkness*, William Hogarth's 'Peregrinations', Thomas Pennant's 'A Journey from London to Dover', and two films, one entitled *Port of London*, dated 1921, and one entitled *City of Ships* from 1948.

Permission was required from the copyright holder for the library material to use the material. The port authority (PLA) allowed him to reproduce the text of the Pennant diary and selected illustrations on condition that the end film had independent distribution. As long as it was shown for cultural and educational purposes only, there would be no charge for copyright. Raban negotiated separately for the clips from the old films that he wanted to use, obtaining an advantageous 'use now, pay later' arrangement with the PLA.

The discovery of these old documentaries brought about an adjustment in his thinking about how to use black and white film. 'I no longer intend to shoot black and white as well as colour. The documentaries I may use are black and white and will therefore be immediately distinguishable from my colour footage. In this respect the monochrome/colour difference overcomes the problem of making "quotation marks" for every insert used' (Raban, progress report).

Documentary helps us to retain historical memory, but the role played by picture archives in documentary projects, and the way it is used, can vary greatly. Music and sound archive are often used to create atmosphere and/or emotional impact, but the issue of authenticity versus filmmaker interventionism impacts upon eventual style and form. Intended usage needs to be carefully considered in advance; detailed negotiation over copyright can be required with official organizations. There are numerous film libraries, both general and specialist, who hold archives and stock shots. The way that a documentary maker plans to integrate the selected archive material into the rest of the film may form part of the discussion, so it is a critical determinant for the future creative direction of the project.

Selecting interviewees and participants

Inevitably, documentary makers are likely to be guided by their own assumptions in a way that will introduce editorial values concerning the selection of participants. These can involve class or wealth, for instance. Options for real-life characters in documentary, as a visual medium, are always influenced to some extent by appearance and how effectively the person communicates. The documentary maker does not always have a free hand in selection; sometimes institutional hierarchy dictates who should appear in the film. In an essay-style documentary, how the argument can be evolved, who should say what, when and how, must all be planned. Therefore, with investigative and current affairs documentaries, one of the main functions of research involving selection of interviewees and testimony is to gauge in advance, before filming, what points need to be communicated in the film and who are the most important players in the given field.

Jane Chapman: *It's Your Choice*

From my own experience, my initial instinctive reaction as to whether or not a person would make a good interviewee has nearly always proved correct. However, this instinct never operates alone or in a vacuum. It is aided by a clear intent that contributes to the bigger vision of what is required. A brief from the client or sponsor will obviously inform my definition of requirement. *It's Your Choice* probably provided the most specific brief for the selection of participants that I have ever experienced. It was not difficult making contact with young people who were taking the training and educational routes that the client wanted to highlight. The challenge with this project came in achieving other requirements: balance between the options, with each character looking equally good; balance between gender, ethnic and class background; balance between geographic areas featured and between types of subjects studied.

Each character in this project had to tell their own story; their interview was used as voice-over with shots of them doing activities, and it was important when selecting the people to establish locations where they could be filmed carrying out everyday actions – activities that provided movement and therefore interest, but which seemed relevant to what they would be talking about. One person sitting at a computer desk for the entire film would not have retained audience attention. Indeed, viewer empathy was a further consideration that the filmic style had to cater for.

Last but certainly not least, the people selected needed to be able to articulate content in a way that suited the brief, without me having to put words into their mouths. As each person was effectively a role model for their particular choice of career route, how they related their own experiences was a central criterion for selection. Documentaries such as this one, in which the interviewees themselves provide the principle discursive element and hence determine the content, mean that the filmmaker has a particular onus to find interesting people who will cover the ground, whilst also setting the pace. This needs to be planned sensitively.

Connie Field: *The Life and Times of Rosie the Riveter*

In *The Life and Times of Rosie the Riveter*, the degree of personal space that the female participants occupy, 'gives an integrity to the testimony which renders it less appropriable by external intentions . . . This places the women themselves as the articulators of the film, rather than as recruits to its project' (Corner, 1996: 128, 130). Field's methods for the selection of interviewees were extensive, thorough and meaningful for content research.

The research effort was twofold and hugely important: selection of interviewees and archive film. According to Field, she made a conscious guiding decision during pre-production to represent 'counterpoint between the way (those) newsreels presented reality and what the women themselves say. We chose that structure and kept with it' (Johnston, 1981: 21). However, the argument and position of the film were firmly grounded in historical facts, which she had established through thorough research on the subject of female wartime work. 'I let the government films and the women express themselves. Although *Rosie* was not scripted, it was carefully planned before shooting, I outlined the history, all the issues' (Rosenthal & Corner, 2005: 157).

Field advertised for participants who had a story to tell and received 700 replies, which she managed to reduce to a final selection of five people. There could have been fewer participants in the eventual film, but the impression of representation of a more general voice would have been lost. Thirty-five interviewees were videoed in order to assess their on-screen potential. 'We interviewed so many for two reasons. First, the response to our press release was overwhelming. Second, the oral histories were a crucial part of the original research necessary for the film.' Applicants were required to have job experiences that were typical of the time, but also, crucially, 'I wanted to find people who could express themselves emotionally as well as intellectually' (Rosenthal, 1988: 229). Anticipating the more general expository function mentioned above, Field also looked for some 'who were conscious of what happened to them in the larger historical framework. To that end, I chose someone like Margaret, who talked about the propaganda and the media after the war' (ibid.: 237). Similarly, Lola, who was a union organizer, was selected because she comes across as a genial person with a wry humour who is able to take on 'the role of spokesperson for women *like* her' (Corner, 1996: 132).

Each interviewee's contribution was intended to cover a three-part content comprising wartime recruitment into industry, experience of this work, and post-war adjustment. Field wanted both critique and celebration. The content that she established through research was both subjective and also expository of a more general history, whereas in some documentaries the latter function is provided by 'voice of God' voice-over commentary, leaving interviewees to supply personal examples to support the bigger theme written as narration by the producer/ director.

Field was also anxious not to show the women as victims, 'I felt *very* strongly about that. I was basically making a film about manipulation, and I didn't want audiences to come away totally depressed and demoralised. So I deliberately chose women who were aware of what had happened . . . the main thing I want to do is to give people back their dignity' (Johnston, 1981: 21). In pre-production, Field chose a setting for each interview that was significant biographically and thematically for each person. 'I was very careful about locations. I don't believe you should shoot an interview with a white wall behind it – the background has to say something. Remember, people are looking at an image, and you don't want the interview to be visually boring' (Rosenthal & Corner, 2005: 152).

The choice of three black women amongst the five elevates questions of race to match those of gender, although Field claims she never deliberately intended to have this black–white ratio. The testimonies of the five women selected clearly demonstrated discrimination against women in general and against black women in particular.

If a story is to sustain the interest of television viewers for a whole half hour, or even an hour, the selection of an individual or family becomes all the more challenging and a critical element in the success of the production. With a biographical profile documentary or a study of the work of an individual, strategic decision making about activities that are to be filmed, or activities from the past that should be featured, need to be made. It is customary to research the entire life of the person, if only to fully understand them, although the structure will not necessarily follow a chronological pattern from birth to death, and not all of this trajectory may be used. There can be a focus on one episode, aspect or part of the person's life.

Author preparing for an interview with fashion designer Karl Lagerfeld for BBC1 series *Europe by Design*

Some portrait films are shot *cinéma vérité*-style, with a crew just following the person who is selected as the subject. Here casting is everything – that is, it can be said that the strength of the film will lie in the importance of the person. The justification for vérité-style may be that this approach will enable the filmmaker to dig deeper and reveal more of the 'real' person. Unfortunately, personalities can be as much on their guard with an observational style of shooting as they often are in a more formal situation, so the naturalistic aim is not always achieved.

Filmmaker Nancy Platt's experiences reiterate the central role in documentary production played by practical considerations such as availability for filming and also human considerations, such as unpredictability. According to Nancy, 'film making is like making up a string of pearls: you attach one, then there is another to thread. Each pearl represents a problem. You solve one, and another arises' (author interview, 2005). On one occasion she had been contracted to direct a documentary for a *cinéma vérité* style television series about disability and everyday life. She had found a US visitor to Britain who was wheelchair-bound. Nancy's intention was to investigate wheelchair access for tourists. The observational approach tends to involve a level of detachment by the filmmaker, who is a 'fly on the wall', not intervening in the reality or influencing the normal events that are being filmed. When the shoot started, Nancy felt guilty that she couldn't talk to the person, or help her when she was struggling. The camera was ever present – more than the participant had expected. The strain of constant observation was too much, consequently the participant withdrew from the filming. Nancy was left with some rushes, but no film to complete.

Luckily she discovered that the week scheduled by the broadcaster for trans-mission of her film also happened to be National Deaf Week, so she decided to find a deaf person. Although time was running out, she telephoned all 10 of the deaf voluntary groups in her contacts book. Eventually, the Jewish Deaf Association helped by putting her in contact with a family of four, who were all hard of hearing or deaf. The son, Daniel, was about to start at a mainstream school. This time Nancy was very careful to explain exactly what the filming would entail, asking the family, 'What would you normally do?' Thus, In terms of advance planning, she ascertained all the anticipated domestic events that would make up the content. The angle was to be the run-up to Daniel's first day at school.

Deciding on levels of reflexivity

Jean Rouch and Edgar Morin: *Chronicle of a Summer*

With the reflexive approach, the people selected to be participants will influence the future direction of the project significantly.

After the project was completed, Rouch said he would never collaborate again with a production partner, because it was too difficult. Yet he admitted that Edgar Morin should take the credit for pre-production arrangements and the development of the idea, for it was Morin who selected the participants (who all belonged to the same political group as him).

> This turned out to be very critical for the film's development, but it wasn't clear to me at the beginning . . . he proposed to make the first sociological fresco film, a film without conventions of stars or leading performers. He wished to deal with anonymous people as much as possible. I told him this was not possible . . . So while we can oppose the star system and what it implies, we cannot deny individuals their humanity and personality. (Georgakas et al., 1978: 17)

Selection of the participants involved a 'concretizing' of the original 'Parisian tribe' idea; it changed in pre-production, becoming now a 'tribe of substance', a 'specialized tribe' of people who actually formed part of the artistic and political avant garde of the time. Participants were no longer to be typical, for as Rouch later admitted, 'In their attitudes you can see what will explode all over France in May 1968' (ibid.: 18). Arguably a selected group will never be absolutely 'typical', and as soon as they have been chosen, as individuals positioned together, they will offer up a more precise definition. Whatever this turns out to be, the act of selection has already given the film its substance.

In situations where content is heavily dependent on the nature of the contribution by participants, how much should they be able to influence the emerging film? Opinions on the level of reflexivity in this respect will vary. The filmmaker must have a vision, but must also be open and flexible to the realities which are discovered during research. On the one hand, these may not match prior ideas and preconceived notions; on the other hand, a project with no filmmaker vision ends up lacking direction. Reflexivity is all about obtaining a workable balance between filmmaker intent, final product and the process of making the journey. This means showing the research and the way both good and bad things are discovered, and this can introduce a level of uncertainty. Too much reflexivity can lead to a documentary that lacks direction and focus.

Ross McElwee: *Sherman's March*

Did McElwee tip the balance too far towards the personal?

McElwee intended *Sherman's March* to be a 'film about a region, to some degree about a way of life'. The project changed substantially during research. McElwee started by following General Sherman's journey through the South during the American Civil War, in order to explore his own ironic identification with the man who fought in a region that he claimed to care for. He had access to people and places because he came from the area, but he states that 'I posit myself in the role of an exiled Southerner living up North who returns to the South again. I both identify with Sherman and find my personality and what my life stands for as being in contradistinction to what Sherman stood for' (MacDonald, 1992: 280).

McElwee's efforts to record Sherman's progress took a new turn when his sister joked that he should use the camera as a way to meet women. McElwee, who operates as a production 'one-man band', had already decided to film some of his relatives, but this new angle of a personal odyssey prompted a subtitle, *A Meditation on the Possibility of Romantic Love in the South during an Era of Nuclear Weapons Proliferation*. The film was to end up as an exploration of placing people, especially women, in front of the camera, but as McElwee admits, 'it was not planned to be as explicitly biographical as it turned out' (Rudolph, 1999: 107).

In his search for love along the path of Sherman's original destruction, the filmmaker also chose to start, resuscitate or end relationships in front of the camera. In general, this man with a movie camera tended to walk in on people without too many prior arrangements. 'I'd steer the conversation in a certain way, and indeed that's what human dialogue is anyway, so why not let it be part of the film?' In the case of Karen, the final portrait in the film, he rang her in advance.

> I said, 'Can I come and spend some time with you? I have my camera and I'll probably do some shooting. I'm making this film about women in the South and about my journey along Sherman's route.' And she said, 'Sure, come.' In one sense she's startled when I walk in the door shooting; she hadn't quite expected that, but in general she's prepared. That scene on the porch when I'm asking her, 'Where have you been for the last year? Why didn't you ever write?' is exactly as it happened. (MacDonald, 1988: 20)

In fact, the reflexive approach means that the extent to which the theme of the film changed (or 'puts itself on track', to use McElwee's words) is actually accurately described in the film itself. This sums up part of the reflexivity triangulation: what the production team normally do in pre-production is recorded in production as part of the content of the film. How comfortably this personalized aspect then sits with the original, discrete content, and whether it has any inherent interest value (discounting the filmmaker narcissism), is open to debate.

Thus, as a result of these changes in approach, *Sherman's March* became a portrait of McElwee's home in Charlotte, a record of his travels in the South and of the women he meets along the route that General Sherman took during the Civil War, but it deliberately reveals more about the filmmaker's own hopes, fears and concerns than it does about history. The camera certainly records personal life, but it also becomes the agent of change.

Arranging permission to film, ethics, release forms and informed consent

Relationships between filmmakers and public are all important, whether the latter consist of participants in the project, or as audience for it, or both. Awareness of ethical considerations during the pre-production planning process should be guided by a sense of responsibility towards participants in the project, and also towards audience and how they will receive the film that is being constructed. People who are required to cooperate will assess the project from the standpoint of how their image will be presented to the public.

Where government or large corporations are concerned, normal practice is to approach the public relations or public affairs department for cooperation with filming. Where sensitive subjects are concerned, sometimes a third party can help: for instance, a voluntary organization may be able to suggest and approach members to obtain their agreement to participate.

When it comes to arrangements for filming, there are times when the documentary maker cannot proceed without prior agreement from the owners or managers of a location, which may be private property. As Nancy Platt says, 'you can't just walk in. You have to fix things first. You have to obtain the permissions and make the arrangements' (author interview, 2005). Professional live performances such as concerts, even if only in rehearsal, will need permission. Private property such as museums, stately homes, public buildings such as hospitals and shopping malls, will also require permission, although filming on the street does not. However, if camera operators put down a tripod in some cities, officially they will require permission.

What the filmmaker says to potential interviewees about the project in order to gain their cooperation can have future repercussions. If the producer/director is not honest about intentions, there could well be complaints and even possibly legal action later, when the member of the public sees that the completed film is nothing like what was described in order to obtain permission to film. Examples of such behaviour abound, and sometimes occur because of a dogged determination by the filmmaker to insert an element of authorial voice that may be at variance with what the people featured actually think or feel.

The fact is that members of the public are not in a position to be able to envisage how the documentary is likely to turn out. Although documentary content can change during the production process as filming and editing progress, nevertheless the producer/director and researcher should be as open as possible with interviewees, and not misrepresent the intentions of the project. It is not advisable for documentary producers to work their way into filming by lying to obtain cooperation, or by falsifying the story when a participant asks what it is about.

Documentary makers need to be sure that they can deliver whatever has been promised as a condition of filming, and that collaborators remain supportive. Sometimes people are reluctant to be filmed, due to previous bad experiences with the media. Some interviewees ask for the questions in advance. Any difficult situation is best covered by a release form. Very often researchers and/or producers carry release forms with them so that anybody who appears in the documentary can sign, especially if they have given an interview. This provides a protection for the filmmaker by preventing participants from turning round later and asking to be withdrawn from the film. The forms usually give the producers the right to do what they like with the images and words. If there are future public screenings or transmissions on television and sales to other countries, the distributor will require these pieces of paper.

Selana Vronti, a first-time filmmaker whose video diary was nominated at the Thessaloniki Documentary Festival (Greece) in 2004, told me about her problem with release forms:

> As most of the young people in Athens and around the world, I went clubbing and I listened to electronic dance music. I bought my own video camera and started experimenting with it, shooting my friends and other people. I was mostly interested in Athenian youth. I just love the power of young people. Also acid house became a major social and political issue over here. I had started with the idea of a doc-drama version, which never happened. After working it a lot in my mind – about two years – I decided that the documentary will be double-faced: a real life story of clubbers and of course the history of the Greek electronic dance scene. I would spend a lot of time with a bunch of clubbers. Just kids going out and having a good time. (author interview, 2005)

Selana ended up with material that was too compromising and intimate to be screened in public. She had wanted the video diary to come across as 'something between fiction and reality' but the real world issue of release forms intervened; she did not obtain legal clearances from her friends, who were now vulnerable because of their appearance in the film. This very personalized film has gone no further.

Even in situations where the people involved are friends, or not likely to be required for filming by other media practitioners, exploitation still remains. Indeed, as Ross McElwee says, 'The problem of exploitation is one that won't go away . . . The single biggest problem I still have, even with the tempered form of *cinéma vérité* that I've ended up employing, is the necessity to avoid exploiting people and setting people up to be laughed at by an audience' (Lucia, 1993: 32–8).

Participants should be fully briefed about procedures and anticipated effects. If the documentary maker withholds information about what is likely to happen, or the particular bias that the film will involve, this could be construed as a form of deception. Informed consent is 'flawed when obtained by the omission of any fact that might influence the giving or withholding of permission' (Barbash and Taylor, 1997: 52). If people are unaware of any potentially negative consequences of participation, they could be letting themselves in for harm in the future, and the filmmaker would then be responsible for putting them at risk. This is an ethical offence. Power relations in a filmmaking situation are not equal, and very often the members of the public involved have no real choice. Arguably, individual documentary makers have a wider obligation to the rest of the film community; we have to live with our consciences throughout and remember that individuals who help us and contribute to the process of project development may well be needed in the future by other filmmakers.

The question is whether the end justifies the means. For his investigative film *Fakes and Pharoahs*, Dermot O'Donovan needed to ascertain the story and to get leads about potential interviewees and locations from the main subject of the story, a character (referred to as JTP) who was in jail. The prison would not allow access to the media, so Dermot had to conduct his research visits posing as a family friend.

> It was difficult to contact JTP in jail, all telephone calls and letters are usually monitored. I therefore resorted to subterfuge. Before each visit I would study my paperwork and consider what I needed to find out. Then I made a list of 10 questions and memorized them, learning them by heart in pneumonic form (by identifying initials and an association with each). I would then raise these in "friendly" conversation. After I had said goodbye to JTP, I would then rush to the car and write everything down before I forgot it. (author interview, 2005)

Without resorting to such tactics, O'Donovan would never have obtained the information and leads.

The way in which filmmakers negotiate with potential participants can be a complex matter, especially if the filming is likely to seriously intrude into their everyday lives. If people do not want to be recognized on camera, there are various technical tricks to retain anonymity, such as lower lighting or back-to-camera shots. There are codes of practice in Britain and elsewhere that cover the ethics of research practices such as cheque-book journalism, interviews without prior arrangement, use of hidden cameras and microphones, the recording of telephone interviews, set-up situations and the interviewing of children. In many parts of the world, for instance countries in the European Union, the right to privacy is guaranteed as a basic human right that should not be infringed. This could also become an issue for the profile documentary maker. If a filmmaker is in pursuit of a potential interviewee as Michael Moore was with Roger in *Roger and Me*, 'door-stepping' is an obvious tactic that carries ethical implications.

On some occasions the entire documentary content can stand or fall on the basis of access given. In this scenario, filmmakers have to face high levels of compromise, which may seriously influence the kind of documentary that can be produced. What sort of shooting is possible in the light of restrictions imposed? A classic Granada television series, called *Decisions*, first brought the secret world of corporate decision making to the television screen, with the inside story of crucial decisions within various British oil and steel companies. Filmmaker Roger Graef had to gain entry to three huge companies and win their confidence, and only obtained permission to film with the following conditions:

1   No scoops. No information was to be released in advance to newspapers, and no one was to be told about any information obtained during filming as a great deal of it was confidential.
2   The filmmakers would only film what they had agreed to cover, but for these subjects they had total access and were able to film at any time.
3   No lights would be used, no interviews filmed, and nothing would be staged.

4   The companies were left with the right of veto over confidential material with the agreement that films would only be released when both sides had agreed to it. (Rosenthal, 1996: 156–7)

Decisions carried a card at the head of each episode saying that nothing had been staged for the camera.

Craig Gilbert: *An American Family*

Gilbert was criticized later by Pat Loud for not explaining things sufficiently in advance. Is this a fair point?

An American Family was one of the first direct cinema series, as opposed to 'infotainment' or 'reality programming', to observe ordinary people, rather than celebrities and other public figures, in an extensive way. A planned seven-month-long shoot created 12 episodes for PBS about the domestic life of one family – the Louds from Santa Barbara, California. The groundbreaking format became a pioneer for 'docu-soap'. By spending longer on the subject than previous documentaries, series producer Craig Gilbert, who had a background as a film editor, television documentary director and former PBS employee, put his faith in the inherent drama that normal folk experience in their everyday lives. The series also 'announced the breakdown of fixed distinctions between public and private, reality and spectacle, serial narrative and non fiction, documentary and fiction, film and television' (Ruoff, 2002: xii).
    The executives at PBS shared the same vision as producer Craig Gilbert.

> Had Jim Day or Curt Davis asked me what I expected to find by filming the Louds for seven months, I would not have been able to answer with any degree of certainty. But they didn't ask that question, because they shared with me a general vision of what life is about and a specific vision about the quality of life in the United States in 1971. They were as convinced as I that if we could afford to spend the money and the time – *time to let things happen* – something fascinating would be revealed. None of us had the slightest idea what the something would be, but we gambled . . . it would say something important and revealing about all of us. (Rosenthal, 1988: 301)

The budget for this 'dream proposal' (Ruoff, 2002: 14) was high: $1.2 million, or $100,000 per episode – but much less than a television drama/fiction series would have been.
    What are the ethical issues involved in filming private lives and how should the documentarian approach the challenge? Gilbert was clear about the intentions of the project: 'I held to my commitment to make . . . a series of films about the Louds, and not about how the Louds interrelated with a film crew from NET. I knew damn well that no matter how we conducted ourselves we could not avoid having some effect on the family. But I was adamant about having to keep that effect to the minimum' (Rosenthal & Corner, 2005: 316). He found that negotiations about filming involved three main aspects. First, privacy. He promised that the camera would never go through a closed door. So, if the family wanted to be alone, they would go into a room and shut the door. Second, the right to withdraw from filming. If the family had a grievance, it would be discussed and if the point could not be resolved, they would have the right to withdraw. Third, how the filming would influence their lives. Gilbert asked them to live their lives for the seven-month filming period as

if there was no camera there. They would never be asked to do anything for the benefit of the camera.

Given the open-ended nature of the arrangements negotiated above, it is debatable whether a fuller explanation would have been possible, but were the family aware that they were somehow supposed to be typical of more general family life? Gilbert, who had worked previously on a film about social anthropologist Margaret Mead, was fascinated by the changing nature of family in the US.

> Human beings do not like to be treated like guinea pigs. If you tell the subjects of a documentary that their behaviour and their lives are being used to make a larger statement about human behaviour and human lives in general, they are more than likely going to be highly insulted . . . More often than not, and certainly more often than has been admitted, documentary filmmakers are unable to tell the whole truth about what they're up to without running the risk of being told to peddle their papers elsewhere . . . The bottom line, as they like to say in television, is that we are *using human beings* to make a point. (Rosenthal, 1988: 292–3)

Gilbert spent several months selecting a family. He maintains that: 'The essential talent involved in the making of a documentary, particularly in the making of *cinéma vérité* films, is the picking of a subject' (Ruoff, 2002: 15). He deliberately chose an upper-middle-class European–American family, because he wanted a family that looked like the ones in television sit coms in the 1950s and 1960s, in order to examine what happens when the trappings of the good life have arrived.

Gilbert went to California because he saw the West Coast as the trendsetting cutting edge of American culture (also the regular sunshine allowed more filming outdoors and with available light), and was influenced by the novels of Ross Macdonald dealing with troubled affluent families whose wealth cannot compensate for their moral shortcomings. When Gilbert found the family, through his contact with the author, and met them, he alluded to a previous, similar BBC series, yet 'talked much, but said little, of his intentions' (ibid.: 18–19).

Responsibility towards the audience

Filmmakers have both participants and audience to consider. Some filmmakers, such as Trinh T. Minh-ha, want the audience to be challenged by what they see. A documentary producer may have a very different conception of his or her responsibility towards the audience from the one that the people being filmed would want. Such is the case with investigative documentaries where the maker's interpretation of the public's 'right to know' is likely to clash with the image that participants would want to project. This can be a constant source of conflict and a recurring theme for Michael Moore. Filmmaker plans frequently push at the boundaries of production ethics, but what is sometimes not considered sufficiently is how audiences will receive the tactics. In very different ways the approaches of Trinh T. Minh-ha and of Michael Moore were both challenging assumptions, even at the pre-production stage.

Michael Moore: *Roger and Me*

How did Moore choose to represent and sustain his main themes during pre-production? How, and why, did this involve ethical considerations about choice of location before filming had even started?

Moore manages to set the pace for the whole of the film in pre-production. The crucial decision was to track down Roger Smith, the then chairman of General Motors, in order to confront him. In most current affairs documentaries, this would amount to a normal behind-the-scenes task, but Moore decides that Roger should be also made to confront the workers of Flint who have been made redundant as a result of the company's policy of rationalization. The very process of pre-production then becomes the main content of the film. There is a continuous emphasis on the difficulty of obtaining access to and information from circles dominated by this huge corporate power.

First, Moore needed to establish his own credentials for what was to be an enormous on-screen role. This meant research for an elaborate opening using home movies, 1950s television clips, GM promotional shorts, newsreel footage and Hollywood feature films, 'with an artistic debt to The Atomic Café' (Cohan & Crowdus, 1990: 27), to demonstrate, filmically, his own background from Flint as the birthplace of General Motors and the United Auto Workers. Roger was to be depicted as having an opulent, bloated corporate lifestyle which can be contrasted with the hardship of the redundant car workers of the filmmaker's home town of Flint.

There are examples of lack of accuracy in research, such as the level of job losses in Flint. Also at stake, as Corner points out, is Moore's questionable choice of interviewees, and most importantly, documentary's own sense of propriety as a form of public communication. (Corner, 1996: 169). In 1993, Michael Moore faced a slander suit by a former county Bar president, who alleged that he was interviewed for *Roger and Me* under false pretences. Moore also faced counts of fraud and false light invasion of privacy because he told Larry Stecco that the filming of Flint, Michigan was to promote the town in response to a magazine article that listed it as the worst place to live. Although Moore denied allegations of misrepresentation, he did not inform Stecco that the intention of the film was to satirize him. (Obiter Dicta, 1993) As a lawyer, Stecco is active in social causes representing the unemployed, but he was interviewed during a lavish 'Great Gatsby' party at the home of a General Motors' heiress. The plush surroundings were to be juxtaposed against earlier scenes of car workers losing their homes and jobs.

Locations for filming the city's wealthy people are deliberately selected to demonstrate outrageous settings, such as a 'Jailhouse Rock' benefit at a newly built prison 'where they're booked and "imprisoned" for the evening – so their fatuous comments and silly behaviour seem even more reprehensible than they ordinarily would' (Cohan & Crowdus, 1990: 29).

Trinh T. Minh-ha: *Surname Viet, Given Name Nam*

'By choosing interviews . . . I found myself closer to fiction' (Minh-ha, 1999: 57).

The filmmaker's pre-planning gained her the practical advantage of not having to return to the country itself. Trinh had a text, which, in content terms, provided a script for re-enacted interviews that filled ' "collective and individual gaps" in Vietnam's history, through unofficial, "undervalued" sources of information such as personal stories, songs, proverbs and sayings' (Minh-ha, 1999: 23). To Trinh, it's a question of experimentation with the interview form, but what will audiences make of it? Hitherto, the interview has been seen as a trusted guarantee of authenticity – direct speech 'from the horse's mouth'.

She wanted to explore popular memory and oral tradition, which 'allows me to offer the viewer songs, proverbs, stories that bring to the fore [women's] . . . oppression, their struggle and highlight how and what people remember of them' (Parmar, 1990: 73). Language would then become central to the artistic exploration for, according to Trinh, it can be enslaving if its workings remain invisible, or empowering if it is allocated space: 'in *Surname Viet*, this space is featured manifestly as presences – albeit presences positioned in the context of a critical politics of interview and translation' (Kaplan, 2000: 326). How was this approach to be 'translated' into filmic form during the decision-making process of pre-production?

First Trinh had to select the participants, then decide how to use them.

> In the casting process, it was important for me to hear about their own life stories before I decided on the voices that they would be incorporating. Within the range of their personal experiences, which were sometimes worse than those they were re-enacting, they could drift in and out of their roles without too much pain. But in selecting them for who they are rather than simply for who they can play, I was not so much looking for authenticity as I was interested in seeing how they would draw the line between the differing fictions of living and acting . . . to a certain extent, interviewees choose how they want to be represented in what they say as well as in the way they speak, dress, and perform their daily activities . . . the second, and even more so, the third, parts of the film, are organized around 'documented' scenes . . . I asked each of them how they would like to see themselves represented, after having been put through the ordeal of incorporating other women's pain, anger and sadness. (Minh-ha, 1992: 193–4)

Trinh has always been heavily dependent on the creative support of Jean-Paul Bourdier for art and design work connected with *mis-en-scène*. She is also quite happy to have someone else do the camera work.

> Since the material is obtained with people whose activities are bound to circumstances that I do not wish to control, to have a cinematographer who may be very different from yourself in the way she shoots, but who understands your sensitivity, is certainly an enrichment . . . The question of having other people work with me on the film does not really raise any problems for me. Of course, it still depends on how one can work with a person, but the collaboration is just another way of working with things that are inside you, with you, and outside of you. (Minh-ha, 1999: 71)

How much pre-production planning was there, apart from the booking of interviews and selection of participants?

> Most of the choices in the film are dictated by what happened during the process of materializing it – the casting of the parts, the rehearsal, the shooting and so on. The script only came about with the film, not before it; and my role as scriptwriter is to provoke a situation in which things are allowed to happen and the choices I arrive at would have to be integral to the specific context of the film since they grow out of its making. (Minh-ha, 1992: 174)

Filming abroad and scheduling the shoot

One of the biggest challenges for television documentary production is the time factor: tight deadlines require quick thinking. Documentary makers who experience the more rigid structure of broadcaster organizational arrangements find themselves having to work around set dates for the availability of crews, budgetary limitations on the number of days for filming and post-production and strict deadlines for the completion of research and hence selection of interviewees. In these cases the documentary-making trajectory tends to involve a discrete separation between the stages of production.

When formulating a schedule for filming in a situation where the number of days is restricted, assessments of how long specific parts of the shoot are likely to take will have to be made in advance. Travel time usually forms a major part of the calculation. If distances between locations are great, or if the requirements for the shoot at any location are complicated, or if there is likely to be a lot of waiting around for an event to happen that is outside the filmmaker's control, then this calculation can be thrown to the wind. *Cinéma vérité* style will require much longer (see next chapter). In addition, time needs to be allowed for the practicalities on site such as loading up and unloading of equipment. Choosing camera positions within a building or big location will take time, as will moving between set-ups, meal breaks, setting up lights, briefing participants before the camera starts to roll and numerous other considerations that can be connected to a particular location.

Filming always takes longer than anticipated, and very often it turns out to be more complicated than originally envisaged. Ideally, a documentary maker will be able to stay with the job until all the necessary material has been collected, irrespective of budgetary and time limitations, but that is rarely possible, and time factors in real life do not necessarily coincide with production schedules. Alternatively, it may be feasible to return later for further shots, as both of the Narmada filmmaker case studies were able to, but this will depend on the nature of the subject.

How far are the differences in approach between these two documentaries determined in pre-production?

Franny Armstrong: *Drowned Out*

Drowned Out was filmed with a more limited time schedule than Patwardhan's, with the disadvantage for Armstrong of having to film in another country with foreign language problems, exacerbated by being relatively new to the subject. Although *Drowned Out* takes over chronologically where *A Narmada Diary* left off, demonstrating that the long and wearisome struggle has not changed very much, nevertheless the filmmaker's approach

Anand Patwardhan with Simantini Dhuru: *A Narmada Diary*

A Narmada Diary captures a period of five years in the activities and life of the Narmada Bachao Andolan (NBA) campaign, which aims to make the social, economic, cultural and moral costs of development more widely known in the face of government intransigence and opposition to the modest demands of the local campaign. The documentary tells the story of Indian villagers

to representation is different. Armstrong chose to catalogue the story of *one* village and in particular *one* family in depth over a three-year period of time, creating a feature-like pace that provides time for the viewer to become emotionally moved by the plight of the main characters.

The main location – the village of Jalsindhi in India's Narmada Valley – selected itself because this was the first human settlement to face the rise in water caused by this particular stage of big dam construction. The protest was all about that village at that moment in time. More important was the selection of a main character or family, who had decided to stay at home and drown rather than be forced to move. Local people advised that Luhariya was the person to feature: 'his house is lowest on the river bank and will be first to be submerged. He is also the healer, holy man, comedian, musician and general centre of attention' (Armstrong, 2002).

The Narmada Bachao Andolan (NBA), or Save the Narmada Movement, helped with the production in a number of ways. Firstly, they advised on what had already been produced – six films up to that point and various books. Armstrong later decided to use some shots of the hunger strike from *A Valley Rise* by Ali Kazini, and some shots from *A Narmada Diary*. In terms of interviewees, the NBA also suggested Indian experts, then later Dr Hugh Brody, an expert from the World Trade Organization (WTO) who had been involved in the report and had recently decided to speak out about it. He had never done an interview about the Narmada before; when Armstrong first visited him, she showed him some 30-year-old photos that took him by surprise, but immediately served to win his trust. The snapshots brought back memories: 'It transpired that he had made student films many years before with my father at college. He was a real star' (author interview, 2005).

Armstrong made three trips in all, returning to England each time to review her filmed material, then deciding what should be

whose 'relatively self-sufficient, egalitarian and environmentally sound culture will be destroyed and a proud people reduced to the status of refugees and slum dwellers' (*A Narmada Diary*: 1997, First Run/Icarus Films). Although both Armstrong's and this film make the point that government resettlement schemes are inadequate, each project reaches the same conclusion via a different route.

The diary format and the decision to catalogue the activities of the NBA provided a definition for the collection of material (i.e. original shooting) about resistance to the enormous Sardar Sarovar dam project. Patwardhan and Dhuru took time to consult the communities that they were working with about narrative content. This primary research enabled them to document events in detail and to be on the spot at the right time. The result was an action-packed range of content, collected by attending every major event for the NBA over an extended timespan. 'Over the years we became very close to the movement and the film reflects this intimacy' (Akomfrah, interview in *Pix*). 'I keep shooting things and eventually some of those things become useful and can be used in a larger film' (Kripalani, 1998: 168). As the project had no deadline, shooting and editing happened simultaneously until a logical end point was reached.

Patwardhan claims that he almost always comes across the main characters by accident. 'That's the advantage of shooting for such a long time' (ibid.). Unavoidably, one of the NBA's most charismatic, fearless and tireless leaders, Medha Patkar, is featured in action. However, an important element of *A Narmada Diary* is the extensive and deliberate selection of a range of other people on the street to interview in addition to the leaders, who are filmed in action, rather than as staged interview 'talking heads'. These ordinary people are the ones that Patwardhan wants his films to communicate with, according to his own political judgement. He has never joined any political party and does not believe that there's only one way of

added during further filming trips, one of which was required by PBS as an update on the story. This process involved shooting, reviewing and rough assembly of some sequences, with research still progressing in order to add to the rough cut.

The main narrative about Luhariya and family is supplemented by background information in voice-over and with 'expert' interviews (including a formal-style interview with activist writer Arundhati Roy) to explain the context to a wider audience. Also featured is Medhar Patkar, who has been dedicated for almost 20 years to the cause of villagers whose homes and livelihood are threatened if the height of dam water and their continued building is not limited. The characters make the same consistent claim that the NBA made in *A Narmada Diary* and continues to make: they would rather drown than leave their homes.

looking at things: nevertheless his sympathies with the democratic left inform all his films: 'if you could provide a significant work . . . I won't call it entertainment . . . but a form that engages people's minds in a way that doesn't oppress them, that doesn't take away their dignity, I think that's worthwhile art' (Gangar & Yardi, 1993: 22–3).

The 'diary' begins in December 1990 with veteran Gandhian Baba Amte marching with other non-violent protesters to oppose the dam's construction. In April 1992, villagers from Manibeli are filmed successfully defying police with drums, slogans and dance. A year later the Morse Report, a review ordered by the World Bank, reveals serious weaknesses in the Sardar Sarovar dam project and another diary event occurs when the global organization withdraws after previously investing $450 million. Further shooting reveals that the government is continuing the train of destruction by persisting in the construction of the dam and the submerging of more land.

Next the camera is on hand to capture NBA supporters led by Patkar beginning a hunger strike in Bombay. It is ended because of a government promise of a review to address issues of rehabilitation and compensation. Once more the camera is there to reveal duplicity as the promise is unfulfilled. This time Patkar and NBA supporters say they'll drown rather than be displaced. Another review is promised, but celebrations are spoiled by a police shooting of a young man.

Again the camera is there to capture the young man's parents state their commitment to keep fighting, just as it is at a five-star hotel in Bombay, where Medha Patkar and others go to meet the World Bank president, who chooses to attend a fashion show rather than meet them. Next the camera is present to capture the discomfort of a Minister for the Environment whom NBA supporters confront. They want to know why the sluices of the dam have closed while the rising water is drowning villages with no rehabilitation for the people. Next the diary registers the aftermath of destruction caused by BJP and Congress activists to the NBA offices.

Franny Armstrong encounters problems of translation/interpretation when filming abroad

Filming abroad tends to demand prior information-gathering about the country, if things are to go smoothly. Efficient documentary makers can check out aspects that require permissions and any special payments, also if there are any particular dangers, subjects which are considered taboo for filming, political sensitivities or censorship. Other questions may include the weather, any health dangers, the customs arrangements and whether a carnet (a customs document listing equipment which must be stamped – forms can be obtained from the local chamber of commerce) will be necessary for equipment. If the producer employs a local crew, they will know all these things. For my project set in Japan (confusingly entitled *Forever England*, a reference to part of a Rupert Brooke poem), I made two filming trips. For the first I took a crew supplied by Carlton Television, together with equipment and carnet. For the second trip, I employed a local Tokyo crew. No carnet was necessary, and they were able to act as translators, fixers and guides in addition to the usual filming skills. The second trip was easier to plan and achieved much more.

Nancy Platt: *Venkatamma's Story*

The filmmaker had to formulate plans without seeing the locations and people in advance. A comparison of the briefing she received with the completed film reveals how she used the information that was supplied via e-mail.

Christian Aid, the clients who sponsored Nancy Platt's documentary short *Venkatamma's Story*, wanted to use the film to brief fundraisers, and also as an example that fundraisers could show to potential supporters in the hope that they would be moved sufficiently to donate towards projects like the one featured. The brief was to show an example of Christian Aid's work in rural India, a project run by a local group called Gramya, supporting residential schools for girls who would otherwise be married young or forced into bonded labour. Clips from the video are screened on the charity's website, and fieldworkers are given copies of the film to show to supporters. The project required a selection of form that would be compatible with the tastes and predilections of the target audience, plus a sensitive and appropriate choice of representation for the content. Nancy also needed to reach the point quickly, because of the short length: 'Corporate is "narrowcasting" – the audience probably already has an interest in the subject, you don't have to capture their attention in the first ten seconds, or state the premise of the entire film immediately' (author interview, 2005).

These are the notes that she made based on the briefing that she was given:

> BRIEF:
> 10 minutes max, personal story, one life, but 1 or 2 subsidiary characters.
> Set in context of Gramya and their issues but through story of Venkatamma.
> Theme – Life before death, turning points and how the organization has promoted that in someone's life.
> Contrast between Venkatamma's roots and where she is now.

The task was to set about transforming this succinct information during pre-production. Platt had to prepare to film in India without a preliminary 'recce', so many of the prior arrangements involved making creative assessments from a distance, based on e-mail correspondence. Although Nancy did not have to select the main character (Venkatamma), or the support character (Sunita), who both came as part of the brief, there were other challenges. The role of the main characters was to demonstrate to viewers that Gramya existed as an organization thanks to Christian Aid, and was doing good work. Nancy had to decide how to film these two people, so she also needed to understand how the organization functioned.

> Clients often know little about the ins and outs of making a film, so it can be difficult to explain to them why, for example, you need a list of possible participants in May when the film isn't being delivered till September. On the other hand, they hire you because you do know about filming, so are less likely to intervene arbitrarily or go on power/ego trips than some commissioning editors. (author interview, 2005)

With corporate films, as Platt says:

> The client will know what they want the film to say and will point you in the direction of people and material for the film. They may have it lined up already. Therefore you don't research the 'angle' or message of the film, it's not open ended, and you don't need so much time to find participants. Obviously there may be times when you are promoting an organization or delivering a message that you don't agree with, or when you see weaknesses that have to be glossed over. (ibid.)

Platt and an English cameraperson travelled to India, having been briefed by their contact, Rukmini, that it would take three hours to the location and that the crew would be spending six hours on travel each day. 'It is very hot and humid, please bring thin cotton clothing', she wrote. Rukmini also provided Platt with background information about the possible locations for filming, so that a schedule and arrangements could be drawn up in advance. From the descriptions that she received via e-mail, Platt had to work out whether the potential shots would advance the story and further the brief for the film.

One such message stated: 'The bridge school [which was to be featured] is located in a small building with 5 rooms. The children live and study in the same space.' The information that Rukmini supplied enabled Platt as director to envisage in advance what sort of pictures she was likely to get. 'Devarakonda town is a very stark place and close to the school are hills and an old fort, which is crumbling down – 13th century I think. You may want to take the children out to climb rocks one day. The children sing many songs and play games all of which can be filmed.' Rukmini also wrote:

> Filming Venkatamma's day. She lives at our bridge school along with 100 girls. You can film her life with us. She goes to school at the local government high school. We will ask for permission to film her at school but I am not sure of permission. If we don't get permission for her to be filmed at school we can film her doing her homework and getting special tuition at the bridge school.

Often with shooting for documentary, the director has to work around existing arrangements. Rukmini's letter continued: 'On the 6th and 7th the children have exams in their govt [*sic*] school and Ventamma [*sic*] will be away for most of the day. I suggest you shoot the rest of the bridge school activities.' Content and aesthetic considerations had to be balanced against practical factors, such as permission to film from third-party organizations, and travel time.

Rukmini's advance notes about the characters helped to inform the off-camera questions that the director was to ask during the filming of interviews, and also provided an option for the background setting. For instance, Rukmini wrote about Sunita, the second story:

> Her mother died when she was very little and her father looked after her. She was married when she was 13 and her husband and mother-in-law ill-treated her and tortured her. She is a Lambada woman traditionally considered to be gypsies but now practicing settled agriculture. She is from Nizamabad district. Her husband was a bonded labourer and could not look after her. She ran away from home one day and wandered around till she was brought to the DDS shelter, which we have set up in Medak district. She stayed with us for a year working with the children there and was interested to continue her studies. To support her rebuild her life I found her the job with Gramya. Initially she worked in one village and now helps to care for the children at the school. She is educating herself with our support and has completed middle school. She will be ready to take her high school exams in another two years. She is now 23 years old. You can shoot her at Pastapur shelter in Zaheerabad if you want a more interesting ambience.

Conclusions

There is a temptation with digital lightweight technology to go for the instant: if it moves, shoot it, then sort out the results later in editing. This can be foolhardy; even the most apparently spontaneous of documentary films are actually well thought out in advance. For some styles, planning in detail is both advisable and necessary. 'Failure here sends you out on the wide ocean in a leaky boat with no charts and few provisions' (Hampe, 1997: 93).

Content is king: no amount of instant or personalized material will compensate for lack of substance within this factual medium. Therefore, filmmakers tend to become experts on their chosen subject by casting the net widely in research, in order to build up a substantial knowledge base. Pre-production is about aspects of advance focus and planning: on the form that the film will take, on the nature of authorial voice, on the ethics of dealing with participants and on the ways of achieving a good product by envisaging problems and approaches before they happen. In essence, pre-production is about taking the steps that will translate the film in one's head into a film in reality.

Summary

Pre-planning pays off later, even if a spontaneous approach is called for. Most filmmakers do thorough research for their subject, and even if they do not use all of it at the end of the day, it serves to inform their subsequent decisions. Content is king; visual 'jazz' is no substitute.

4 Shooting and Collecting

The argument

Audiences do not automatically see on the screen what the director sees on location: the image has to be constructed. Therefore the purpose of shooting is to collect pictures and sound for editing, for films are made in the cutting room. Filmmaker approach, intent and directorial control will determine the nature of the material, to the extent that the range and scale of interventionism, as exemplified in case studies, becomes a central issue.

If the filmmaker has already formulated a definition of intent, as examined in previous chapters, then it is easier to measure progress and to assess during the shoot whether there will be a film worth sorting in the edit suite. The experienced filmmaker always thinks ahead to the next stage, thus, during the shoot, the way it will 'go together' will become a constant consideration. Documentary filming requires a unique level of flexibility combined with an overview and strong sense of purpose. It is an eclectic undertaking in which personal approach tends to outweigh formulaic technique, nevertheless practicalities contribute to the success of the aesthetic, so they too are mentioned here.

Ethical considerations are constantly emerging during a shoot: how far can the filmmaker go? How far should he or she participate or influence the shooting? Is it ethical for a filmmaker to engage in dialogue with interviewees to further an argument? How should the filmmaker represent the witnesses? The aim of the documentary maker is different to that of the participants; for example, the latter may want to clear their name in a legal case, as in the now classic *Thin Blue Line*, whereas director Errol Morris's aim was to make a good film (Nichols 1991: 45).

What are the rights of the interviewee? Legal safeguards such as protection from slander or libel may exist, as well as the right to privacy, but they are not guaranteed. Informed consent should protect participants, but many filmmakers choose to ignore it, saying that the free speech and free press, which allow journalistic intervention in pursuit of the news, also apply to them.

Considering the role of director

Documentary directors need to have the sort of mentality that can handle no script at all. They have to improvise when events in the real world turn out differently on location from the way that was expected. The role of the director is to foresee problems and to solve them. The director must make decisions about where to begin, what sequence is intended, or where to place the camera for the shot to be framed, and he or she must have the overall vision of what is needed, including the mood that is required during each scene. Consistency of focus needs to be mirrored by consistency of style. Style is normally established at the beginning of the film, and tends to remain a constant.

Filmmakers working for a broadcaster are usually subject to a higher level of financial and deadline control. Even grant-aided films tend to have a limited number of filming days: Connie Field could only afford one day for each of her key profile interviews in *Rosie the Riveter* (see case study later in this chapter). Without the combined pressures of a tight schedule, the controlling influence of the broadcaster commissioning editor and the budgetary constraints involved in a limited number of shooting days, there is a danger of aimlessly overshooting. The nature of the project will usually supply its own form of discipline for shooting, as the case studies illustrate. I would agree with Hampe: 'Yes, I'm in favor of shooting a lot of footage, but always as an active, decision-making participant in a process of communication that begins with an idea and ends with an audience (1997: 5).

Nancy Platt: *Venkatamma's Story*

Platt explains the challenges and discipline provided by the format of this documentary short and its associated web clips.

In *Venkatamma's Story*, the style of shots was influenced by the requirements of a short film. For instance, Platt didn't shoot any pans, because she felt there was insufficient time for shots that move gradually from one point towards another. Sequences were short, with less coverage in each than would be expected in a longer film. Less is more: the working challenge of this short consisted of 'having the same components, but less of them'. It was hard work achieving the concentrated approach, as the filmmaker explains: 'If I hadn't captured the actuality in short 1 to 15 minute chunks whilst shooting, the whole pace would have changed. There was no time for atmosphere shots, just the essentials' (author interview, 2005).

There was no chance to develop an argument through the short interview contributions, so interview technique had to ensure that the people with whom Platt talked gave answers that could be used in a short web clip. The informational bites had to be approximately three minutes long. The question she put to them in order to elicit a suitable response was, 'tell me what you're doing here and why'.

Nancy Platt sums up: 'You're delivering a piece of information that still requires a narrative, but isn't as big. You're saying to the audience "here's this thing, that's all". Most of my time when shooting was taken up with ensuring that the right people were in the clip' (ibid.). The economy of this length of documentary requires a certain discipline and focus from the filmmaker, and brings the added pressure of trying to ensure that the small amount of film is still packed full of little gems.

Shooting a lot of material is easy, but when *not* to film can also become a difficult decision, especially if one is capturing a one-off event. The wrong decision could mean that an element of what is happening could be lost forever. During the filming of *Europe by Design*, the five-part series made by my company Chapman

Clarke Films on commission for BBC 1, I visited French government offices in Paris to capture an interview that had been arranged with the Minister of Culture. In the next room at the time was Lionel Jospin, who was then Minister of Education. He was doing a book launch for his memoirs and I was introduced to him. The PR people suggested that I might like to conduct an interview with him. I politely declined because we were there for a different purpose and a tight filming schedule did not allow time for the luxury of gathering additional material that was not required for the story. When he later became the next French leader, current affairs departments worldwide would probably have jumped at the footage, but I had wanted to concentrate on the task in hand, however short-sighted this may now appear in retrospect.

In a situation where there is such a lot of footage, filmmakers tend to keep records on location – shot lists if possible – so that sequences can be found more easily (with time codes) later in editing. This is especially important when one considers shooting ratios: that is, the amount of material shot compared to the amount actually used in post-production and the completed product. Why do filmmakers shoot so much more than is actually needed? The answer is not simply that digital video is cheap, or even that the director keeps the camera rolling just in case something interesting happens. Most often it is because there must be enough shots to satisfy the requirements of the editor. This means that reaction shots as well as action need to be covered, and that there must be close-ups as well as 'GVs' (general views).

Sometimes a plan to edit in a certain way is just not possible when the material is reviewed during editing. If there are no alternative shots, it will not be possible to try other edits because there will be no material to do it with. Therefore it is better to shoot the entire action, not just the bit that the filmmaker thinks he or she may use. This means, for instance, when people are filmed walking, it is better to start and end with them out of shot, if possible.

Editors like choice, so, when shooting, a documentary director will usually keep the editing options open. Lack of cutaways is a common mistake which editors constantly complain about. Cutaways allow the filmmaker to intervene in post-production, for instance, to help condense time and shift point of view in a sequence. It is therefore advisable to obtain shots of important aspects in several different ways: by covering it more than once, the editor will be able to choose the best parts and will have more scope in the way it is reconstructed effectively.

The director's task is to guide the viewer via the directing; the viewer must *want* to see the next shot that is shown because it is logical to do so. So, the best action shots flow naturally from the sense of the film. Of course, the documentary maker creates that sense in the first place, so it is important to ensure that the action advances the film and reveals something about the characters.

The director is the final decision maker for what goes in the film and must take full responsibility if anything goes wrong during filming. It is possible to be open to suggestions, as long as this is not misconstrued as documentary making by committee. The director will understand focus and message, which are under-written by the original intent concerning the project. Hence, he or she is the unifying factor, the person who has an overview that is retained throughout the entire production.

Nancy Platt and camera operator recording 'atmosphere' shots, to be used as 'cutaways' in editing

Franny Armstrong: *Drowned Out*

Director Armstrong's experiences reveal several challenges: physical hardship during filming, foreign language problems and an ethical problem relating to the potential of deliberate performance by participants for the benefit of the camera.

On the first day of Armstrong's initial shoot in the Narmada Valley to film *Drowned Out*, everyone was in the water protesting. She joined them to shoot the action. She was up to her waist, with batteries and passport in her pocket. The batteries got wet, and then she was left with only the one which was already in the camera. There was no electricity in the village to charge it. She and all the protesters were arrested, so Armstrong spent the first night of filming in jail.

Nevertheless, on this first visit, she managed to capture the protest scene, plus an interview with Arundhati Roy.

> I learnt a lot. There were other logistical problems as well. I got ill lots of times because there was no clean water. Basically, I

Anand Patwardhan with Simantini Dhuru: *A Narmada Diary*

Patwardhan's directorial approach is flexible and content driven, involving a clear attempt to provide a narrative of political activity by placing people in the frame in a way that empowers them. Interview technique is particularly interesting, because it lacks the formality of traditional current affairs style, yet retains a serious dramatic tension by capturing moving conversations 'on the hoof' during marches or with other forms of activity in the background. The shoot for *A Narmada Diary* involved capturing events 'which over time acquire political and cultural significance' (Akomfrah, interview in *Pix*). 'I rely on found material, found interviews and found images, so there are self-imposed limits for creativity. I am not creating interviews, I am doing interviews. I might ask questions the way I like but I am not telling the interviewee what to say' (Gangar & Yardi, 1993: 23).

Patwardhan captures actuality music, as performed on location by the protagonists. He refers to the function in post-production

was running a film production on my own, in a language that was not my own, with no electricity. But whenever I felt low, I only had to look at what these people were losing to realize that I should stop whining and get on with it. (author interview, 2005)

Armstrong made three trips to India for *Drowned Out*, with the final one paid for by PBS.

The Supreme Court verdict had changed things, so I had to finish the story. This time I had a rough cut and knew what was missing. I had a list of shots that I wanted to get, and 6 weeks on my own. Most of the eventual film is from this trip because I was a better cameraperson by then. Having a rough cut was a good way to work, it made for a better film. (ibid.)

With *Drowned Out*, language was the biggest problem. There were seven dialects in this part of India: 'A nightmare.' The NBA recommended translators, but she found that these would be middle-class people who might not want to stay in a tribal village, roughing it. Others were not available. She couldn't find one single person who could speak English and the local tribal dialect, Bhilali. They had to go to Hindi first, then, with another translator, to English. Therefore she had two translators at a time, and as the interviews were being conducted, the interviewees got bored with waiting before the next question, because of the time delay.

When Armstrong returned, she devised a different way of working. This involved working out the questions in advance, the interpreter writing them down, then the person answering; but Armstrong didn't know what was said, and had to ask the translator 'did you get this point? or that one?'. The translator inevitably said yes, even when they didn't. Although she had asked them what they had got, it wasn't until she returned home and had the material translated in the UK that she realized what the answers really consisted of. At this point she vowed never again to shoot in a foreign language.

of these sound extracts as: 'Playful moments where you can get out of being immediately literal and are able to jump' (Akomfrah, interview in Pix). As one cineaste has observed, almost all of Anand's films use a popular song to illustrate an argument or provide moments for cutting together a set of shots which would otherwise not cut together (ibid.).

Patwardhan distinguishes between the capturing of reality, which happens during filming and the filmmaker creating something, which happens in post-production. 'The documentary may create through editing, through juxtaposition of images, but I don't create in front of my camera . . . I would not like to manipulate the actual event though I may comment on the event' (Gangar & Yardi, 1993: 23).

Armstrong agonized over whether the participants decided to face death because she was there with her camera. Would they still have taken the same stand if she had not been present? 'If you recognise that the camera or your own presence is an incentive for the behaviour, then you are clearly implicated' (Barbash & Taylor, 1997: 57). The answer to this ethical issue emerged at the end of 2003 when Armstrong returned to the Narmada Valley to shoot an update for the PBS contract. This piece of filming is featured as an update on the *Drowned Out* DVD. In her absence, and without camera presence, the villagers had been submerged in water up to their necks, still wanting to die, rather than give in.

The authorities had prevented them from doing so by beating and arresting them, and removing the people to 'police camps'. The family featured by Armstrong lost all their land and their house and were forced to move to higher ground in the hills to avoid further flooding because of the dam construction. But their story of suffering will continue as long as the waters also continue to rise. 'Eventually there will be no more hills', say the Advisasis, who are still forced to keep on moving upwards. Armstrong's interviewees were saying the same thing as a different set of villagers had said in Patwardhan's *A Narmada Diary* five or so years earlier. The answer to her ethical dilemma is rooted in the on-going history of the valley protest.

Representation: aesthetics and practicalities of sound and shots

It is impossible to avoid instinctive audience interpretation of the language of shots, given the widespread acceptance of the conventions of the film genre. What does each one say, emotionally and visually? The camera operator may go in really close when an interviewee is about to cry, or pull out from a higher and higher angle as the audience distance themselves from a scene that is about to finish. Practice makes perfect when it comes to most camera and sound techniques. This book assumes that the documentary maker can already operate equipment, or has somebody else to do so, or will consult a proper manual, especially for information on basic battery care and how to work the four basic controls on a digital camcorder: sound, focus, exposure and zoom.

At the beginning of a shoot, the viewfinder and the monitor must be adjusted and a white-balance check must be carried out. It is advisable to use a tripod for steady shots and also to always have additional sound gear, such as a directional or gun mic; manufacturers often skimp on sound (Watts, 2004: 149). Sometimes with equipment that is not professional standard, the sound quality is particularly bad. The built-in camera mic is adequate for non-specific sound or for voice recording in good conditions where the person is at a distance of no more than two metres.

Documentary makers sometimes neglect sound, then realize after the event that extra neck microphones or radio microphones (for recording two-way conversations) would have helped. Audiences will tolerate the occasional bad shot, but if they cannot hear and therefore understand the sound, they will lose patience with the film. It is often just a question of using headphones so that one hears in the same way as the recording, keeping the microphone near to the interviewee (whilst still out of shot), and watching that the volume needle on the external mixer does not oscillate too dramatically. The purpose of location sound recording is to collect material that will be required in order to build a soundtrack later. When a sound operator arrives at a location, he or she will listen to the ambient noises, then take a level and do a test run before going for the main recording. The reason for such preliminaries is to get it right. It is virtually impossible to remove an intrusive background noise from a recording later on if one wants to retain the main part of the recording, which may be an essential interview.

Even when the director knows that certain shots will be overlaid later with music or post-production effects, he or she will still always record synchronized

Nancy Platt on location in India, operating sound as well as directing

sound on location. There is nothing to lose, for it costs no more, and may reduce the need for expensive dubbing later. Wild tracks or 'atmos' can be used to fill holes in the tracks that may be created in editing when an unwanted noise is cut out. For post-production systems that are geared to multi-track, one or two channels can be used for the main sound and a separate channel for background noises.

If the images merit enhancement, good sound will bring a picture alive. People who are new to a camera are often beguiled by the power of the zoom: in fact, editors detest zooms, unless they are accompanied by other options (at the beginning or the end). 'Zooms work best when they are motivated by the action in the shot, or combined with another camera movement, or progressively reveal content in a scene' (Watts, 2004: 136). 'Godard said every edit is a political statement, by extension I think every camera movement is a political statement. You opt to zoom in because you're after something. You've got to be aware of the political implications of every camera movement, every edit, every decision to shoot as opposed to not shoot when it's real life that you're filming' (Ross McElwee in MacDonald, 1992: 275).

How much care and craft is appropriate for documentary making? Responses vary, but quality should not be seen as a value-added luxury but rather as a way of enhancing content. If a director wants the viewer to see the same as he or she sees, it has to be made to happen: it will not happen automatically. Filmmakers will choose almost instinctively to shoot in eye-catching places; they will study the available light for the best position, think and look around the action, and consider shooting higher or lower, using shots involving windows, doors, reflections or mirrors, for instance. During a shoot, the other aspect of quality which constantly emerges is lighting, or lack of it. 'Just because something seems simple does not mean that it does not deserve to be used with care and respect. It is possible, for example, to light beautifully for mini DV, just as it is possible to shoot without any regard for the lighting' (Ellis & McLane, 2005: 329).

Filming Luhariya on the banks of the Narmada River: low level close-up creates viewer empathy

Like sound, lighting is often taken for granted – a mistake when one considers how it can influence mood and atmosphere. Artificial light gives a yellow tone, whilst natural daylight is bluish. If there is both natural and artificial light in the same area to be filmed, it is easier to eliminate the natural light by drawing a curtain, or by moving the set-up so that a window no longer forms part of the background, than it is to apply blue filters on the lamps or orange filters over the window.

Highlights need to be in the right place. The contrast between darker and lighter parts of a shot also has to be right and may require adjustment, using the ND (neutral density) filter. Hard light will deepen shadows, giving a dramatic impression. Soft light will lift them in situations where excessive contrast may not look right. In situations where they are losing light, camera operators have to guard against loss of quality when they apply 'gain' by using the camera's built-in light booster. Although the white balance will ensure that colours are constant, if light is coming from more than one source, it is safer to adjust manually.

Every shot is important as it contributes to the story or moves it forward in some way. For instance when composing a shot, the camera operator will avoid static subjects and shade, knowing that the eye is attracted to points of interest such as movement and light within the image. When the shot changes, the eye will want to continue focusing on the same part of the screen for the next shot, rather than flicking to another part of the screen. Therefore to avoid a jump cut and to achieve a smooth edit, the points of interest must be in the same part of the screen, even when changing the shot, if they are to be joined together.

Hand-held work is a skill in its own right, if shots are to be steady and even. To a certain extent this is a quality issue: almost every professional cameraperson claims that they are really good at hand-held work, but not all of them are truly successful. The unsuccessful ones sometimes inadvertently make the viewer feel seasick. Shaky shots are a question of choice. For instance, William

Franny Armstrong keeps the camera steady for hand-held work

Raban made a film about the English Channel using 35 mm for the cinema, shot on the high seas from a small vessel. When viewed theatrically on a big screen, *Continental Drift* deliberately creates a feeling of seasickness, but this is called for because of the content. As with *Thames Film*, Raban effectively used the movement of the boat as a tracking shot, which would normally move over the ground.

Moving shots require the operator to have a good eye and a steady hand. For Raban, the movement of the boat meant that a dolly was not required. On land a wheelchair, a trolley or a track would have been used, or a Steadicam for smooth moving shots. Moving shots can be difficult to cut in and out of, and it may be advisable to shoot alternative versions at different speeds as it can be difficult to know what speed will work best for editing.

A tilt up or down can be used for movement, or a motivated pan, which follows the action to see what will happen next. The camera can start on an object such as a tree then pan or tilt to reach the subject. Alternatively a pull or throw focus can be a good means of changing either from background to foreground (or vice versa), or of introducing a new piece of visual information. Either a narrow depth of field, or two objects that are different distances from the camera will be required. It is a good idea to practise such movements in advance.

The sort of shot and the position of the camera must be considered for each set-up. Composition and framing are subjective creative skills, although there is an accepted universality about the language of shots. If filmmaker intention is to achieve calm, detached shots, then a tripod will be called for. If it is a feeling of distance that is required, with people condensed, a long shot will be called for, whereas tighter framing with close-up has the opposite effect: it increases the emotional impact of the visual. Of course, if framing is too tight, then the

Franny Armstrong creates a feeling of distance by positioning camera and tripod high for a wide shot

viewer can miss the edge of the shot because of 'cut-off': some cameras therefore indicate 'picture safe' and 'title safe' areas in the viewfinder.

If more depth is required, something in the foreground can be displayed – if a leaf or tree foliage are used, the effect is called 'dingle'. Shadows create depth, but when a director wants to increase dramatic impact, a reduction in depth may be called for. For example, in two-way interview discussions, tension will be conveyed by moving the camera further away, then zooming into a two-shot which enhances the apparent drama of the debate.

I once produced an educational history (documentary) television series entitled *The Manufactured Landscape* about the Industrial Revolution in Britain. We filmed several scenes involving vintage steam trains, and had to consider the positioning of the camera to give a range of shots. The majority of views that people see are from eye level, so visuals at other levels add interest value. First the camera was placed low down, in between the tracks right in the middle of an empty railway line (which can be dangerous). When the train appeared in the distance, it looked to the viewer as if was coming towards the camera, which was very dramatic. Needless to say, we were in contact with the driver, so could make it stop before it ran us over! A shot of something coming towards the camera is always more exciting than a visual of an object moving away from it.

We then wanted to film people crossing the track and decided to move position. When the camera was to the side of the track, the people appeared to move from the left to the right of frame. We then decided to move the camera to the opposite side of the track, thinking that these alternative shots (right to left) would intercut. In fact this did not work, because the shots were taken from different sides so the changes in direction on screen were confusing, and the background was also different. We were actually committing the technical mistake of 'crossing the line' (a film, not a railway, phrase!). It would have been better to

How to avoid 'crossing the line': author filming a steam train with crew

do one master shot, then some close-ups, or two shots of people: these *would* have intercut.

Most shots are outside looking in, but sometimes it is important to tell a story from the inside looking out. For this, the director uses POV (point of view). For example, director Dermot O'Donovan made his documentary *Last Among Equals* from the disabled person's perspective. 'I used POV (point of view) from a wheel-chair for example and ALWAYS shot at their level. Sometimes I could only inter-view a relative or carer.' This last point provided a further consideration in terms of director interventionism: he needed to set up the shot sympathetically to the disabled person, who would be in the frame, but not taking part. 'I was deter-mined not to "talk down" to contributors. Sometimes it was impossible to achieve a variety of set-up shots and cutaways if the disabled person was immobile' (author interview, 2005).

Camera POV can become a central distinguishing feature of a film, in the way that William Raban used small boat POV as a naturalistic way of shooting for an entire film. He also used pace very effectively: this is influenced by camera angle, focal length or length of takes, as well as the behaviour or action that is covered.

William Raban: *Thames Film*

How does Raban use his camera and was this influenced by archive footage? Why does he eschew the sticking plaster effect of post-production special effects? What is his approach towards sound?

Thames Film was now changing rapidly. Previously, the film that Raban had planned was to consist almost entirely of actuality captured from his boat; now that he knew which archive pictures interested him, Raban was looking to locate the sites and views on the riverbanks in order to match the present-day visual where possible. First he had to identify the position that the original visual had been created from, then align it to the present view, in order to achieve what he calls an 'interplay of contrasts between present and past' (author interview, 2005). Then the old pictures could be filmed under the rostrum camera, matching the pace, movement and style of the live action by running the same speed for the rostrum camera so that it took over seamlessly from the live action shot.

Many documentary makers select archive to fill gaps that appear later in post-production, with the result that it is too late to film the original footage to match the pace and style of archive image. Post-production effects such as dissolves or wipes are then used to smooth over the lack of visual, but Raban does not agree with this approach.

A small boat ebbs and flows with the river tides and the camera is close to the water surface, drifting with the tide in order to shoot the point of view of the river itself and 'using the movement of the river current to regulate the direction and speed of the visual scan' (Raban, 1998: 16). The low camera movements that go with the flow of the boat create the impression of a huge living organism with its own force, whilst also capturing 'giant shapes and structures that fill the mind with awe' (Ackroyd, 2004). Although he went with the flow, each shot still needed to be carefully composed.

Raban operates the camera himself and is clearly influenced by Vertov's reflexive, creative experimentation. In *Thames Film* the boat provides the movement: he uses it where on land it might have been a track or dolly and he argues that, by steering the tiller, his partner effectively controlled the framing of the film. When I asked about his camera 'style', he immediately stated that he hated that word, because it implies the affected. 'I never use it. I prefer the word "idiom", which is better because it suggests a way of working, and for me naturalism is important' (author interview, 2005). Although use of lens and filters can add value to the scope and range of aesthetic production quality, his naturalistic approach means that he would not use colour filters to affect the image. Yet polarizing filters are acceptable to him because they control reflections in the image and reduce the contrast ratio, which means that one can fit the image more closely to the 'gamma' of the film.

How does Raban know when to stop and start a shot? He concedes that he thinks about editing when he is shooting, because 16 mm film is expensive, so he has to exercise restraint. For him, the flicker of the camera shutter is like a metronome or pulse that provides a natural pace and rhythm. He looks for the end of the movement when it comes to a natural resting or cutting point. He often uses shots to their full length in editing, which means that he is shooting to the length that is required. 'Vertov talks about that – he's my hero', he enthuses. 'I am trying to foreground the physical and visual elements of the medium: framing, perspective (dependent on the focal length of the lens) movement of the camera, movement within the frame, dark and light, colour, contrast. I see all these things as being central to the formation of the kinetic structure. Sound is also central to this too' (ibid.).

Raban did not shoot any synchronized sound, only separate wild tracks, recorded from the boat on a walkman audio cassette and DAT, which enabled the sound to be post-produced using a non-linear system. *Thames Film* does not have any interviews. On one occasion he risked being capsized as he recorded a giant pile driver from the boat with his engine turned off. He was so intent on getting the recording that he failed to notice a large ship approaching. The vessel hadn't spotted his tiny 20-foot boat!

> Sounds need to be selected with as much deliberation and care as the images. I want to record both natural and mechanical sounds from the river with special attention to their acoustical space. I heard a power grinder on the steel hull of a lighter barge. It was half a mile across the water. The sound resonated off the river, was blown on the wind and deflected by warehouse walls. The space made it sound like the bells of St Paul's Cathedral. (Memo to Marion, 2 January 1984)

William Raban braves all weathers, and studies the light carefully

The observational mode/hidden camera?

Direct cinema proponents argue that the observational style presents a challenge: how to ensure audience understanding of the storyline *without* using commentary. The filmmaker's eye must be used to dig below the surface for an insight that will emerge from the banality of everyday domestic situations, with narrative potential in the shooting. This shifts the burden to the filming stage. Therefore, it is not enough to simply turn on the camera and hope for the best. Direct cinema techniques are hard work and can be fraught with difficulties. The time spent following a subject intensively, but not knowing if or when something will happen which is of interest from the filmmaker's point of view, can be expensive. Usually direct cinema methods mean that the filmmaker has to find the purpose of the film during the edit. During filming they simply follow a hunch that something might happen if they shoot enough footage. As one writer says: 'I guess the same rationale supports the argument that if you leave monkeys long enough with a typewriter, they will write *Hamlet*. It seems obvious that one must have a clear concept before embarking on a film, yet many *cinéma vérité* filmmakers ignore that at their own peril' (Rosenthal, 1996: 225).

The style, even today, appears open, raw, direct, un-manipulative, more intimate than the well crafted but static news documentaries. To follow a subject, capturing situations without any prompting, intervention or interviews by the director or cameraperson, neither a researcher nor a reporter is needed. There is no pre-structuring of the story, no commentary to write, and the evolving film will be built in the edit suite. For this to work, a huge amount of footage is required, and the story (if it could be called that in advance) would require plenty of incident. Subjects in the early days tended to be confined to music concerts, personalities, crises and some events in politics.

It is possible to overcome the problem of waiting for things to happen by planning a schedule in consultation with the characters. It should centre around specific happenings within their regular routines, rather than creating events for the purposes of the camera. Clearly documentaries thrive on action, conflict and performance, so the filmmaker needs to look for scenes that reveal opinions, activities, arguments, passions and particularly human aspects of the personality. To detect these, the director needs to be a good listener and to have a sensitive approach to what is happening around the camera – to the extent that he or she can anticipate, recognize a pattern to events and be ready.

Even when filming is in the intimacy of someone's home, as *vérité* often is, the action may be jumping around, but the sync dialogue has to be captured whilst the filmmaker also tries to anticipate where it will be next. Sometimes the cameraperson will move in anticipation, then find that it has proved to be the wrong move, so the camera has to move again, without losing too much of the sync dialogue in the process. At some point the camera will probably have to break off from that subject again, in order to get cutaways, but during the time spent on this, the director runs the risk once more of missing an important piece of sync dialogue. The purpose is to try and understand, whilst also capturing, the nature of the scene that you are in. The fact that you are in the midst of it, but not controlling it, is what differentiates the method from other documentary techniques which also strive to capture the heart of a specific action.

In observational films synchronous sound and long takes are necessary in situations where speech is overheard indirectly as participants engage with each other rather than speaking directly to the camera. This has the effect of locating dialogue in a specific moment and historical location.

> Each scene, like that of classic narrative fiction, displays a three-dimensional fullness and unity in which the observer's location is readily determined. Each shot supports the same overall system of orientation rather than proposing unrelated or incommensurate spaces. And the space gives every indication of having been carved from the historical world rather than fabricated as a fictional mise-en-scene. (Nichols, 1991: 39)

The crossover between fiction and documentary in terms of shooting style has changed. In the past, drama techniques were seen by broadcasters as a vehicle to achieve higher audience ratings by introducing elements of entertainment values into documentary approach. These days, fiction uses documentary camera techniques, such as following rather than anticipating the action, encouraging a vérité style of moving and speaking rather than blocking the action. 'fiction's search for realism has honoured documentary's perceived closeness to "real" life, flattering by emulation' (Search & McCarthy, 2005: 16).

Sometimes fictional techniques can be difficult to sustain in a documentary situation. If the original intention was to capture 'a day in the life', if the camera moves elsewhere, that feeling of same day, same space, will be compromised. Continuity therefore plays a crucial role during the shoot. Some people say that an experimental documentary maker doesn't need to worry about this in the same way that a feature film director would, for instance. But it is often necessary for flow and to bind the film together: 'The main problems here are maintaining correct screen direction between shots and proper continuity between sequences' (Rosenthal, 1996: 134).

Craig Gilbert: *An American Family*

Details of the filming process reveal ways in which Gilbert was able to make decisions from behind the scenes, influencing the final product in terms of what was NOT captured as well as elements and activities that were filmed.

Gilbert describes the observational method as 'a highly specialized technique which demands a kind of sixth sense understanding between the person who is doing the shooting and the person who is doing the sound.' His crew (who took the final credit as 'filmmakers') – Alan and Susan Raymond – were a married team who obviously had this knack. They arrived at the house at 8 am and left about 10 pm, although they only started to 'turn over' when they thought there was something interesting about to happen. Gilbert did not want any other production staff present, so he kept away from the house in the daytime, but stayed nearby to discuss progress with the Raymonds when they were not shooting. He was in regular contact on the telephone and had a daily meeting with the crew, in addition to liaising with the family.

> Since the moment to moment decisions as to what to shoot and what not to shoot were up to the crew, the arrangement was not always a happy one. But there was no viable alternative . . . Because life has a tendency to repeat itself – which meant that if Alan missed something I wanted the first time, he could get it the next time it happened – I think that over the seven-month period he and Susan recorded an extraordinarily accurate picture of how the Louds lived. (Rosenthal & Corner, 2005: 313)

In terms of lighting, intrusive cables were reduced to a minimum by the use of photo flood bulbs, inserted into the regular light fittings in the house for the duration of the shoot. Obviously, this lighting was brighter than normal, but Gilbert claimed, 'I do not want to imply that having their daily lives recorded for seven months was easy or normal for the Louds, or without problems. It wasn't. I am simply trying to point out that it was not as disruptive as many people, including the critics, believed' (ibid.: 314). Neck mics and a boom pole would have been equally intrusive, but the pay-off if these are not used is poor quality sound. On one crucial occasion when Pat and husband Bill are rowing in a restaurant, the dialogue between the couple is virtually inaudible.

Decisions concerning what *not* to film were equally challenging. During the filming period, Gilbert opted *not* to film husband Bill spending time with his mistress.

> God knows, I was tempted. But in the final analysis it seemed to me that doing so would put us in an impossible position with Pat and seriously endanger the completion of the series. From time to time Bill and Pat and the kids would ask to look at various pieces of film, and I didn't want to have to lie about what we had shot while she was away. After Bill and Pat had separated, there was no need to continue this self-imposed limitation. (Ibid.: 315)

Gilbert's authorial voice emerges subtly in terms of what sound *is* recorded, as well as what is missed. It is likely that the presence of the camera over such a long period motivated a certain sense of performance by the participants, increasingly attuned to the requirements of the filmmakers. During yet another row Pat says to Bill, 'Too late now. You know that song? That Carole King song: "Too Late Baby"?' Then in a later episode, after Pat has announced she is leaving Bill, and is languishing depressively by the pool, upstairs her daughter is putting make-up on, whilst listening to another Carole King song (with very apt lyrics), entitled 'Will You Love Me Tomorrow?' Was this a lucky artistic break for the filmmakers, or a deliberate choice by participants for the benefit of the camera? Ruoff comments: 'Although documentary makers imply in interviews that such incidents simply happen and are just happy coincidences, their use clearly demonstrates an authorial intention on the part of the makers . . . The music provides an editorial perspective for interpreting the images, which is the function of narrative film music in general' (2002: 84–5).

The crew also shot the Loud family looking at old home movies and photo albums. This allowed a departure from the immediate 'here and now' that can be a limiting factor for observational films, and, as with the music example, provided further range for editing. Again, one wonders whether the family would have engaged in such visual nostalgia had the camera not been present. The next chapter analyses the editorial intervention involved in the assembly of such material.

Sometimes I am asked by students whether they should use hidden cameras. Invariably I advise against it, usually on ethical grounds as an invasion of privacy (the right to privacy is a basic human right, grounded in law in most civilized societies), practical grounds (what do you do about release forms, for instance?) and because there is usually no real need. Most broadcasters have carefully constructed rules about hidden cameras, which have been devised for sound practical reasons, and from their own experiences, including clashes with the law. They have every right to be suspicious of the motives of a filmmaker who suggests the use of a hidden camera, even if he or she argues that the 'public has a right to know'. 'A very thin line separates the behavioural scientist from the Peeping Tom' (Hampe, 1997: 234). Every case study example in this book contains powerful images that were all collected openly. That speaks for itself.

However, the investigative filmmaker may be forced to use hidden camera techniques for part or all of the film. Current affairs television cautiously uses the technique, but often the experiences on location are difficult, as Dermot O'Donovan related to me in an interview about the filming of *Fakes and Pharaohs*. This local documentary was shot partly undercover in the Middle East, with what he refers to as 'much skulduggery', involving clandestine meetings with 'various crooks'. O'Donovan as director, a cameraperson and an accomplice (fixer) all posed as tourists to work undercover in Egypt. They split the PD150 equipment between three separate bags, managing to capture shots of the antiquities special police on a long lens without being detected. When they were challenged by the police, who asked why they needed a tripod and a whole five minutes to take tourist snapshots, they replied that they were members of the South West of England Camera Club.

The accomplice's role was to introduce Dermot to JTP's (the subject of the investigation) Egyptian contacts, which proved difficult. 'We were nearly rumbled several times. Clearly, we were not going to get JTP's Egyptian contacts to sign release forms. In the end, none showed up.' The accomplice let Dermot down: they did not acquire any interviews in Egypt. 'The three potential Egyptian contributors were either on the run from the police or intimidated into not co-operating.' The undercover aspects and the visit to Egypt had been a costly experience without significant results (author interview, 2005).

Reflexivity

How can reflexivity be used on location as a form of reactive camera work that allows participants to influence the film? The answers are several, and reveal a lot about the triangulation between filmmaker, process and final product. Available options are best examined through case study analysis, for it is difficult to be prescriptive. Every situation will be unique. Yet there are certain strategic choices to be made.

The filmmaker does not have to be on screen to be reflexive. Neither does he or she have to concede all power of decision making to the participants. The sophisticated and often beautiful camerawork used by Rouch in *Chronicle of a Summer* demonstrates that spontaneity and flexibility do not necessarily also mean lack of thought and care in the composition of shots, or in the quality of the sound.

Jean Rouch and Edgar Morin: *Chronicle of a Summer*

How did Rouch and Morin use their powers of filmmaker intervention, and how did this influence the final product?

Rouch was pioneering the use of more portable synchronous sound equipment which enabled filmmakers to participate by stimulating conversations, provoking encounters and conducting interviews. 'The possibilities of serving as mentor, participant, prosecutor, or provocateur in relation to the social actors recruited to the film are far greater than the observational mode would suggest' (Nichols, 1991: 44). Rouch believes that the filmmaker shouldn't even try to be objective; the truest documentary is the one that is the most false, 'from the moment that the person who makes the film assumes the responsibility for it and signs it' (Levin, 1971: 139). As he readily admits, he took his cue from Vertov, who abandoned all pretence of filmmaker non-interventionism in *Man with a Movie Camera*.

> At the beginning of *Chronicle of a Summer*, I was afraid because the people were paralysed in front of the camera and they couldn't say anything. But very quickly I discovered that the camera was something else; it was not a brake, but . . . to use an automobile term, an accelerator. You push these people to confess themselves, and it seemed to us without any limit . . . the camera is, let's say, a mirror, and also a window open to the outside. (*Movie*, 1963: 22)

> When I make a film, I edit in the camera. I see the film in my viewfinder . . . The camera deforms, but not from the moment that it becomes an accomplice. At that point it has the possibility of doing something I couldn't do if the camera wasn't there: it becomes a kind of psychoanalytic stimulant which lets people do things they wouldn't otherwise do. (Levin, 1971: 135)

During the shoot, while some of the participants and the filmmakers were having lunch, the conversation turned to anti-Semitism. This prompted Rouch to decide to ask about the tattoo on the wrist of Marceline, a Holocaust survivor.

> I knew the Africans did not comprehend our concern about anti-Semitism . . . the Europeans began to cry and the Africans were totally perplexed. They had thought that the tattoo was an adornment of some kind. All of us were deeply affected. The cameraman . . . was so disturbed that the end of the sequence is out of focus. I stopped filming to give everyone a chance to recover. Now, is this a 'truthful' moment or a 'staged' moment? Does it matter? (Georgakas et al., 1978: 18)

Rouch was disturbed at how everything can suddenly run out of control when the camera encourages participants to expose themselves. What are the ethics of creating a personal drama in this way? It is possible to argue that such intense encounters pose more of a threat to the participant if the filmmaker remains separate and 'objective' through withdrawal. Rouch and Morin used the device of showing themselves making the film so that the viewer could not then dismiss the experience as 'fictional'. Ironically, this same decision also raises questions of the boundaries between documentary and fiction.

Rouch asked Marceline to talk about her memories while she walked the streets of Paris. He gave her a tape recorder and a microphone, so the situation was artificial, yet:

> I suddenly discovered that this released a series of confessions that Marceline had never made during direct, face-to-face interview, simply because she was suddenly in a totally different element. [It was] . . . deforming in a good sense because it stimulated something she would never had said without it. That's what a documentary does: it reveals these exceptional moments when, suddenly, there is in effect no camera, no microphone. That's a revelation, a staggering revelation because it's totally sincere – and totally provoked. And totally artificial, if you like, because you asked someone to walk in the street and talk. (Levin, 1971: 137)

On location at Les Halles, the shot begins with a close up of Marceline talking to herself. As her voice continues, the camera pulls back slowly, revealing the beautiful and impressive old buildings (since demolished to make way for the Pompidou Centre). The buildings, that used to look like a railway station, provoked Marceline's memory of her return from the concentration camp, when her family came to meet her at the station, but her father was absent. As she becomes smaller and smaller, the enveloping space symbolizes the isolation and loneliness of her memories.

Just as the soundtrack is manipulated for expressive purposes, so also the camerawork is varied and carefully composed to create texture with light and dark, and movement. During the outdoor activities, the camera floats with the subject, whilst in a tense interview scene with Marilou, it is close and still, allowing an intimacy with all the hallmarks of a psychoanalytical session. 'The camera stays on her when she stops talking, letting her hands and face speak in a touching and painful way.' The camera acts to free her, whilst also freeing the filmmakers 'to participate actively in the situation, even to provoke situations, without feelings of guilt' (Jacobs, 1979: 440).

In this film, Rouch uses more close-ups, mainly interiors, than in his previous films about Africa.

> When we began the film, the camera was still on its tripod. I thought the effect was much too static, so I began to move it as people spoke. How they looked and what they did with their hands seemed important, so I did close-ups. . . . Remember, I didn't know these people personally and they began to speak of very intimate problems. I was somewhat embarrassed by that. The first Marilou sequence was shot right after I met her for the first time. In the second, we were alone at Marceline's flat after dinner. She was talking so nervously that I had to react. So I took big close-ups, to try to get inside. I was very upset by the experience. (Georgakas et al., 1978: 19)

'With Morin, we were so enthusiastic about this process that we were filming all the time. We stopped in October, but there was no reason to stop ever. The film could have been without an end' (*Movie*, 1963: 22). They found that the reaction of the participants to seeing themselves in the first cut was so interesting that they decided to film their reactions to the final cut. The film ends with Rouch and Morin walking through the halls of the Musée de l'Homme, talking about their reactions to the whole experiment. By showing participants their own footage, and filming this, 'he initiated a moving self-examination in his participants and a desire to go deeper. The results show Rouch's radical curiosity, his sympathy with the ordinary person's need to find meaning in life, and his willingness not only to question the medium but his own authority to use it' (Rabiger, 2004: 75).

When the unexpected occurs during filming, the smart response is to turn this into a positive creative feature. For *Europe by Design*, episode four, we were filming in the former East Berlin quarter of Prenzlauerberg. Since the collapse of communism, the area had become run down, and there were numerous disputes over the ownership of property due to the fact that people who had had their houses confiscated by the Nazis, or had fled the country and abandoned them at the time, were now able to reclaim their properties, subject to certain evidential paperwork. We were in the area for an interview with a local councillor, when suddenly an unanticipated drama erupted in front of our eyes. A fleet of fire engines raced onto the scene, sirens blaring. Director Martin Clarke took an immediate decision to follow them at top speed in our crew car, camera rolling. He then used these exciting shots for the opening scene of the documentary.

This sort of flexible, speculative shooting which is responsive to the location represents a form of problem solving through the process of filmmaking. As soon as a person picks up a camera, there are choices to be made: the question is then 'where do you draw the line?' However, speculative shooting does not equate to unplanned shooting.

Interviewing, authorial voice and use of presenters

There are no hard and fast rules about the backgrounds that a filmmaker chooses for interviews, but there are issues to consider from the technical standpoint that interviewees may not be aware of. How will the background contribute to the overall feel of the film? Is it likely to prove too strong, and therefore distracting from what the person has to say? The choice should enhance the mood of the film at this point, and may be influenced by the fact that the interviewee is more at ease in certain locations than others.

Exteriors can appear more natural than interiors, and exterior cutaways usually make more sense, but factors such as weather and time of day may militate towards interiors. In some cases the story, rather than the need for lights or the problem with extraneous sound, may also become a factor. I once interviewed a resident who lived near Gatwick airport, and who was leading a campaign against the construction of a new runway because of the noise hazard. Her back garden had planes constantly in motion overhead. For once, this intrusive sound was exactly what we needed to illustrate the point of her message.

Camera angles for interviews are best kept simple: medium close-up offers the advantage of then being able to move in closer for more intimate or critical content in the reply. If the interviewer is positioned next to the camera and asked to look and talk to the interviewer, this will give a full-face framing of the interviewee and ensure a constant eye line. Shifty eye movements give the impression of nervousness or dishonesty!

For interviews, there are choices in terms of camera position which will have an implication for the style of your film. The interviewee can look directly into the camera, in which case they are addressing the audience with no apparent intervention and will appear to have more authority. Or they can be captured slightly more obliquely by the camera, so that it appears they are talking to a person off-screen: this is more informal, relaxed and anecdotal. Here the interviewer sits slightly to the side of the lens and interview questions can be cut out during post-production.

When interviewing the veteran fashion designer Karl Lagerfeld, I employed the 'tell me' gambit. By prompting him in this way, I obtained usable, self-contained statements. Obviously, the interviewee must name the subject in their answer rather than referring to 'it'. Instead of formal, written questions (which sound stilted and should therefore be avoided), prompts such as 'what about the . . .' will give the filmmaker a self-explanatory soundbite which can be used in editing, or intercut with other contributions, without the need to introduce the situation using voice-over narration or commentary links.

I only ever ask one question at a time, and it will only contain one single point. If the question consists of several parts, the interviewee will inevitably forget, or ignore one of the elements. If I had started my question with 'why did you . . .?', then the interviewee would most likely have answered 'because I . . .'. This would only have represented *part* of a sentence, so the answer would be unusable as a self-contained statement.

Alternatively, the interviewer can appear on screen, so that the two-way conversation features the presenter or reporter as well: this is necessary for a confrontational dialogue. Walking interviews are a good idea if using an on-screen presenter – they provide both movement and the impression of a natural conversation. Radio mics will be required.

For some projects, an on-screen presenter (often scripted by the director/producer if they are not a journalist or subject specialist) can personalize the experience, enabling a dialogue with participants, contact, shared experience and involvement, especially if they address the viewer by using the second person. However, presenters who are only present for a small part of the filming can feel left out, so it is important to keep them informed and to make them feel part of the team.

In fact, a presenter can fulfil a number of different functions, depending on how strongly they are featured: it may simply be for 'top and tailing', or it may be in a more complex fashion. Dermot O'Donovan employed actor Edward Woodward in *Fakes and Pharaohs* for a very comprehensive role as an on-screen narrator, both judge and jury. Woodward told the viewer things that interviewees had not mentioned. He moved the story on with his links, and provided crucial information for which there was no visual evidence. Where actors tend to score over journalist or 'expert' presenters is in their ability to hit precisely the right tone of delivery straight away, and consistently. O'Donovan believes that, 'Actors know how to pitch it just right' (author interview, 2005). However, international sales distributors prefer films without an on-screen presence as it reduces the requirement for dubbing or subtitles.

It is better to use the medium to show, not tell. Therefore, the director will want to film an interviewee doing some activity before or after the interview: walking into their office, fetching a file from a cupboard, entering the building, or some other form of lead into the interview. This can serve several useful purposes: it provides shots over which voice-over can be used to introduce the person before coming to the first extract from their interview; it also provides cutaways which may be necessary as edit points, enabling a filmmaking style that shows activity and movement whilst also conveying a sense of location and context for what the person does. The participant's voice-over from the interview can be used over such shots. This was the style used in *It's Your Choice* (see chapter 2).

Cutaways will also be required if a group discussion is being filmed, as the camera will not always reach the correct person immediately. People will probably interject in an unpredictable fashion, even if they are asked to not talk over each other so that edit points are clean. Usually editors prefer to avoid using the section of a shot that shows the camera finding a fresh position, so cutaways of other people listening, their hands and reactions, provide useful fillers for smoothing the way. It may be helpful if the director also shoots part of the discussion a second time, focusing on speakers not listeners. A second take provides choice in the edit suite.

Sometimes during interview situations, the answers that people give during the warm-up before the camera arrives are better than when the camera is rolling. Although the interviewer should run through the topics to be covered (if this is a formal interview situation), there is always a danger of over-rehearsal so that the participant burns out in advance. Nevertheless, the interviewer must make the person feel at ease and less suspicious of the process; the eventual performance will benefit from the empathy that has been created. Famous people are more likely to be cautious in their comments in case they are sued, or adverse publicity arises as a result of what they say. Whatever the apprehension or otherwise, the filmmaker always has an obligation to provide the interviewee with information about how long the filming is likely to take, what is expected from them, and what the practicalities are likely to be.

On occasions the director may have to make some fairly unreasonable demands on them for the purposes of filming, such as requesting that they move furniture in order to accommodate the camera movements, remove noisy jewellery, or stop their nervous gesture; jingling coins in trouser pockets is a frequent habit! However, there are situations where interviewers will not want to be too deferential, because this may inhibit them from asking the hard questions. If the documentary is an investigative or current affairs adversarial style, the filmmaker does not want to get too close to interviewees. In more formal situations, the interviewees sometimes ask for the questions in advance and may want to adhere to only those questions. However, prepared answers will destroy the normally spontaneous, natural conversational style; documentary interviews should not amount to a written speech!

The interviewee may also want to view the rushes and have a veto over the final edit. I never grant the veto, and most filmmakers would agree. Showing the rushes is fine, and is likely to happen anyway if the filmmaker uses playback with a monitor on location. Whether to accept these sort of restrictions will depend on how desperately the interview in question is needed. If only this particular person can answer the point, and the rest of the content will collapse without this contribution, then the filmmaker may take the view that something is better than nothing.

Connie Field: *The Life and Times of Rosie the Riveter*

The interviews in this film allowed for the unfolding and development of the participants as characters. What sort of technique best elicits such responses?

The priority during interviews was to obtain the personal reflections, then as a secondary consideration, any more general impressions. Repetition between the contributions had to be avoided. Because Field had recorded interviews beforehand, when it came to filming, she was able to ask questions that would elicit specific stories that she knew already. Each woman was given the time to develop their reflections so that anecdotes could be included.

Field never asked direct questions: 'they were broad questions, not leading questions . . . "Oh, tell me that story again . . ." ' (Rosenthal and Corner, 2005: 160). Questions were not used and the interviewer was never in shot. Each interviewee had a different and appropriate background setting, which Field considered 'says something about what they were talking about . . . [for example] we shot Lyn on a ship as she used to build ships during the War' (Tammer, 1981: 359).

Each interviewee was filmed with the same eye line, slightly offset from direct address to the camera. The filming set in the present gives depth to the contributions. In terms of the directness of the film's argument and how this is addressed, the interviews were not shot to present a hard, interrogative question. Field could have adopted a tougher current affairs approach by introducing 'experts' on aspects of wartime policy, who could have addressed points that the female interviewees made, but this would have given a different feel, introducing an element of more general discussion, which would have detracted to some extent from the potency of the profiles. Instead, Field allowed viewers to follow an unfolding of personal self-awareness by the women, whereby the personal became the political during the course of the film.

As is often the case during the shooting of interviews, a person will offer up a little gem at the very end when the crew are about to 'wrap'. The statement that Lola makes at the end of the film illustrates this tendency: 'I had done with her. I asked her a very simple question, like "What happened to you?", and she said what she said' (Tammer, 1981: 409). Better late than never!

With 'softer' themes and profiles, it is important to build the trust and confidence of the participant. Sometimes the interviewee will need to be convinced that the filmmakers are going to be fair and non-judgmental to their case. In formal interview situations, the more the person feels they are having an intimate encounter and can forget the presence of the camera, the better. The arrival of the production team can seem like a formidable disruption (although a one-person crew will be less disruptive) and can make interviewees nervous. A good crew will be as unobtrusive as possible and allow the interviewer to establish a rapport with the interviewee. Part of that bond involves the submerging of film-maker ego in favour of the interviewee's.

During the interview the rest of the crew (if there are several people) should keep away from the sight of the participant, so it will help if the director and camera operator have a kind of hidden code for communication, as their voices must not be heard on the recording. A tap on the shoulder will indicate that this is the time to zoom in on an emotional or important answer, or to use a close-up on a repeat of that same question. Use of frame should be agreed in advance, and most professional camera operators will ask the director or reporter if they want a change of movement during questions. The filmmaker needs to decide how involved the audience should be at this point – the tightness of the shot depends on this strategic decision. Conversely, the wrong length of zoom at the wrong time will make the answer difficult to edit.

Eye contact is important, especially in close-up; the interviewer should keep constant eye contact with the person while they are talking. Shifting eye movement on screen makes an interviewee look nervous; constant blinking tends to indicate potential dishonesty. Interview technique requires sensitivity. It takes judgement to assess when to ask more and when not to, especially if the answer is very personal and sensitive. Sometimes silence is the best policy: this in itself can prompt the interviewee to say more. Anand Patwardhan, for example, knows from experience and because of his firmly defined filmmaker intent, precisely when to continue rolling the camera and when to cut.

The dilemma is that the interviewer will want emotions and drama, anecdotes and colourful examples, as well as facts. Facts can be presented with graphics or voice-over narration, but there is no substitute for individual human feeling. However, this may be an intrusion into old wounds and tragic memories. As one writer expresses it: 'In the name of the public good we delve into people's lives, invade their privacy, and expose their souls' (Rosenthal, 1996: 152).

On the content side, the more a documentary maker knows about the subject involved, the easier it becomes to conduct successful interviews. Even without having done a research interview first, most people will ensure that they know as much as possible about interviewees: then the questions will be more focused. There is an ethical dimension to the handling of content; as Patwardhan states, documentary does not mean putting words into the interviewee's mouth. The best parts of an interview are when clear truths emerge spontaneously, referred to by Jean Rouch as 'privileged moments'.

Earlier questions can be more straightforward – background information to set the context, for example. It is better to ask clear, concise, open-ended questions. The filmmaker may have to ask the same question again at the end of the interview, if the first answer needs amplification. 'Tell me again about how you did . . .' will result in a more succinct, relaxed, useable answer the second time round, especially if the point is important but the interviewee stumbled during the first take. Yet according to Patwardhan, the second take will be acting. Is this ethically justifiable in the interests of the film?

Operating solo on location

A 'one-person band' who directs, shoots and records will have less time to think about situations on location than a crew will. This means that more, not less preparation will be required. On the one hand, a disadvantage of going solo is that one does not have feedback from other production members on location, which helps to formulate ideas and to clarify the focus of the story. After all, the process of having to explain things to a production team is one way of gauging if one truly knows what to do next! On the other hand, a solo director can take his or her camera to a 'recce' and shoot preparatory shots as a record, and will find that access is easier. Being unobtrusive is useful in documentary situations where one person alone can get inside the action, whilst several people may stand out and move around more slowly.

One-person operations are more democratic and can provide an ideal way of getting into the media industry because commitment and capabilities are transparent. In addition, certain styles of documentary, such as video diaries, investigative journalism pieces, low budget films, wildlife films that may take a long time to capture subjects, fly-on-the-wall and films that are shot in confined spaces such as inside cars, all lend themselves to one-person shooting and recording.

Yet there are practical disadvantages to going solo: very few people are equally good at all of the skills required. Experienced specialists work faster and more efficiently, usually with a higher-quality result. Sound may suffer without a separate person holding a mic and watching levels. It can be useful to have others to help carry equipment, park cars, or watch out for intrusions whilst shooting. Camera equipment can easily be stolen on location. McElwee is a one-man crew, but says he would not necessarily recommend this to others: 'Sound quality suffers, and I often find it difficult to do basic things like changing the focal length on the zoom lens, because my left hand is holding a microphone' (Rudolph, 1999: 107).

Anand Patwardhan: *In the Name of God*

*Patwardhan is a 'one-man band' on location. **In the Name of God** involved a risk-taking investigative persistence, with camera work clearly at the service of content, led by an idiosyncratic interview technique.*

In the Name of God was shot on film, with a ratio of 8 to 1, but these days with DV equipment, Patwardhan's ratio can reach 100 to 1. He simultaneously acts as a solo news camera operator, interviewer and director by mingling with the crowd, in their midst as part of the fray. He uses a hand-held camera in a way which suggests a more informal, participatory style, without sacrificing quality:

> the films are unpremeditated. They have a very long gestation period. If I was doing a shoot which was well organised and over a short period of time, then I could afford to have a cameraperson . . . Sometimes I'm so concerned about the content of what's being said and so involved in what's happening that, being the cameraman, I have done the minimum to get the story told. Slowly I'm imposing a discipline on myself saying that OK, this was the exciting bit but I also need to get into where we are and what other things are happening – it's like having two cameras, one camera which covers the main subject and one camera which picks up on incidental things. (Akomfrah, interview in *Pix*)

> There are advantages and disadvantages of being both cameraperson and editor. By narrowing down the point of view one can get more focused, but one can lose it on crucially tangential moments. Sometimes I miss the joy of discovering a new viewpoint; at other times I'm thankful that the shot I really wanted is there without the filter of someone else's eye. (Goldsmith, 2003, ch. 10: 11)

The subject matter that Patwardhan deals with is potentially dangerous, and the way that he follows events while shooting raises the issue of risk-taking by the filmmaker.

> Although I am outspoken, the risks I take are far smaller than those taken by some of the people I have filmed. I'm protected by my class and caste, by the fact that people know and support me. So I have a responsibility to use my privileged position to speak out against fundamentalism. If a Muslim did this, he'd be finished. Nor can a working class person do as I can. (Goldsmith, 2003, ch. 10: 14)

This risk-taking is not analogous to a war reporter, for instance: 'unlike many war correspondents, I am not titillated by it . . . I am more interested in analyzing the causes of the situation so that the film can be useful . . . I don't think filmmaking is an heroic activity. It is a way of analyzing a situation to arouse people's thinking' (Gangar & Yardi, 1993: 21).

The way that Patwardhan stays with his national themes for a long time is reflected in his technique:

> Over that period you run across exceptional people, who do not necessarily speak very well but whose experiences are very important for the film. So that in terms of framing them, that's quite unconscious. When I like somebody, or when I get into it, there's probably technically something which I can't define, which is not pre-planned. Maybe something happens and my respect for the person gets translated direct to the camera, or the cameraperson, in the framing, and everything takes a form. (Akomfrah, interview in *Pix*)

'I stay on the characters after they finish speaking. The camera doesn't switch off immediately, it lingers on. I find that a good way of staying focused and yet providing the space' (ibid.). 'On long interviews, for instance, I knew when to turn the camera off and then on again. What started out of necessity soon became enjoyable. I've grown to like the direct eye contact that is achieved when one shoots and interviews at the same time' (Goldsmith, 2003, ch. 10: 11). 'When you are doing interviews, you waste lots and lots of footage, but if you are the cameraperson you can switch off and then on again whenever things get interesting' (Akomfrah, interview in *Pix*).

The people in the street that Patwardhan stops to interview often add an uncanny spontaneity, humanity and simplicity to the theme. An interview with a seamstress from a neighbouring village provides the information that people who were born there have been evicted from their hutments and nobody cares, but in contrast, the place where Ram was supposedly born makes people care. Destruction of a temple and other buildings can be repaired, but the lives of the many poor people killed in the riots cannot be restored. These striking comments explain the reasoning behind the filmmaker's argument that the poor have a 'growing resolve not to let hatred and intolerance in the name of religion win over reason and humanity' (Chatterjee, 1997: 33).

During his street interviews Patwardhan repeatedly stopped different people at random to ask them the same deliberate, interrogative style interview question – 'When was Ram born?' He explains the reason:

> There is the whole question – is it a temple or a mosque? There are people who believe that Ram was born in this spot and are willing to kill for it. But when I asked them when was Ram born, they had no answer to whether Ram was born millions of years ago or thousands of years ago. So that extreme logical perversity became revealed through one question . . . On the bridge to the mosque–temple in Ayodhya there are these guys who are so angry that they reveal they are quite happy that Mahatma Gandhi was murdered. They think it's perfectly all right – that he deserved to die. Normally the fundamentalists would hide this deep nastiness. But if you catch them at the moment of passion and they reveal that, then the audience can see where it's all coming from. (Akomfrah, interview in *Pix*)

'In documentaries there is no acting. The difference between documentary and fiction film lies there. If you say something once and if I ask you to repeat it – the second time is acting' (Sharma, 2002: 286).

Objectivity/subjectivity?

Ross McElwee: *Sherman's March*

Ross McElwee challenges the concept of objectivity with his personalized style.

McElwee's one-man operation is extended to his role as the protagonist and narrator, on camera. 'The camera is a catalyst, and it does intensify and force things. You're after something with the camera.' In addition, McElwee has no script for guidance. 'It is very, very difficult to work without a script or the preproduction that most documentaries have. It is also invigorating and quite exciting when it works out' (Rudolph, 1999: 108). 'I make the films in the present tense. They capitalize upon the spontaneity of the moment. It's not scripted. It's not rehearsed. This isn't "Take 3". It's the one and only time it happened. You either get it or you don't' (Rhu, 2004: 8). During the shoot, McElwee created a film personality for himself 'based on who I am, but it isn't exactly me . . . It's difficult to know yourself and to know how you're presenting yourself to the world' (MacDonald, 1988: 23).

Like Rouch, McElwee believes that 'versions' of truth emerge as people react to the artificial presence of the camera, but he extends this approach by foregrounding his own presence to such an extent that he becomes the content in his own right, although he is responding to the people that he films. Whist admitting that films like this are 'a tad indulgent', he draws our attention to the blend that he has evolved:

> In all the Godardian hue and cry about objectivity and truth being captured by a camera . . . I've missed the idea of subjectivity. Somehow melding the two – the objective data of the world with a very subjective, very interior consciousness, as expressed through voice-over and on camera appearances – seemed to give me the clay from two different pits to work with in sculpting something that suited me better than pure *cinéma vérité*. (Lucia, 1993)

There are pros and cons when it comes to abandoning the so-called 'objectivity' of classical observational style in favour of a more up-front personalization:

> Often, you've given up the observed detail that reflects the depth and multileveled complexities of the world, both visually and sociologically. What you're getting instead is a self-reflective complexity that turns back on itself. Occasionally, in *Sherman's March*, however, there are moments when I was able to step back and observe what was going on. The scene with the survivalists is an instance of that. (MacDonald, 1992: 275)

By making people aware that it's only a movie, he is using this technique to draw them in. The dichotomy became apparent when McElwee stated on screen that he wanted Karen to fall in love with him, yet he appeared to be using the camera to end the relationship. The truth is far from clear: 'If I really wanted her to love me, would I not have put the camera down, and convinced her of my seriousness in doing that?' (Lucia, 1993: 34).

> We have to keep in mind that this is a film about real people and real events. It's a documentary, not a fiction, and there are certain issues of privacy one simply has to respect. But the sexuality being alluded to and yet not directly revealed adds a subtle tension to the film that I hope works in its best interests. (MacDonald, 1992: 281)

As Nichols says, documentary 'calls for specific ways of being among and apart from those ultimately represented in words or film' (Grant & Sloniowski, 1998: 13). As stated in previous chapters, the ways that this can be achieved are both varied and complex. The issue of potential objectivity or subjectivity arises with every documentary style. It is worth considering, for instance, whether direct cinema (observational mode) is any more objective than *cinéma vérité* as used by Rouch. Barnouw summarizes the differences as they relate to location behaviour. The distinction helps to identify the choices for the director, which are still relevant today:

> The direct cinema documentarist took his camera to a situation of tension and waited hopefully for a crisis; the Rouch version of *cinéma vérité* tried to precipitate one. The direct cinema artist aspired to invisibility; the Rouch *cinéma vérité* artist was often an avowed participant. The direct cinema artist played the role of uninvolved bystander; the *cinéma vérité* artist espoused that of provocateur. (Barnouw, 1974: 254–5)

Conclusions: ethics, good and bad faith during filming

If only shooting was as easy as Anand Patwardhan claims: 'There are no scripts – no arduous briefings. You film people. You ask them what they think and they tell you. You get on film what is happening – the reality of the moment as it is . . . My 'style' of documentary filming is simple – you just film the truth' (Sharma, 2002: 286). Yet ethical judgements are complex. There are a range of issues to consider on location when collecting material.

Digital technology may have made it easier and cheaper to shoot larger amounts of material, but that is only an enabler, not a solution. The easier it becomes to step out of one's front door with a camera and to enter other worlds with the intent of capturing some form of reality, the more an ethics of production is required. There are no absolutes other than a need for an inherent sense of fairness and respect for the people to be filmed, and a permanent desire to seek at least a perception of truth in all situations.

What are the ethics of camera presence? When should the filmmaker turn the camera off and stop rolling? Is the existence of a crew actually encouraging a situation, drama, or conflict, that would not arise if filming was not happening? In other words, are participants being encouraged by the documentary maker to stage their story in a certain way, perhaps a more exciting way, for promotional or entertainment purposes, and in the process abandoning the sense of reality on which the genre depends? What happens when the filmmaker deliberately sets out to subvert that sense of reality?

Michael Moore: *Roger and Me*

From the production standpoint, does Moore show bad faith towards participants during filming? Does he treat interviewees as either victims or oddballs whilst enhancing his own on-screen image? Are his interview techniques designed to wrong-foot vulnerable social actors as well as the rich and corporate players?

The on-screen image that is cultivated is full of a kind of irony, invective and comedy that can only be conveyed by the filmmaker posing as the man in the street with a personal, 'amateurish' grudge that combines with autobiographical polemic to form a distinctive authorial voice. During the filming, Moore is regularly on screen as an active enquirer. As we follow his present-tense investigations, entertainment value is derived from the process of trying to squeeze information out of a closed corporate power. However, the filming effort of the crew themselves is not shown: Moore's David is seen to be fighting alone against the General Motors Goliath.

Moore's own interview comments, as exemplified below, show his intent to break with the order of events. Methods of production clearly influence audience expectations of what information they believe they are receiving and how they should assess it. The approach to the filming of several encounters with interviewees is questionable from an ethical standpoint. As an example, the 'Pets and Meat' woman, who remains anonymous, is filmed in a way that focuses on her as a remarkable, strange character, in a way that emphasizes the grotesque and detracts from the context which would provide the real reason why this should be so. The woman raises rabbits and slaughters them (which we see on camera) to be eaten.

> His own responses to her remarks about the 'butchering' and the 'fryers' and 'stewers' are calculated as *performance* to camera; the bonding with the viewer serves to objectify the woman as weird in a way which is also darkly comic. She is positioned within the scene to play this role, with little if anything by way of an empathetic viewing relation being developed through Moore's presence alongside her. The later sequence amplifies this mode of depiction ... The way that Janet, the 'colours consultant' is depicted for her comic value is also an example of Moore's 'bad faith'. (Corner, 1996: 162–3)

Critics have referred to this sort of behaviour on location as a 'cheap shot strategy', with his badgering of the beleaguered beauty queen contestant as a further example that ultimately says 'more about Moore than it does about Miss America' (Cohan & Crowdus, 1990: 28–9).

Moore's *vérité* investigative-style interviewing involves 'switching them into a line of enquiry which they have neither prepared for nor find it convenient to respond to. Repetition and emphasis reduce the opportunities for playing safe and introduce further harassment into the improvisation of answers' (Corner, 1996: 165). Interviewees are prompted by Moore's leading questions, such as 'don't they feel that a lot of unemployed are just lazy? ... too many of these people are simply set up for laughs. Moore may boast of his working class roots ... [but he] seems only too willing to use ordinary working people for his own comic ends' (Cohan & Crowdus, 1990: 27).

Sometimes when the filmmaker arrives at the location for filming, he or she discovers that the story is not quite as they had envisaged in advance or as they would like it to be. Then the question of ethics arises once again: should the director attempt to show the situation differently from the way they actually find it?

Filmmaker Nancy Platt refuses to depart from the 'truth' as she finds it. During research she had been told that 'bonded labour' was an issue in *Venkatamma's Story* (see earlier case study), but it turned out to be not quite as exploitative as she had imagined. 'It was an arrangement, they were doing the family a favour. I showed it as it was. I couldn't make it more dramatic without lying. In this film the children aren't all skin and bones: but you shouldn't need that in order to prompt audiences to donate to charity' (author interview, 2005). The media is full of the stereotypical third world images of people as horrendous victims of war, violence and famine. Whilst certainly not denying that such things exist, by being truthful, Platt is also presenting a more positive and complex image. The people in her film display subtlety and dignity, demonstrating once more how central issues of representation can become to the business of shooting.

Challenging the borders of documentary during the shoot

Some filmmakers are determined to create a hybrid form when shooting that borrows from documentary, but does not necessarily adhere to all the standard tenets and definitions. I believe that this is unnecessary: the real world has sufficient interest and complexity within it to allow for plenty of scope without also taking on this particular creative challenge. However, those filmmakers who decide to create a hybrid in order to confuse the viewer need to think carefully about the nature and integrity of the undertaking, especially in terms of what reaction audiences will have.

Trinh T. Minh-ha: *Surname Viet, Given Name Nam*

Trinh allowed the subjects to move in and out of frame, subverting the formality of the interview itself (Nichols, 1991: 53). Is this still documentary?

> What is offered to the viewer in this [first] part are long socio-autobiographical criticisms whose unconventional length and use of spoken language allow each woman her own space. It is, for example, at the difficult pace of her English utterances that the story of her life is unrolled, and the film structured. Lighting, setting, framing, camera movement, shot duration, and the use of visualized words are other strategies indicative of the carefully constructed nature of the interviews. I wanted to keep the re-enactment ambiguous enough in the first place so as to solicit the viewer's sense of discovery . . . (Minh-ha, 1992: 205)

Trinh claims that 'interviews in which a camera and a microphone are set up to catch the "spontaneous words" of a woman while she is having lunch, for example, are no less staged than the re-enacted ones . . . but [the staging is] more via the situating, framing, editing and contextualizing' (ibid.). These latter sections were no easier to shoot than the re-enactments, because the women found it difficult to talk about their own lives.

> Since the memorization and the rehearsal of the re-enacted interviews in English was such a hardship for the women, I thought that the change to their own voices and to their mother tongue would be a relief. But to speak 'spontaneously' and 'freely' in front of the microphone proved to be impossible. It was another form of 'acting natural', another ordeal altogether. (Minh-ha, 1999: 57)

Summary

Documentary filming amounts to the collection of raw material, both sound and pictures. When interacting with the real world, directors need to be flexible, to have an overall vision, and a sense of ethics, which extends to integrity in dealing with participants and good faith with the eventual audience. Every shot matters, and should be thought about carefully. A good filmmaker will set a high store by quality and constantly take stock of what is needed rather than shooting aimlessly. It is important to ensure that the editor has plenty of choice in the next stage.

5 Shaping and Editing

The argument

The editing process consists of reviewing the pictures and sound that are available, selecting the best parts, and ordering them into a narrative by narrowing them down, with a view to achieving the maximum impact on screen. The one word 'editing' covers a complexity of purposes, issues and tasks. It's often said that a documentary is either made or at least sorted out in the edit suite, a process which can be both creative and rewarding, but also painful. The filmmaker becomes aware of the parts that work and the parts that do not, and also what is missing. Now the director faces the music and is forced to focus on his or her chosen methodology in order to see it through successfully. In doing so, he or she will be inviting the audience to interpret and assess what they see.

Introduction

The editing process usually divides into two stages, offline and online (with film, rough cut and fine cut). Technically, the purpose of the offline edit is to create an EDL (edit decision list), to identify the matching point on the master during the online edit. During the offline a rough assembly edit comes first as a loose compilation of the shots that the producer/director wants, in the order of the script, allowing for trimming later.

When viewing the rough cut the filmmaker therefore checks the structure, logic and effectiveness, for there will be a definite shape to the film and it will be approaching the final length, although probably still a little longer than would be intended for the final version. It's important to question the point of every shot, especially during the fine cut stage. Thus, the rough assembly edit is gradually transformed into the final rough cut, with a real structure, rhythm and pace.

Representation

In post-production final decisions are made about form and representation, using the available material; decision making involves value judgements, ethics and craft considerations. Combinations of picture and words can be contentious, such as juxtaposition that may require choice and interpretation, offering the viewer opposing ideas and moods with great economy.

Juxtaposition and counterpoint can also be used in editing 'to stimulate imagination when the conventional coupling of sound and picture is changed'

(Rabiger, 2004: 438). However, this has to be constructed carefully, for the viewer may find it difficult to differentiate between the evidential claims of sound and image separately (Corner, 1996: 28). There is a fine balance between gratuitous manipulation by the filmmaker, and creative interventionism. The possibilities for decision making are enormous, provided there are good rushes to work with, and if the editor and producer/director have a symbiotic working relationship.

Outlining the editing process

The material that the filmmaker has will dictate how far he or she can now deviate from original intentions, which may have been scripted previously. The raw material needs to be reviewed, everything must be systematically logged and assessed and can be viewed while it is being loaded into the editing machine. A window print dub for review is done in real time by digitalizing or 'capturing', so it can be a lengthy process. Records are needed of all the raw materials, which will be derived from a variety of sources such as archive film, newspapers, stills and interviews. This exercise in taking stock enables the filmmaker to assess whether pick-up shots will be required.

Video must have time code, and if there is none, it must be added. Part of the preparation of materials during post-production usually also involves making transcripts of interviews. If there is dialogue in a sync sequence, it may not be necessary to obtain a transcript – the editing script can summarize the content with, for instance: 'sync sequence in office, Jane talking to editor'.

It is a good idea to make a provisional editing plan. For my project with shooting in Japan, *Forever England*, I was given VHS editing for a week. I had the shots logged with burnt-in time code and a written description of the shots. I could

Author selects 16 mm archive film

decide whether there were any sections that I definitely would not want to use, and which therefore did not need to be digitalized. This enabled me to make loose sequences, without being too selective at this point, and then take the time code (VITC) on to the computer. The editor was able to follow the suggestions that I made after a paper edit. This is advisable if the editing script is out of date, or if there is none because the project is a *vérité* film and only partly scripted, or if the documentary maker needs to assess how to build dramatic meaning.

After logging all the sources, obtaining the necessary transfers and viewing the rushes, sound and pictures need to be selected, structured and layered. There may be additions such as special effects, titles and graphics to create. These will be compiled with a soundtrack, which itself may go through a process of sorting and enhancement, as sound effects, music and narration may be added. Video editors like to lay a rough sound commentary early on as a 'guide track', along with sync sequences which will have their own soundtrack. This first assembly will mean that the material has been compiled in roughly the right order, with shots topped and tailed, but without any definitive cuts having been made.

Approaches vary according to the nature of the material and intended style of the film. One way is for the editor to make loose sequences then digitalize the sync sequences as cut. The correct relationship between sequences will help the process of representation and understanding. Selected parts of the interviews can be used as a sound guide track for the over-laying of shots, although it is advisable to build a structure visually. The process is like a funnel, first with a loose assembly edit where the shots and sequences that have been selected are all joined together in an order which evolves a narrative. Then the filmmaker chips away at it as a cut-down version, until it becomes a final version, even shorter. Every shot should move the story or the action on. If it doesn't, then it can be dropped.

The more material there is to review, the more difficult the decision making about what to cut out. Many direct cinema documentaries are shot at a ratio of 40 or 50 to 1. An emotional attachment to certain parts of interviews, sequences or individual shots, sometimes because they were difficult to obtain, can lead a director to hold on to material in a way that may be stopping the flow. This will only render decision making more difficult. If an interview is not used, it is usual for the producer/director to send a sensitive letter to the interviewee. The person may be eagerly awaiting the final film in order to view their personal contribution. From the filmmaker's point of view, their help, or their organization's support, may be required again in the future.

It is perfectly normal to rethink and rearrange many times. Sometimes the structure that emerges is linear, sometimes it is not. Either way, the filmmaker can always play around with it. Only then can something approximating a finished product emerge. This may have to be shown to a sponsor or commissioning editor for approval, possibly resulting in further changes, before they approve it. Then there can be an online edit, a sound mix or sound sweetening, an audio layback and a complete video master edit.

Dziga Vertov: *The Man with a Movie Camera*

When considering how to edit sources together, the filmmaker should be guided by more than simply the need for a narrative. Vertov defined the essence of a range of considerations.

Vertov called for montage before, during and after shooting a film, which Nichols argues is a form of control (1991: 13). It was not enough to show 'separate frames of truth' on the screen, these had to be organized so that the whole was also a truth.

The most difficult task facing the editor is to find a formula 'expressing in the best possible manner the essential theme of the cine-thing' (Geduld, 1967: 114). The viewer will assess various factors: 'At the same time that we perceive the movement which determines the relation between images, we also take into consideration, between two adjoining images, the spectacular value of each distinct image in its relations to all the others engaged in the "montage battle" which begins' (ibid.).

Vertov believed in a fluid montage style, establishing large patterns of sequences, organized into a rhythmic visual order which he named 'intervals', but these were not 'scenes' as we find in fiction: 'Montage means organizing film fragments [shots] into a film-object. It means 'writing' something cinematic with the recorded shots. It does not mean selecting the fragments for 'scenes' [the theatrical bias] or for 'titles' [the literary bias]' (Michelson, 1984: xxix). The viewing order of the 'intervals' is constructed according to 'the movement between shots, upon the visual correlation of shots with one another, upon transitions from one visual stimulus to another.' The chief correlations, according to Vertov are between ' "planes" [close-ups, long shot, etc.], "foreshortenings" [cuts], movements within the frame, light and shadow, recording speeds' (ibid.).

Proceeding from one or another combination of these correlations, the author determines: '(1) the sequence of changes, the sequence of pieces one after another, (2) the length of each change [in feet, in frames] . . . Moreover, besides the movement between shots [the "interval"], one takes into account the visual relation between the adjacent shots and of each individual shot to all others engaged in the "montage battle"' (Michelson, 1984: 90).

Working with an editor

The advantage for a director of working with a separate editor, who may see the film differently, is that this input can be inventive and bring a new creative eye. 'He or she is there to support what is right, challenge what is wrong, and put new energy into the whole process' (Rosenthal, 1996: 166). Particular sequences may have been difficult to achieve, but the editor will not want to know *how* the shots were obtained. It is not the process of gathering material that is important now. All that matters at this stage is what can be seen on the screen.

The filmmaker can fall in love with the material that he or she took such pains to shoot, so that there is no fresh, critical eye. Sometimes the director may feel special sympathy towards a certain character, maybe because he or she has been through a formidable experience or set of circumstances in the presence of the crew. Again, the editor will not be interested in this kind of 'back story', only the performance that has been captured by the camera.

The editor could well make suggestions that the director hadn't thought of, which can then be incorporated into the editing script. Rosenthal quotes the example of the classic *vérité* Maysles film *Salesman*. The concept was to follow four Bible salesmen around until something happened. The filmmaker brothers didn't have a clue what the final story was likely to be about. This emerged during the editing. Editor Charlotte Zwerin is quoted as saying:

> David and I started structuring a story about four salesmen, very much in the order the thing was filmed . . . it took a long time because we started off in the wrong direction. We took about four months trying to make a story about four people, and we didn't have the material. Gradually we realized we were dealing with a story about Paul, and that these other people were minor characters in the story. So the first thing was to concentrate on Paul, and go to the scenes that had a lot to say about him. That automatically eliminated a great deal of the other stuff we had been working on till then. (Rosenthal, 1996: 225–6)

Jean Rouch and Edgar Morin: *Chronicle of a Summer*

I cut with an editor at my side, and he tells me what he sees, and if he doesn't see something, then what I wanted to put in isn't there, and if he sees something that I don't, then I have to take that into account – which I find invaluable. (Rouch, in Levin, 1971: 134)

The editing is creating the form, but I've never made a film where the editing didn't conform to what I wanted to do. It's a question of honesty. From the moment that a documentary filmmaker changes the sense of the film he wanted to make in the editing, it's bad, it's false for me. And generally bad and false at the same time. (Levin, 1971: 135)

Rouch believes that most films require a form of narration, though this can come in several forms, even asking interview questions and retaining them in the final version will act as a form of narration. 'I think it's very difficult to have a commentary without narration . . . *Nuit et Brouillard* is a profoundly human film precisely because the commentary is there, because there's a guiding hand' (ibid.: 138, 142).

At the time, Rouch's film was not particularly well received in the United States. One critic felt it was less powerful than contemporary American *vérité* films because it appeared to have been manipulated arbitrarily both in shooting and editing. Others have argued since then that 'it is this very manipulation which makes the film still work today and achieve poetry as well as fact, artistic form as well as realistic content' (Freyer, in Jacobs, 1979: 438).

Deciding on authorial voice, subjectivity and objectivity

In the early stages of editing, overall approach is more important than considerations of length. The question of where the voice of authority lies will be finally settled. If the documentary maker does not consciously make choices about how authorial voice is to emerge, the film will seem to lack focus and direction. The producer/director will find themselves clarifying an editorial stance which is brought into focus by the writing of narration, the selection of interview sections and sync dialogue. It may lie in voice-over (referred to as 'voice of God'), or with the presenter who may also be the filmmaker. Levels of personalization have to be decided upon as another important element of interventionism. The presenter may represent a broader, institutional source of authority.

Alternatively, authorial voice may rest with the interviewees and participants in the film. It is possible to achieve subjective exposition with a number of different speakers, or at the opposite end of the spectrum, to achieve 'objectification' and distance through a more formal 'voice of God'. Using interviews as testimony, levels of apparent truth/objectivity or of partiality/subjectivity can be influenced by visual and sound editing and by the juxtaposition of testimonies.

The filmmaker has a choice of evidential sound styles: testimony via observed conversations, but here both purpose within the film, and quality of performance by participants, will vary; or testimony via interviews. Use of interview material as voice-over can 'refocalize' visual portrayal, encouraging viewer empathy. This is the evidential sound style that we selected for the careers information film *It's Your Choice*, with participant profiles.

Emile de Antonio: *In the Year of the Pig*

De Antonio had more than 40 hours of material to edit (Lewis, 2000: 88). Every piece of film was time-coded and edge-numbered as it arrived in New York. His fascination with obscure images of Ho Chi Minh and others made it difficult to let go of shots and make cuts. 'I can't let go of a single frame . . . and every cut hurts. *C'est ça'* (Lewis, 2000: 88). The filmmaker would paste sections of interview transcript onto his cardboard paper wall noticeboard (see chapter 3), with ideas of images, then try the soundtrack on the edit machine with different shots, 'so the process was always one of collage' (Rosenthal, 1978: 9). He had covered two whole rooms with paper before he constructed a scene.

With the parts of the interviews that he had selected, he was able to construct a basic structure (Eisenschitz & Narboni, 1969: 48, author's translation). Yet that structure was still very loose and long: the scene about Ngo Dinh Diem was a 60-minute assembly at first, but was finally reduced to 15 or 16 minutes. De Antonio constantly experimented with combinations of pictures and words, changing them many times. 'I've got a good visual memory'. He made structural plans, but they were never as detailed as his own memory (Ciment & Cohn, 1970: 30, author's translation). At the same time, he assessed what was still needed, and continued to shoot more interviews. 'I realised that there were big gaps, so I found other people' (Eisenschitz & Narboni, 1969: 48, author's translation).

The filmmaker's argument in the film is not expressed in voice-over commentary, but instead from interviewees, from the selection of archive and from the arrangement of evidence (visual, oral, and their juxtaposition) in post-production. 'All the attitudes that we tried to show in the film, like American racism, I showed in the most revealing way that I could, such as the following phrase: "One dead American is worth 50 dead Chinese (Vietnamese)"' (ibid.: 49). We only hear the filmmaker's voice once during an interview.

Historical reconstruction is based on oral history, witness testimony and archive footage. It was not until some years later that de Antonio came across the films of Esther Schub, who pioneered compilation film methods in Russia during the 1920s. Unconsciously, he had followed in her footsteps. 'I was overwhelmed', he remembers (Rosenthal & Corner, 2005: 158).

De Antonio's use of some of the interviews as voice-over with illustrative historical shots is well illustrated by early archive of rickshaws, with interview voice-over, 'not talking about colonialism, because the image explained colonialism – but explaining what was behind colonialism . . . what the French were trying to do . . . at the same time I was weaving the life of Ho Chi Minh in and out of the whole film right down to the end where I film Dan Berrigan, who had just come back from Hanoi' (ibid.: 96). Berrigan's interview voice-over is matched carefully to archive visuals when he says, 'the Vietnamese know what it is to have a leader who leads a simple life'. Ho is surrounded by a group of children. 'I used another shot they gave me of where Ho lived, which was a small space with a tiny typewriter and one extra Vietnamese suit hanging there, and you know it wasn't bullshit' (ibid.: 97).

The archive footage that de Antonio used of the battle of Dien Bien Phu includes shots taken from a fictional reconstruction: 'Still, it was beautiful footage and I think I used it well, because I cut from that to the real footage of all those white faces surrendering to yellow faces, which is one of the symbols of that war' (ibid.: 95). At the last moment during the editing process, he was offered some footage of General Patten, which prompted an entire recut of another section of the film.

Both beginning and end of film were important. 'The music, the noise you hear in the film is really a helicopter concerto, it's written by a young man who studied with John Cage, his name is Steve Addis' (Kellner & Streible, 2000: 217). With its noise of blades, the 'concerto' is difficult to identify without an image of a helicopter on screen. Yet Vietnam veterans amongst the film's audiences immediately recognized the sound, and instinctively ducked at the sound (Lewis, 2000: 105). 'You're cutting away and always trying to make two or three things happen at the same time, and those who get it, get it and those who do not get it, do not get it, and it doesn't really make any difference anyway' (Rosenthal, 1978: 9).

The ending was carefully put together in editing in order to make a statement. First de Antonio had used some old footage of Vietnamese charging at the camera, but he dropped it in favour of a more American ending, 'a more suitable ending, a politically coherent ending' (Lewis, 2000: 88).

> I had an ending, and we were ready to go to mix, and the ending was all right. But it was wrong. It would have worked, but failed to make the point I wanted. The editor and I stayed so late, she cried. It was a miniature nervous breakdown, but then I had what I wanted. My work has to do with sweat. (Kellner & Streible, 2000: 94)

Shots of wounded and disabled American soldiers are followed by a shot of a statue of a young man who died at Gettysburg, which is reversed and put into film negative,

> to show, in my mind anyway, that our cause in Vietnam was not the one that boy had died for in 1863, and then I added a kind of scratchy version of *The Battle Hymn of the Republic* . . . The temptation of the compilation film, though, is the high, jazzy moment, that plateau moment that you want in there even though maybe it doesn't belong. (Rosenthal & Corner, 2005: 97)

Assembling, structuring and fine cut

Although some films can be assembled in the order that they're shot, and the diary format tends to dictate this approach, each documentary maker has their own idea of what structuring entails. The order in which information is communicated can be a difficult challenge. The main criterion tends to be what works creatively with the available material, usually in the interests of creating a logical narrative flow. With good editing, the flow that is created makes the audience unaware of the process of compilation, yet allows them to interpret whilst actively viewing.

Sometimes a prior paper edit helps. If a project has been shot *cinéma vérité* style, there probably was no intended structure, in which case editing will take much longer. There can be huge amounts of material to review, video's cheap and easy flexibility compared to film has the downside of encouraging a 'shoot everything that moves, then sort it in the cutting room later' approach. Even if there was no intended structure, there should have been some form of concept which can act as a guide to editing. With this in mind, it is possible to edit scenes one at a time. When there is a variety of scenes, connections, lines of dialogue and meaning should emerge that will provide a logic for links from one scene to the next.

Methods of structuring are dependent on the nature of the project. In observational work, editing is not directed towards a rhythm or the building of a temporal framework so much as aiming to create or enhance the impression of lived or real time. With the interactive (reflexive) mode, editing aims to maintain a logical continuity between viewpoints or reactions and conversational exchanges, usually without commentary to help join the fragments together. Some films are about the interaction itself.

As Dai Vaughan points out, technicians try to keep the quality of 'real time' that they themselves experienced when watching the rushes. 'Editors of this sort of film spend a good deal of their time trying to find the piece which "tells it all in one shot". But this tendency to work with larger elements means that frequently the story takes longer to unfold' (Vaughan, 1976: 32). The longer a shot is held, rather than subordinated to an extrinsic structure, the 'more reliably may the viewer guess at its "integrity"' (ibid.). However, if a take is held longer than is strictly necessary for reading the visual, this will serve to call attention to the shot itself. This is a technique of reflexive mode editing which makes the viewer aware of his or her relation to the text and of the text's problematic relationship to that which it represents. Editing increases this consciousness of cinematic form.

Craig Gilbert: *An American Family*

In observational documentary, there is normally no external music, voice-over commentary, re-enactments or inter-titles, or formal interviews. In fact, Gilbert departed from some of the norms. The family later claimed that the editing betrayed their story.

Documentary editing always involves selection, condensing and creating – how else could the volume of material be handled? There were 300 hours of rushes. The shooting ratio was 25 to 1 – normal for *vérité* filming. Post-production lasted a whole year, with up to 20 people involved, including 3 editors, 2 assistants, a coordinating producer and Gilbert as the producer. This latter team spent the first three months viewing for five days a week, six hours a day. Then they took a week to discuss their reactions and how each of them felt the material could be made into an interesting series of hour-long episodes, running chronologically. Gilbert then started a paper exercise of dividing the rushes into episodes, and at first came up with 30, then reduced this number to 24 and finally to 12.

The ethics that the team adopted as guidance was that personal judgements, likes and dislikes about what they had seen, should not influence decisions; the rushes were a record, and how they were structured in editing should reflect the 'characters of the individuals, the lives they led, or the events they participated in . . . I was asking the editors to let the material speak for itself rather than, as editors are trained and paid to do, create something out of the material' (Rosenthal & Corner, 2005: 320). This had implications: if a scene was boring, it should not be made less so by the tricks of editing; speech impediments should not be edited out to increase clarity; events should not be compressed through editing, but should be communicated as far as possible in their entirety. According to Gilbert, one editor had difficulty in not trying to make the family less objectionable through her editing, which contravened this brief. She left the team because of differences in approach.

Observational documentary is often criticized for not taking the past into account, but this is not the case here. Scenes of the family looking at home movies and photo albums were edited together with background music. Music, also abhorred by direct cinema protagonists, appears in the background when son Lance goes to Paris (predictably an accordion). Gilbert also broke with proscriptions in order to strengthen the narrative drama when he used voice-over, recorded during post-production, of parents Pat and Bill. As one of the production team says, 'we wrenched the convention of not telling you, by telling you up front that she was driving down to speak to her brother about the divorce' (Ruoff, 2002: 87). The inclination to flag events before they happened rather than to let them evolve during each episode in strict observational non-interventionist style was enhanced later by the plot summaries in television guides, such as 'Producer Craig Gilbert hints how the family's summer separation may have deeper roots'. Ironically, Gilbert decided during post-production not to take a director's credit because he did not want to undermine the inclination of viewers to see the series as a 'recording of real life as it happened' (ibid.: 112, 116). In fact, the imperative to enhance the sense of narrative during post-production had the effect of making the presence of the camera appear to be the cause of events, and the actions of the family to appear as the effects of that same presence. Lance coming out as gay and the parents' divorce were most often cited as examples of this.

Long duration of a series (12 hours) may not resolve ethical questions, only postpone or extend them. 'We knew that to some extent the family had been affected by the presence of the camera despite our best efforts to minimize this effect; we admitted this in a statement that appeared at the beginning of episode 1' (Rosenthal, 1988: 292–3). As Ruoff concludes: 'Paradoxically, the more documentary producers remove conventional traces of authorial presence – such as on-camera narrators, voice-over narration, scored music and interviews – the more problematic their influence becomes' (2002: 116).

With documentary, the order that information is communicated, and how much of it at any one time, is a dominant issue in editing, centring as it does around the construction of a narrative. The structure of the narrative is often formulated around a crisis. As in fiction, an unstable state emerges during the beginning, in the middle a problem grows in either strength or complexity, then at the end there is some form of resolution. Although editing techniques commonly found in fiction, such as continuity and montage editing, are frequently used in documentary editing, because documentary structure is normally reliant on evidentiary editing, the classic techniques of continuity editing are often changed.

Documentary requires that an *argument* be advanced, and to do so, time and space can jump about. 'Instead of organising cuts within a scene to present a sense of a single, unified time and space it organises cuts within a scene to present the impression of a single, convincing argument in which we can locate a logic' (Nichols, 1991: 19).

How to introduce the dynamic/problem/question without gazumping the whole film can be difficult. As Nancy Platt explained: 'Sometimes in editing, a need arises to use a particular contribution *before* the person has been introduced in context as a character. There is a problem with laying out the story early on, without giving it away too soon, so some soundbites can't be used too early' (author interview, 2005).

With fiction editing, it is only montage that can join diffuse aspects of time and space to give the impression of one continuous argument. In narrative technique, the classic unity of time means that events occur within a fixed period and move towards a conclusion with a sense of urgency or suspense. This structure is the one that *vérité* tends to create.

Documentary structures following an expository or essay approach create a dramatic involvement around the need for a solution to the 'problem'. This can be an issue or challenge that the filmmaker has devised: 'the felt need itself can be as much a product of expository organization as of narrative suspense' (Nichols, 1991: 38). A structural pattern can emerge:

1 The opening: this should be catchy and attention-grabbing.
2 Explanation, exposition: the purpose and problems to be dealt with. This is best kept short, otherwise it can become boring.
3 Evidence related to the theme: this is the middle, which builds the story. Sometimes there are recurring themes. For instance, in *Roger and Me* Michael Moore regularly cuts between a business or government optimistic decision to a 'reality' such as the sheriff evicting people from their homes. Dramatic conflict or tension can be built via such editing.
4 The resolution: the point towards which all evidence is leading, e.g. the point at which in *Roger and Me*, Michael Moore finally confronts Roger Smith.
5 The ending: the point after which nothing more needs to be said, the final sequence.

The opening sequence is especially important. In post-production the editor will also be searching for the symbolic shot that encapsulates the message; the selection of order and, in particular, the way the opening sequence is constructed will enhance this. The opening sequence acts as a 'hook' to hold audience attention, indicating the nature of the participation that is required of them. Viewers will then perceive a sense of direction and suggested destination for the journey which they are embarking upon.

Connie Field: *The Life and Times of Rosie the Riveter*

Rosie the Riveter demonstrates a way of reconstructing the past in the present using interviews, whilst adding a visual presentation of history using archive footage.

The production and editing of this project took a year. Field had already worked out what was to be said, and what she calls 'the emotional curve'. She also decided that a chronological approach would achieve the greatest impact. Editing set the pace and involved decisions on final content. 'But when I sat to edit, I found it very hard; I had too many things in my head. I had picked the individuals for so many different reasons and they had so many things to say'

(Tammer, 1981: 409). She called in another filmmaker to help with the interviews and the shape of the film, which was crucial given the distinct viewpoint which emerges from the structure and the way information is offered.

> I believe in presenting the material in an analytical structure that's accomplished in the editing room, if possible, and in letting people deduce for themselves – aided by an analysis you give in the way you structure the material . . . This meant no narration so that the material could speak for itself . . . I think the disembodied voice of a narrator distances people from the material. I believe that audiences are intelligent enough to get the point, even subtle points. (Rosenthal & Corner, 2005: 155)

'The audience then deduces. The film doesn't tell people what to think, particularly' (Tammer, 1981: 409).

On the one hand, Field found that specific personal references in interview material worked better than more general comments. 'If she spoke of *the* black experience, it didn't work as well as when she gave a specific experience from her life' (Rosenthal & Corner, 2005: 157). On the other hand, because there was no 'voice of God' commentary, Field also needed some of the interviewees to make more general comments, such as the observation Lola, an ex-welder, makes about her wartime work. 'It felt good to make something, to be alongside other people. I hope for that feeling again, but without a war.'

The main element of this film is the juxtaposition of female case study interview material next to archive footage of media propaganda about the war effort. 'Many telling points are scored simply by juxtaposing the idyllic WASP world of the media with the women's own memories of childcare problems, racial discrimination, union busting and safety at work – or rather lack of it' (Johnston, 1981: 21).

In editing, contemporary songs were added to the soundtrack, and the mixing of these three elements was used to create a distinctive pace and interest value, with regular movement between archive footage and interview profiles. On each occasion that the editing returned to one of the women, her story was advanced, to the extent that one character – Lola – who opens and closes the film, makes 17 appearances in all. She fulfils a role of general narrator as well as an example of personal experience.

All of the personal experiences emerge, through editing, as evolutionary: gradually, we observe the development of female self-awareness. This reflexive process of participant reflection comes from the fact that the participants are able to provide in-depth, intense interviews. Because they are allowed the time in editing to develop as characters, they take on a role that goes beyond that of the conventional interviewee, whose individual experience is curtailed in post-production because it is used to exemplify a more general argument provided elsewhere, by somebody else. 'I was very conscious of wanting the audience to feel the experience, for it to have an emotional impact . . . If I was using people *just* for information, I could have used some of these stories which, for whatever reason, didn't carry the emotional weight that matched up to the events they were describing' (Rosenthal & Corner, 2005: 152, 157).

She decided to use the archive footage in two different ways. First, as visual illustration for the voice-over testimonials of the interviewees, where their comments have a more general relevance. Such descriptive sequences integrate the accounts of interviewees with archive images. The second way in which archive film is used provides an amusing contrast which demonstrates discrimination towards women. Here Field retained the original male commentary on official film from the period as soundtrack, which gives an impression of both manipulation and condescension. These are then intercut throughout with the original interview testimonials of women. The contrast between 'official' information and the reality of women's lives introduces an element of comedy tempered by a wider theme of media and propaganda, as the film first encourages women into the workplace, then urges them back into the home as the men return from the war. The contradiction between the propaganda and the women's experiences escalates as the film progresses.

An example of how creative editing can be used to integrate past and present is provided by a scene about the news of Pearl Harbour breaking via the radio. The editing moves from one interviewee's account of hearing the radio bulletin, to archive sound recording of President Truman delivering the broadcast. The visuals first show members of the public listening (including some fictional archive footage), then each of the female case studies apparently listening in each of their individual interview locations, followed by visual footage of the President speaking. This sequence of cutting and use of sound with pictures provides a sense of past and present which demonstrates that recollections can involve both closeness and distance.

In terms of how the messages are conveyed, the impact of Field's authorial voice is no less effective for being indirect: 'the provocation of the viewer, by sharp contrasts and intensities of recorded experience, towards the thinking (and feeling) which will lead to politicisation of an issue and, if it is historical, to its placing in relation to the present, is more effective than an explicit treatment' (Corner, 1996: 138).

Originally Field had planned for a 90-minute film, but when she distributed advance marketing leaflets at trades union and community group conferences, the feedback she received was that this was too long for them to use at meetings, allowing for discussion afterwards. She made it shorter, which meant that some of the more complicated points had to be cut out.

During the fine cut, the beginnings and ends of shots will need to be trimmed so that the cuts work. Editors normally avoid cuts between one static and another and between the same size of shot on the same subject (see previous chapter). Cuts on action are smoother and there is no requirement for another shot of the same thing just because it is available; as long as a shot is working, it can be held on screen. Whilst reviewing the storyline, it is also a good idea to check if there is a better shot that can be used, or if changing the order will help.

Responsibility towards the audience

The viewer will expect to engage with the film text through 'teleological devices' that are structured in editing either around expository problem-solving, or around narrative suspense. The way that a documentary film is put together will be dictated by what exactly the maker intends the audience to make of the viewing experience. Most viewers can sense the filmmaker's attitude, which will be revealed in a number of different ways:

> the way subjects are framed, the shots they're juxtaposed to, the images their voices are laid over, how long they're allowed to talk for and what about, the revelation of a camera pan or tilt, whether the style disguises or discloses the filmmaker's authorial presence – in all these ways an audience pieces together clues. (Barbash and Taylor, 1997: 50)

The more production circumstances vary, the more important it becomes to always retain a vision of how an audience will receive the message that is likely to accompany any given combination of words, sounds and pictures. After all, what is selected will probably only represent a small section of an event, but it will be edited to suggest as much as possible about what happened. 'It has to be presented to your audience with the ring of truth. And that means paying attention to verisimilitude . . . [this] can mean trying to get into the heads of your audience to see how a sequence will appear to them' (Hampe, 1997: 76).

Franny Armstrong: *Drowned Out*

For *Drowned Out*, Armstrong had shot various Indian expert interviews, but cut them out altogether in favour of expert interviewee, Hugh Brody, because he said things better. She deliberately edited Brody so that his statements start off moderately and calmly, then progress – 'he has his own progression' (author interview, 2005). Thus his contributions became increasingly tendentious.

She adopted a structure for *Drowned Out* with a linear narrative of the steps in the resistance of the villagers as the floods approached, intercut with interviews to provide a more general understanding of context and the problems with 'big dam' construction. The dilemma that Armstrong faced was how to order information at the end of the film. In reality, a ruling from the Supreme Court came first, followed by a government ruling. But for the purposes of the narrative structure, the Supreme Court verdict was the crunch point, and everything thereafter was resolution. Armstrong wanted the Supreme Court verdict as the end of the third act, which would be logical, but not chronological. By changing the order, she sacrificed current affairs accuracy, but gained emotional impact that served to enhance the general spirit of injustice that the film was intended to expose. She explains, 'I wanted to make a long term film, therefore chronology was less important than the bigger significance' (ibid.).

Anand Patwardhan with Simantini Dhuru: *A Narmada Diary*

The need for a chronological diary approach creates its own narrative, although Patwardhan starts the story with archive film because audiences need to reflect on the fact that when Nehru referred to dams as the 'temples of the future', he did not anticipate that they would later become 'the implement and symbol of an unjust and unsustainable form of development – one that increasingly seeks to uproot people on a global scale' (Sharma, 2002: 290). Thereafter, actuality footage is used to progress a narrative that catalogues a story of struggles, triumphs, defeats and confrontations with power elites. He took pains to consult with the activists involved about editing decisions. 'I still never cut in shots just because they look good, unless they help with clarity in some way. This is not to say that every shot must have an immediately recognizable function, but I'm suspicious about art for art's sake and impatient with self-conscious "art"' (Goldsmith, 2003, ch.10: 8). 'My habits were formed with film, so I'm a bit of a purist. I almost never use dissolves, preferring straight cuts, not much layering, no background music, few audio tracks, and very little colour correction' (ibid.: 12).

Patwardhan does not want to personalize his approach by using narration, an option that is open to him, but he rejects:

It would have been nice if I'd found the diaristic voice of: 'Here I am. This is happening to me.' But I felt uncomfortable saying that I am important to this event. I was caught between not wanting to have an objective voice-of-God narration, saying: 'This is how the world is', and not wanting to say: 'This is how I see the world and this is all coming through me – through my interrelationship with the people that you see.' It's obvious but I didn't want to have to state it in the voice . . . It's diaristic but it's not confessional. I haven't got to the stage where I want to bare my soul on camera. (Akomfran, interview in *Pix*)

His projects are intended to create public discourse. As such, he has achieved a level of personalization which works well for his purposes.

The documentarist needs to ensure that the real substance of what the person is saying is selected, even though the editing process abbreviates the answer. But how far it is wise to consult with participants, or how far the filmmaker should have free licence, is central to debates about creative independence versus what can amount to a form of public relations. A decision concerning which part of an interview to use raises a point of honour towards the interviewee, for there is an obligation not to misconstrue and to portray the whole person to the audience, rather than a distorted impression of them. If an interview is edited tightly, the person can be cut off. They could be edited to deliberately say something that they do not believe. If quick moments in their life or an episode are reassembled, they could be trivialized. Parts could be omitted that complicate the position, give a context, reduce or increase the drama by juxtaposition next to another person.

The ability of edit structure to change perceptions of time and place probably offers the strongest potential for filmmaker manipulation. As this function is inherent in the medium (Chapman, 2005: 123), the issue in post-production is one of degree, level of mediation and how the maker wants the audience to read the edited film. Juxtaposition of interview extracts for political, satirical or conflict effect can make the viewer reassess a statement in the light of a second one. Sometimes the discrepancy between the two can cause surprise or insight, or humour. The filmmaker may need to rearrange the order of comments to structure a particular argument, again in the interests of how the audience is to receive the information.

Michael Moore: *Roger and Me*

In the end credits, there are nine names listed under 'legal'. How the film was put together goes some way to explaining the mix of litigation with filmmaking.

Structure is obtained during editing, and the approach that Moore adopted favours an expositional narrative with a sequence of events connected to what happened to Flint throughout the 1980s. This is achieved by a combination of investigative *vérité*, interviews and heavily ironic commentary over library film depicting events in the town's recent past. In editing, there is juxtaposition of scenes of deprivation with scenes of affluent 'society', whilst the continuing effort to interview Smith acts as a dramatic device, narrative framework and 'apt metaphor for corporate indifference to the public interest' (Cohan & Crowdus, 1990: 28). Although Moore used many of the basic elements and techniques of documentary filmmaking – archive footage, 'talking head' interviews, news clips – it is the way that these are compiled in editing that achieved the effect of what has been described as 'a personalized, freewheeling, satirical broadside against the callous and irresponsible actions of a giant corporation' (ibid.).

While Moore decided to follow a narrative structure in the exposition of a storyline centring on what happened to Flint, he also opted to use a form of compression that misrepresented the chronology of events by 'occasional adjustment of facts to suit narrative shape and pace' (Corner, 1996: 155). For example, there is a discrepancy in the facts as depicted after the *Great Gatsby* party in 1987. The evangelist who is shown visiting the city actually did so in 1982. There is also no attempt to dispel the impression that Ronald Reagan's visit to redundant car workers happened during his presidency, when in fact he was a presidential candidate. Similarly, three major civic development projects are depicted as happening concurrently with the lay-offs when in reality they had already finished before the event. These points were put to Moore in a long interview for *Film Comment* (Jacobson, 1989: 16–26). It is evident that the filmmaker was aware of the chronology of the civic developments and of the fact that the job losses quoted in his film had actually been spread over a longer period. He has drawn on events that happened throughout the 1980s, but, as the interviewer puts to him: 'you're playing fast and loose with sequencing' (ibid.). Moore presents the alternative choices in terms of the accuracy of events:

> Should I have maybe begun the movie with a Roger Smith or GM announcement of 1979 or 1980 for the first round of layoffs that devastated the town, which then led to starting these projects, after which maybe things pick up a little bit in the mid '80s, and then *boom* in '86 there's another announcement, and then tell the whole story? . . . then it's a three hour movie. It's a *movie*, you know: you can't do everything. (ibid.)

Moore's interviewer at the time outlines the expectations of the audience for documentary presentation: 'We expect that what we are seeing there happened, in the way in which it happened, in the way in which we are told it happened' (Jacobson, 1989: 22). These expectations of the audience 'need to be recognised by documentary filmmakers, even if their subsequent plan is, openly or otherwise, not to meet them' (Corner, 1996: 168). There are obligations when it comes to accuracy and honesty, even when a documentary is made, as this one was, outside the institutional framework of television where journalistic codes of ethics are more widely discussed.

Sometimes manipulation is used positively to excite audience emotions in support of protagonists. In his television film about a Leonard Cheshire home for the severely disabled, *Last Among Equals*, Dermot O'Donovan used an archive song over the opening titles. After the titles, he allowed the point of the old song to emerge gradually. He started with Leonard Cheshire footage from 1960s' film, at this stage with the song, entitled 'Home from Home' as period background music only. Then he introduced modern actuality, and thereafter he intertwined the two stories. 'The song was actually sung by a Leonard Cheshire patient called Lenny in the 1960 film, so by using this as theme music I hoped to elicit emotional response when the audience eventually saw and heard Lenny singing on screen, just before a commercial break. I wanted there to be tears' (author interview, 2005). When a high point in editing is created just before the television adverts, it is to ensure that viewers return after the break. In this case it worked. Why?

Lenny was a wheelchair-bound young man in his twenties, totally paralysed from the neck downwards, but he could still sing on stage, in front of a concert audience. The care home and the people in Dermot's film were the centre of his entire life, hence the relevance of the song's title. Standard journalistic methods such as narration would have explained Lenny's circumstances to the audience more quickly, but the emotional impact would have been lost. By 'showing' gradually, not 'telling' immediately, the audience became involved in a moving experience, with an impact that had been created through the pace of editing.

Writing voice-over narration

Commentary is conversation, not literary prose, therefore verbal padding and erudite phrases should be avoided. In fact, many documentary makers prefer either not to use narration, or to try to keep it to a minimum. Yet voice-over commentary can provide a framework for understanding the unfolding story. Although, as the old saying goes, 'a picture is worth a thousand words', narration can be still be applied sparingly to bridge shots. It is useful where abstract, propositional matters need explaining and where disparate visuals require linkage.

Editors are usually sceptical about commentary. Why? 'The mere existence, especially if placed over synchronised sound, indicates that the original is not worth our entire attention' (Vaughan, 1976: 33). Images will become illustration if commentary is used to add information. Obviously it can be used in various different ways, nevertheless 'commentary can scarcely fail to sever the indexal bond whereby we read the images, and not some verbal significance invested in them, as our prime source of information. Therefore editors tend to support writing that will "focus attention upon or feed significance into" the shots' (ibid.: 32).

If a film has plenty of sync sequences and *vérité*-style scenes, there may be no need for commentary, or maybe only a very small amount. In this case it will act like the spine to a book, helping to 'stick the film together', and if necessary to flag up the location of time – for instance, to create that same day, same place feeling which may be required. However, with 'pure' *vérité*, even a studio introduction will detract from the approach of the film, because to explain amounts to interpretation. Similarly a long caption at the beginning, or super-imposed captions for people and/or places will have an effect, because the material can then be read as the demonstration of a thesis. 'The sabotage is the more insidious for appearing in the guise of essential data without which the films might prove too dense for comprehension: but sabotage it nonetheless remains' (ibid.: 33).

Conversely, if the documentary has an essay style, commentary will be an important element to contribute to the overall message. Historical, social, politi-cal and current affairs films all tend to use commentary. An assessment of the need for narration should always be made in conjunction with picture and sound, as they will need to be integrated, for it is the effect of the final combina-tion of all three that really matters, not the narration in isolation. Some pictures only take on meaning with narration, but it's a question of balance between the elements in the film.

Narration can also help to move the film along, providing direction, as well as supplying the viewer with the required five w's (what, when, where, why, who), if they do not appear naturally. Ideally, a symbiotic but not repetitive relation-ship between the words and pictures should emerge. This is best achieved when words are written to picture, so that they enhance the pace and rhythm of the shots, and the flow of the film. Specifics work better than generalities. Wildlife documentaries provide a good example: with judicious choice of adjectives that add texture and colour, narration gives it meaning, brings it to life, gets inside the scene.

Ross McElwee: *Sherman's March*

It's a very strange, reverberating experience, as an editor, looking at the footage of your life years later . . . trying to restore some version of the life that you feel is due to it, that you feel relates to how you experienced it at that time. It's a little, in that way, like medicine. In some metaphorical way, you are trying to revive the patient, to bring the patient back to life. (Rhu, 2004: 8, 9)

McElwee spends an enormous length of time in constructing his voice-over narration during post-production, revising constantly. He inserts insightful reflexive comments like: 'My real life has fallen into the crack between myself and the film.'

'I deliver monologues. I try to create an almost literary voice-over. I think this enables the film to achieve a subjectivity it wouldn't otherwise have' (MacDonald, 1992: 281). The reflexive nature of filmmaker comment on production technique was enhanced in post-production by the decision to ask Richard Leacock to narrate the opening: an ironic homage, given the fact that Leacock's own direct cinema filmmaking techniques always stringently avoided use of commentary.

During editing, McElwee decided that he wanted viewers to be aware of the thin ethical line he had trodden during filming. The scene where Karen tells him to put down the camera was retained: 'I could have just dropped the whole scene, and the film would have rolled along to a more graceful conclusion . . . It's obnoxious what I'm doing in the film, and it's meant to beg the question of, "What do I think I'm getting away with here?" To some degree I am taking advantage of people' (Lucia, 1993: 35).

For the five half-hour films in *Europe by Design*, we developed a way of working whereby we would send the presenter a VHS of the rough cut, with a paper edit script that indicated a sketch of the subject matter that, as producer, I wanted covered in commentary. The presenter would then reword the script, adding his own thoughts and wit. A classic example was the opening sequence to the first film, when he arrives by helicopter at an isolated hilltop residence in the South of France. He is introduced to the eccentric architect who has designed the sprawling mansion without a single straight wall: everything is circular. As he and the interviewee crawl into a low-level round site office (the house is still being constructed), voice-over makes a joke about hobbit holes. The Tolkien analogy had never occurred to me when I selected the location!

Writing voice-over narration involves finding the raw material for commentary – interesting facts – and presenting them imaginatively. The voice-over can tell both a personal and a general story simultaneously; sometimes what is required appears to be almost self-evidently natural, to the extent that, when the structure is almost in place, the narration will virtually shape itself. Narration is composed for the ear, so it can sound like a conversation with the viewer, using simple words, short sentences and sounding clear and understandable, otherwise the effect can be to distance the audience. Over-use of narration can encourage passivity.

For some projects, if the film is to be 'topped and tailed' with an on-screen presenter, they are also scripted by the director/producer if they are not a journalist or subject specialist. A presenter can personalize the experience, enabling shared experience and involvement, especially if he or she addresses the viewer by using the second person. The writing skill involved when a presenter needs to be scripted involves not merely composing words that suit his or her personal style, but also the tone and style of the film. Dermot O'Donovan wrote the commentary for his film about disability, *Last Among Equals*, for actor Jane Asher to deliver in the sort of language she would use – 'concerned but *not* schmaltzy' (author interview, 2005).

When O'Donovan wrote the voice-over for Edward Woodward in *Fakes and Pharaohs*, he tried to write in the style of the actor's earlier role in the *Enforcer* television drama series, set in New York. Then he said to Woodward, 'personalize it'. One example of this technique emerged when the presenter came out with a single word in summary, after recounting the protagonist's (called JTP) appeal against his jail sentence: 'rejected'.

The need to avoid being verbose and the requirement for economy come across well in the conclusion to Raban's *Thames Film*, demonstrating that, if well used, narration can enhance mood and provide focus, helping the audience to appreciate the full significance of the content: 'The river journey unwinds a distant memory, each moment has a particular meaning and relation to the past . . . On this journey time is exposed: the past and present form one continuous pattern of unfolding experience.' This choice of words sums up, but doesn't specifically refer backwards; that does not work because it assumes the viewer has seen and remembered everything that appeared previously.

Nancy Platt: *Venkatamma's Story*

The final running time is only 12 minutes, so commentary is very economic in the way that it is used as an introduction to the theme, the setting, the organization and the characters. Platt admits she 'did not have the luxury of being able to make it breathe: but I did have the luxury of not having to shoot so much' (author interview, 2005). Sentences in the authentic editing script, as used by Platt and reproduced below, are very short and purely factual: any emotion and the strong human interest comes from the images and from the participants themselves, captured in interviews and sync sequences. Commentary therefore enhances the pace and style, it does not kill it or go against it.

Children, buffaloes, animals, Venkatamma washing her face	Children's song
	VENKATAMMA SYNC: My name is Venkatamma. I like to play, but I like to study as well.
Venkatamma skipping rope Series of shots of girls playing	VENKATAMMA VO: My friends' names are Sarita, Lata, Sharada, Santosha, and Amaravathi. COMM: Thirteen-year-old Venkatamma is one of 120 girls who live at this school run by Gramya, a voluntary organization in Andhra Pradesh, south India, and a Christian Aid partner. In this culture, daughters are seen as an economic burden on the family, and many of these girls would be married early, given up for adoption, or sent out to work, were it not for this school.
B&W RECONSTRUCTION of story	VENKATAMMA VO: I was put to work, looking after cattle in the fields. One day nobody brought me any food, so I went home to eat. But the cattle ran off and trampled the farmer's crops. He was angry and didn't give me any food for two days, and whenever I asked for some, he beat me. That was when I ran away.
	VENKATAMMA SYNC: I went to my sister and her children were going to school. I said I wanted to go to school too, but she wouldn't send me. I cried and cried and I refused to eat anything for three days until she agreed, and then she brought me to the Gramya school.
Teacher and students at Bridge school Exterior Gramya office Rukmini working inside	COMM: The school Venkatamma was fighting to go to is the Bridge school, so-called because it helps girls bridge the gap in their education. It was started by Gramya, a group of experienced women activists concerned about the desperate situation for girls in this area.

CAPTION: Rukmini Rao Founder member, Gramya Girls in classroom	RUKMINI SYNC/VO: A Bridge school is a place where we bring children who have never been to school, or who may gone for a year or so but now the girls are ten and eleven and can't go to regular school. So we provide them with an opportunity to live together and to study intensively, so what they would learn in regular school in 2 or 3 years they learn with us within a year.
Girls in classrooms Girls eating Venkatamma eating with friends	COMM: The school has five rooms. All the girls live here, they sleep on the floor of the classrooms and eat in a yard next door. It's a primary school only. So along with the other older girls, Venkatamma moved on to the local state high school, though she still boards here.
	RUKMINI SYNC: We try to link up with government institutions because we do believe that the government has a responsibility to ensure education for all.
Venkatamma studying with friends Walking through town with friends	VENKATAMMA VO/SYNC: In the morning I wake up around 4.30 or 5.00. I study for an hour or two, and at half past six I wash my face and eat breakfast and then I walk to school with my friends.
Ext school English class – Venkatamma reads poem	Venkatamma reading poem.
Girls at government school Sunita teaching at Bridge school	COMM: Gramya's commitment is not limited to the education of girls. They try to create opportunities for adult women to develop. Back at the Bridge school, for example, they employ Sunita Dharavath as a teacher. Yet she started life very poor, with little education, and unhappily married at the age of 13.
School play – opening song Audience watching	COMM: The girls and Gramya workers have devised this educational play. It shows the unhappy life of a child sold into bonded labour. It's a common practice here. Debt-ridden families take children out of school and send them to live and work away from home, for as little as £25 a year.
Venkatamma in play, scolded by landlord, crying, singing a song	VENKATAMMA VO/SYNC: I play the part of the bonded labourer. I have to do all the cleaning in the house. One day the landlord scolds me for not cleaning the floors properly, and he beats me. So I start crying.

School play Audience Venkatamma singing	COMM: The poverty here is so extreme that families not only send children to work, some sell their girl babies for adoption, or are even driven to kill them in infancy. Gramya's aim is to support poor and tribal women here, so they can fight for their rights, and the rights of their daughters. The story Venkatamma is acting out could almost be her own.
Aunt and uncle's hut Venkatamma sweeping up in front Others making baskets	COMM: When she was only six, her parents left in search of work, and she hasn't seen them since. She and her brother and sister went to live with their aunt and uncle. Their tribe, the Erukula, is among the poorest of the poor, living by raising pigs and weaving baskets. Venkatamma's aunt and uncle got into debt, and had to send her to work to repay it, tending cattle and buffalo in a village hours away. She was only nine years old.
CAPTION: 'Ramulu, Venkatamma's uncle'	RAMULU SYNC: We had no money to live on: we had no choice. We have to eat, and we thought if she works we can earn some money and we can get her back.
Venkatamma sweeping	COMM: But it didn't work out that way. Because this was a turning point for Venkatamma.
Sunita teaching	SUNITA VO/SYNC: My husband and my in-laws were all alcoholics. They made me work, and whatever money I brought home, they drank it up. I thought about it, and I decided that I had to get away from them or I'd kill myself. So I ran away.
Sunita teaching	COMM: Sunita came into contact with Gramya through a women's shelter.
	SUNITA SYNC: After coming to the school here, I started to study along with the Class 7 children. I took the exams, and passed. And I got an A grade.
Sunita reading with two girls	SUNITA VO/SYNC: I feel like these are my own children. I spend all my time with them, and it makes me really happy. I want to buy some land and build a house. I want to study and become a Hindi scholar. So I want to develop my life, and keep teaching here.
Rukmini talking with women in *sangham*	RUKMINI VO/SYNC: We have come here and we have started working with the communities, helping the communities to bring about change for themselves because we believe they can only change themselves and we can help in that process.
Women's group, sitting in circle Shots of women in group	COMM: Gramya's way of mobilizing the community is the *sangham* – local women's groups. All these women form *sanghams* in their own villages, and keep a lookout for vulnerable girls who could come to the school. They've learned how to be activists on their own behalf.

Sangham women	RUKMINI VO/SYNC: They influence men to send daughters to school, they improve their own agriculture, they try to earn money by working as a collective, which they would not have an opportunity to do as an individual.
School play, girls singing CAPTION: 'We are the children of labourers but we won't be labourers ourselves'	
Tug of war	VENKATAMMA SYNC/VO: In the last scene of the play, the children pull me to one side and the landlord tries to pull me back. But finally the children win – I get away, and go back to school with my friends.
Audience at play Ext tent	VENKATAMMA SYNC/VO: We put on the play in ten or fifteen villages, the whole drama troupe, and the teachers. And after that we got 40 or 50 children to go back to school.
	RUKMINI SYNC: Christian Aid has been supporting us very generously over the last 4–5 years and it's because of their support that we have been able to function as an organization. So Christian Aid makes all of this possible for Gramya.
Venkatamma and friends drawing on the ground	COMM: One girl can go to this school, and board as well, for only £5.50 a month.
Montage: Girls in class Girls playing game Lunchtime Classrooms	RUKMINI VO: We hope that in the future that most of the children who are with us today will go to school, will go to university and will find work which will give them a decent wage and give them an opportunity to live a decent life.
	VENKATAMMA SYNC: I want to get a good job, and I want to get married. Whatever work I do, I want to feel proud of myself.

For rough cut approval, *Venkatamma's World*, with the editing script above, required a response from three different sets of people in Christian Aid: the officers for that part of the world (India), the department that had commissioned the film, in this case the Churches department, and the media (Broadcast, Digital and Print) department. However, these three different groups were not difficult to please.

Creating pace

Pace is central to the way that audiences respond to a film, for it can set the mood as well as the energy level. Television producers are so conscious of pace that they tend to announce the story up front: 'This is the story of so and so.' They demand movement and action. As filmmaker Dermot O'Donovan says, 'Current affairs is now push, push, facts, facts. They've lost it. These days, it's no more than a series of vignettes strung together: done and dusted within 3 minutes, then move on. There's a resistance to picking up a theme and staying with it, for fear of losing the audience' (author interview, 2005). Television cutting styles usually dictate that the shot has to change every two or three seconds, working on the premise that this will beat the channel zappers. The 'either/or' soundbite approach is also very common in television current affairs documentaries.

However, it can be more interesting to let things goes unexplained for a while, as a means of attracting audience attention by intriguing them, then following up later with an explanation. Sometimes a filmic, slower pace will allow a documentary to breathe. Otherwise the viewer could find that the concentration of argumentation is too much to take. The best way to check if the flow and pace of information is workable is to sit back and look at the film as a viewer would for the first, and probably, the only time. At the same time, it is also more respectful to the audience if they are able to formulate their own conclusions. As Dai Vaughan explained:

> Ultimately it is a question of rhythm . . . What is required is an editing style which will invite a rhythmic response founded not upon the rate of satisfaction of prior expectations but upon the interest engaged by the shots – a style in which rhythm will be perceived as legitimating the action simply because the action itself will be the prime component of the rhythm. In this way, perhaps, we may succeed in extending to our subjects an existential courtesy matching that which we extend to our viewers in declining to pre-empt their interpretations. (1976: 20)

Anand Patwardhan: *In the Name of God*

In this film, Patwardhan built a complex tension through the editing process: 'We are made aware that many options were jostling to become reality; we get to understand how this option (a mob will attack a mosque) becomes the logical recourse in a perverse chain of reasoning. How is a narrative constructed that amounts to a 'trajectory of rage which leads to an outcome'? (Akomfrah, interview in Pix).

'I do have a tendency to overshoot . . . and then have the nightmare of editing vast amounts of material that is all over the place, but this also makes the film more multi-dimensional than before' (Goldsmith, 2003, ch.10: 12). Patwardhan has stayed with the subject of religious fundamentalism in India, 'The horror of that violence has kept me occupied for a decade . . . There was supposed to be one film. The material I was shooting became too complex so I had to separate it into three films which add up to a total of five-and-a-half hours. So you can imagine how much more material there was.' (Akomfrah, interview in *Pix*).
    Patwardhan's unashamedly subjective editorial control is content driven.

> Quite often I cut out very fast on the people I don't like because then I just get the punch-line, the nasty bit that they've said and then I juxtapose it to something else. But, when it's a sympathetic person that I'm talking to, I tend to stay on that person for longer because that

person has other dimensions from the immediate dimension of what is being said and that has a visual dimension – it's a way of saying that we don't want to leave you right now but we have to do something else. (ibid.)

I now find that my films work better when I provide breathing-space, moments which are connected but are not absolutely dictated by the story. There's a lot of intensity in different sections of the film and you need to have time to absorb what has happened before moving on to the next thing. In that sense I do find I use more of those moments now than I did before . . . I also don't cut as fast because I find it disrespectful of the person I am talking to. (ibid.)

I've been editing sequences which held together. For instance, when I did the interview with the woman from Rajasthan . . . I edited her, kept the things that I thought were important, left it as a chunk and then moved on. As I'd shot over the years I edited different sequences, boiling it down to what was important, but not necessarily at that point connecting them all up. Other things I just left separately. Over many years a whole mosaic developed. Then basically, six years after I had started shooting, it all fell together, the pattern began to emerge. (ibid.)

I knew when I was shooting that this was important and that was important, but I didn't know exactly how they were connected to each other. (ibid.)

I choose moments that are very clear in themselves and then string them together. I'm always looking to find the moment of greatest, the most obvious contradiction which anyone can see, focus in on it for a while. (ibid.)

It's really the juxtaposition of real events and people who are speaking. So nobody can dispute that Bal Thackeray [leader of Shiva Sena] didn't say that, because you can see him saying it. And it's not even edited in such a manipulative way, where I've taken one sentence from here and one sentence from there and created a third sentence which he didn't mean. I've been careful to keep the sense of what is being said intact. All I've done is juxtapose it . . . So in that sense the film 'editorializes' but it doesn't distort. (Kripalani, 1998: 170–1)

Nevertheless, Patwardhan has also been criticized for having a post-production style that tends towards black and white, 'an either/or analysis' (Sharma, 2002: 292). He is also criticized by one reviewer for lack of transparency in the way he has presented interviews. 'Sometimes the viewer does not know who is conducting the interviews, on what basis the interview questions have been constructed, and whether the interviewees are willing or unwilling subjects. In a few cases the interviewer actually badgers the speaker' (Richman, 1994: 1035).

Use of music

Although the documentary maker will find that some picture sequences can be cut to the beat of the music, for other parts music may not be added until the film is close to the online or final edit. Opinions vary as to how important music should be: I believe that it is important not to be over-dependent on it during post-production. Usage will depend on the intentions of the project and the target audience.

Martin Clarke studies the script before briefing musicians for the composition of an original score

William Raban: *Thames Film*

'The film's dominant paradigmatic structure lies in its inserting into contemporary views of the Thames shot from a boat making its way downriver, historical images of the same sites taken from engravings, old photos and archive film footage' (Chanan, 2000). By mixing contemporary footage shot from a boat with historical archive footage, Raban was able to structure a reflective essay on time and change: 'time regulated by the effects of tide, daylight and seasonal change' (author interview, 2005). The narrative works on three different, yet interdependent levels: a narrative of the journey undertaken in the film, individual anecdotes and stories about parts of the river and a largely visual narrative about change in general. 'The inclusion of rostrum and archive material helped to lend a structuring hand to the editing process, because to a large extent each engraving, photograph or film clip was linked to a specific location that I had captured on film' (ibid.). Using the words and following the 1787 route of the Thomas Pennant diary, Raban edited the film around the original 66-mile journey – the completed film was also to be 66 minutes long. This Pennant document turned out to be a pivotal find because it provided the key edit points.

Raban cut on the second or third frame of the prints and stills, which, despite creating a slight jump, still achieved the seamless precision that he was aiming for between live action and rostrum archive. 'I don't think that the ways in which film communicates are sufficiently understood. For me the kinetic structure is very important and this has to do with the whole way that patterns of movement are set up on the screen in relation to moments of relative stillness' (ibid.). His naturalistic approach means an attempt to avoid optical effects in post-production, such as fades or wipes as sticking plaster between shots and sequences.

During post-production, Raban felt there was something lacking. He needed a strong image to tie the whole film together – a sort of visual book spine to complement the content spine provided by the Pennant diary journey. At that time, he was in Madrid at a screening of his earlier films. He visited the Prado and came across the Bruegel painting *Triumph of Death*. The painting made a huge impression on him and he dreamt about it two nights later. In his dream, the images moved in combination with music from Bach's *St Matthew Passion*. He thought about actually doing this in the film. He already had other associations between the Thames and death, for instance the eighteenth-century engravings of the gallows that he had researched and shot. Although this particular work of art does not depict the Thames, people in earlier times thought that England was joined to the continent of Europe. I asked him whether the inclusion of the painting gives too strong an emphasis to depressive, negative elements of the past? He answered, 'I find the *Triumph of Death* an incredible funny painting – it relieves the film' (ibid.).

Raban edits his own work. His naturalistic philosophy also means that he doesn't like to use sound effects libraries, preferring to record his own original, authentic effects. 'While I cut the mute picture I am hearing the sound in my head and getting an idea as to how the track crosses the picture cuts so that in a way I am developing two parallel though not necessarily synchronized channels of picture and sound' (ibid.).

Sound was to function primarily for atmosphere and historical effect. When post-producing the sound, the cross-mixing had to reflect the conflict between natural and man-made environment in order to achieve an equilibrium between picture and sound that would enhance the senses. A dominant sound in the post-production effects, used to great effect, is that of a repetitive pile driver. 'The sounds, as well as the images, of the river are of great importance. There is a continual clangour, a loud lament, with the sound of machinery fighting against the lap of the water and the cry of the seagulls' (Ackroyd, 2004).

All of his sound effects were original, although these were mixed with a soprano singing extracts from Bach's *St Matthew Passion*. He tried to let the sound of the documentary 'loop' between shots, in order to obtain a resonance between past and present. 'Then I laid a series of guide tracks to assist the fine cut. I took each sound and processed it. This meant that I could rationalize the final dub to simple cross-mixing and setting levels on the sound. This was much cheaper and gave considerably more control than the conventional dubbing route' (author interview, 2005). In retrospect, Raban regrets not shooting *Thames Film* on 35 mm because the sound quality is so much better.

However, he was able to use 35 mm sound tracks from two archive films. One of these old documentaries in the PLA archive – *City of Ships* – by Harvey Harrison (1948), showed the docks at their busiest, with a compatible approach to shooting: 'These shots can be lifted without destroying that film's integrity. Most of the film is shot from a moving camera (much from the water) and so will relate visually to my material' (Raban, progress report). In contrast, the 1921 film showed the opening of the Royal docks with flickering, fast moving pictures. 'Both these films present a now forgotten image of London's dock trade' (author interview, 2005).

Part of the atmosphere of sound for *Thames Film* is also built by the BBC Radio 4 news clip with the story of a tug called *General Seven*, going down. T. S. Eliot's voice delivers his celebrated words on time together with the various layers of sources, each serving to underline the visuals of time: from the eighteenth-century brick warehouse at Free Trade Wharf which has since been demolished, to photos of it from the late 1930s, with children on the shore below it.

In general the use of scripted words is economical and does not drown the pictures and natural sounds. For example, Raban had come across an amusing historical story in Hogarth's 'Peregrinations'; the same anecdote of a man dying also appeared in Pennant's diary. By fusing the two accounts and rewriting them more succinctly, he was able to use it in narration, delivered by actor John Hurt. The combination of testimony in the soundtrack between the journey made in 1787 and today, with Eliot's poetry, rich sound effects and commentary, with a small amount of music, all provide a collection of audio textual material that is diary-like, 'a record that contains and contrasts past and present whilst generating new meanings from the tension between the two' (Luxonline, 2005).

Thames Film starts with the *Triumph of Death* and ends with the present actuality of people crossing the river over London Bridge. This latter occasion is the only time the camera goes onto land, but ironically none of the people are looking at the river. 'I remember that David Curtis was positive about the rough cut viewing at the Arts Council. He wanted the film to end out at sea but later he changed his mind on this and could see why I brought it back into the centre of London' (author interview, 2005). With this ending, Raban is making a statement: 'Raban initiates a socio-political critique of policies leading to the social neglect of the city' (O'Pray, in Curtis, 1994: 157).

Time pressures

Post-production can be a stressful time. Where there is a fixed schedule with a deadline, burning the midnight oil during post-production is a commonplace phenomenon. Often the work turns out to be more complicated than antici-pated, but shortage of time can prevent the filmmaker from considering other ways in which the material could be presented. Although digital technology has increased the flexibility for editing images, equipment can break down and then technical back-up will be required. Sometimes the older digital equipment turns out to be a lot more stable and to provide fewer technical problems than the newer designs.

Showing rough edits to clients, sponsors and audience trials

For sponsored films, commissioning editors and clients normally view the film in advance, and give an opinion as to whether the material is really working in the way it has been put together. The rough cut that is shown can be in varying degrees of readiness. It is advisable to have the editor control the sound levels, which may still be unequal. It should be possible to show the film to a small group of people, without having to make any verbal explanations to talk them through it. Receiving reactions, and therefore criticism, can be traumatic when a documentary maker has lived with every detail of a project for a long time. There are a variety of points to check. Do the viewers understand the theme and issues? Did they feel it was the right length, what was the reaction to certain parts and people? What did they emerge with in terms of understanding? Whether or not the filmmaker makes changes according to the suggestions of others will depend on his or her assessment of the situation and who exactly is right.

Jane Chapman: *It's Your Choice*

Sometimes the screening process with commissioning editors or clients can involve approval by a number of different people, especially for corporate films. Chapman Clarke Films' *It's Your Choice* had to be shown to two different government departments, in a two-way, live video conference, as everyone was based in different parts of the country. In research, one of the participant profiles that I had selected was a female Anglo-Chinese medical student; she had been chosen from over 100 students. She turned out to have a tremendous on-screen presence. So what was the problem?

The answer was oblique, rooted in government policy. Young people who previously would never have applied for university were now being encouraged to do so, and a top medical school was seen as too elitist, an unobtainable role model requiring very high entry qualifications. I defended my choice of participant by arguing that doctors were badly needed, and that this personable, intelligent, successful young woman would act as an inspiration to viewers, and that, anyway, extended opportunity should not equal mediocrity in filmic terms. Some people will always stand out more than others on screen. The clients did not ask for her to be removed.

I talked to one producer who had experienced serious problems at this stage of post-production whilst working on a contract for a foreign television station. The first viewing was postponed by the commissioning editor by 10 days, which had a devastating effect.

> Everybody took their eyes off the ball . . . key to the crisis was the lack of a properly regulated timetable, which forced a decision about hiring time for the offline equipment. We extended the hire period and decided to continue refining the offline. The first viewing was now held almost at the end of the time allowed for the offline, rather than two thirds of the way in. The commissioning editor hated the film because it didn't have the 'hard edge' that she had wanted. (author interview, 2005).

At this point, the team regretted taking up all the allocated offline time *before* the commissioning editor viewing, a problem that had been compounded by the fact that they had misinterpreted the commissioning editor's wishes. 'The commissioning editor did not like the whole structure and concept of the film and requested a major re-cut'. This content crisis had arisen largely because of bad communication attributable to language difference. Now there was no time and money left for making the necessary changes. Meanwhile the team were putting in extra time to make major changes such as removing some interviews and substituting new ones, which also entailed a total rewrite of the commentary.

Online edits

With non-linear editing, it is possible to experiment with all sort of mixtures of sound and picture *before* you make the final EDL (edit decision list), but editing machines never actually assemble the completed film. Furthermore, the offline system of editing is below broadcast standard, so the filmmaker will then take the EDL to an online set-up where the film will be assembled from the original recordings to broadcast quality. 'In digital editing, each succeeding image is considered to be a clone of the original, because each generation is re-created using the digital code of the original. Nevertheless, the better the original, the better the copies' (Hampe, 1997: 204). During the online, playback is achieved immediately by retrieving the shots on the EDL from the computer memory.

Subtitles and other visual/optical effects such as wipes can be added during the online process. Accurate and appropriate subtitles are difficult to produce successfully and probably best done by professionals.

Conclusions: ethics, editing and manipulation

Digital technology has made ethical considerations more urgent in the light of 'the amazing new possibilities for fraud' (Rosenthal & Corner, 2005: 5). This consideration has to be balanced against the fact that filmmaker manipulation during editing can be both necessary and inevitable. Whether or not it is deemed to be unethical will depend on documentary maker intent and respect for the bigger truth of the reality that has been captured, and for audience understanding of this.

If the documentary maker is using juxtaposition to manufacture a form of controversy between protagonists, then the technique can be highly contentious. As Patwardhan says:

> There is no getting away from the fact that filmmaking is manipulative and the filmmaker retains control in over a hundred different ways. Even the famous 'jump cut' is merely a statement. It's the director's way of saying: 'I'm trying to manipulate you.' But manipulation does not begin and end with the seamless cut. One is always choosing to use one camera angle over another, and deciding from amongst so many variables. The ultimate truth of a film does not depend on formalistic gestures, but lies in a realm between the filmmaker and his conscience. (Goldsmith, 2003: 12).

Whatever the documentary maker decides on in post-production can be contentious. As the phrase goes, 'you can't make a silk purse out of a sow's ear'. The raw material to work with must be good in the first place: no amount of special effects can disguise bad shots, poor-quality sound and boring participants. From the jumble that first arrived in the cutting room, the editor tries to construct a seamless whole. If the viewer is not conscious of how the film is being constructed, and is drawn into the content, the filmmaker will probably feel that editing has been effective.

Challenging the borders of documentary in editing

Trinh T. Minh-ha: *Surname Viet, Given Name Nam*

In editing, Trinh structured the interview footage to express 'the play of the true and the false, the real and the staged. In the first part of the film, the interviews were selected, cut and blueprinted for re-enactment.' With these, she retained each as an autonomous story with a 'certain length of speech'. Editing is used to emphasize the empty space between filmmaker and interviewee. In the second part, the viewer is presented with a series of 'real' interviews with the same women; 'the editing of these last interviews comes closer to the conventions of documentary as the statements are chopped up, redistributed, and woven in the filmic text with footage of the women's "real" life activities' (Mayne, 1990: 8). By demarking some of the differences between the two approaches to interview, differences in length, mode of address, camera work, use of English, Trinh hoped to draw viewer attention to 'the invisibility of the politics of interviews and, more generally, the relations of representation' (ibid.). Gradually, she inserts devices to suggest that the interviews are less and less 'natural': for instance, the reflexive voice-over is heard with the synchronous voice, thinking aloud the politics of interviews. A tension that had been present throughout the production came to the fore in post-production. Through editing, the unease between what is heard, read and seen emerges for the viewer: 'not only do you have to listen to these Vietnamese faces speaking English, but you also have to understand a different sound of English' (ibid.).

Trinh's use of archive was not intended to construct a linear history of Vietnam, but rather to stretch filmic and historical time. This is exemplified by the end sequence of what she describes as, 'step-printed images of a group of refugees in the 1950s floating amidst the sea on a raft, seen with comments on the contemporary condition of the "boat people" and more recently yet, of the "beach people" . . . It materializes the fragility of life . . . re-photography displaces, and displacement causes resonance' (Minh-ha, 1992: 209). Similarly, Trinh uses some very grainy black and white images of three women moving slowly. The same images appear on three occasions throughout the film, each time slightly differently. On the third occasion they are presented as they were originally shot, with a (male) journalistic voice-over referring to them as captured prisoners. According to Trinh: 'A multiple approach to the same image is at times useful to cause resonance in the very modification of the material' (ibid.: 210). Some documentary makers would question the ethics of changing historical archive in this way during post-production.

Karl Nussbaum: *Thanatos and Eros: The Birth of the Holy Freak*

Nussbaum goes beyond documentary to create a multi-media collage which bridges the two film worlds of narrative and experimental film by using elements of both. In post-production, Nussbaum combines 'bits of history (personal and historical), pop culture, Greek mythology, Jewish cultural tradition, biblical stories, classic monster movie and film noir genres, religious versus scientific systems and evolution of historic art movements – a world of contrasts and opposites to provoke visual conflict and illustrate emotional growth' (author interview, 2005).

> The narrative collage style I have developed draws from the way [Holocaust] survivors and disturbed people tell their stories – fractured, searching for order or understanding. Hundreds of details, memories, and connections are all seen at once, flowing like a dream . . . Keeping the audience's senses hyperactive through dissolving layers of pictures, music, story, and editing, I hope to overwhelm the logical mind and stimulate an emotional experience. (ibid.)

Many layers overlap creating unusual juxtapositions or run simultaneously as contrasts; often the picture and sound are not connected linearly, but refer backwards or forwards to other pieces in the film, creating visual and aural connections over time. One of many emotional/conceptual arcs concerns reality versus film; documentary versus mythic filmmaking and how the viewer inherently knows the difference just from looking (ibid.).

Summary

Editing, which encompasses a range of tasks and considerations, is critical because most films are sorted in the cutting room. The process is a creative one when the filmmaker must assess the material objectively by trying to understand the audience's viewpoint when they see the documentary. A degree of manipulation is inevitable, because editing changes time and space, but there are ethical obligations not to misconstrue and to consider the effect of the way visual and audio elements are intregrated.

6 Obtaining Public Reaction

The argument

A documentary as a completed statement becomes a 'free floating entity' (Barbash & Taylor, 1997: 536). The afterlife of a project is important on two levels: the personal, and at the level of the wider documentary community. The first entails feedback and audience reactions that can be useful to the individual as learning points for the future; the second enables discourse with the wider documentary making community through participation at festivals and with distribution activities. Theatric screenings with an audience, which can be a special interest or community group, fulfil an essential function because of the feedback and discussion. There should also be an altruistic aim to strengthen documentary's public profile: 'We need to reposition the . . . documentary in our cultural life and rediscover its range and power' (Search & McCarthy, 2005: 4).

Introduction

'Making a film is only half the battle. Showing these films is the real thing. Otherwise, what's the use of spending all this time and energy?' (Goldsmith, 2003, ch. 10: 11). Anand Patwardhan's words would seem to express a truism with which, in principle, no sane documentary maker would disagree. Yet producers often move on quickly to the next project, especially in situations where they do not have the distribution rights and need to work as freelancers, or where broadcasters and distributors deal with sales. 'We believe that filmmaking and film marketing are two halves of a full circle. A film that never reaches its audience is little different from a film that never gets made. It just costs a lot more' (Jill Godmilow's proposal for *The Popovich Brothers*, in Rosenthal, 1990: 30). This is precisely the reason that grant-aided foundations, for instance, are so keen for the projects that they fund to be screened publicly.

Almost all documentary content can find appreciation amongst some interest group or set of viewers in some small corner of the world. Whether or not this happens depends on subject matter, production craft and quality as contributory factors, along with identification of markets through imaginative, persistent and flexible distribution tactics.

Commissions: reactions from television and corporate sponsors

Although the rest of this chapter discusses promotional experiences and options, assuming that the documentarist has some decision making power over how

The producers of *El Documento* hired a cinema in London's Leicester Square for a screening as a condition of the funding

the film is exhibited, some mention should be made first about commissions. If the maker has no distribution rights, or rights have not been cleared, he or she will not be able to control the screening arrangements.

Before a film is transmitted on televison, broadcasters will prepare their own promotional trailers, usually without consulting the documentary maker, as Dermot O'Donovan experienced. 'The Carlton promo producer cut a short trail for the programme which did not show ONE SINGLE disabled person!!!' When O'Donovan enquired why his film about the severely disabled, *Last Among Equals*, was promoted thus, 'they explained that such shots would not entice an audience. This deserves much more discussion' (author interview, 2005).

Strangely, given television's high profile, once the completed product has been delivered, feedback is generally difficult to obtain. What about the ratings figures? These do not necessarily equate to viewer satisfaction or stimulation. In the case of our primetime BBC 1 documentary series, *Europe by Design*, executives were more impressed by the high audience satisfaction results, which are measured separately, than by the average 3.85 million ratings. The first transmission took place during the summer in an early evening Sunday slot whilst the regular incumbent – the *Antiques Roadshow* – was on holiday, so our series was a filler. However, it did beat other long-running British television war horse series such as *Equinox* and *Panorama* into fourth place for national factual programme ratings. There were no complaints, and the BBC granted Chapman Clarke Films the right to distribute the series worldwide for three years outside UK terrestrial television. We achieved 42 different sales to 30 countries.

Similarly the clients never provided any feedback for our corporate film *It's Your Choice*, although we informed them that we were submitting it to the New York International Film Festival. It won the 'best careers film of the year' award.

Congratulations were muted, yet we had fulfilled our function as producers by delivering the product to the client, on time and on budget – the bottom line for what a commission requires.

Nancy Platt did not receive a detailed response to *Venkatamma's Story*, only the comment that her film was 'subtle'. However, it clearly has an enduring value; web clips from the film are still available for viewing on the Christian Aid website <http://www.christian-aid.org.uk/video/501collector/index.htm>.

Success can be accompanied by dissatisfaction, for what pleases some people displeases others. A local television documentary that I once directed, entitled *Cider People*, went on to achieve the highest ratings of the season in its prime time 7 pm transmission slot. Nevertheless one of the companies featured in the film – Taunton Cider (part of the Matthew Clark multinational drinks conglomerate and rumoured at the time to have been a shareholder in the television station) – complained to the broadcaster about the ironic way that they were represented. I had introduced some offbeat humour through juxtaposition in editing. I never again worked as a freelancer for that particular broadcaster.

Festivals

If a maker is entering a documentary, as opposed to merely attending and viewing, festivals need to be selected carefully. Some are free of charge, others require an entry fee for films that are submitted. They all have juries for different categories, so the trick is to choose the appropriate category if one wants to do well. However, some filmmakers object in principle to being put into boxes: 'Festival categories have always posed problems for me; I have to decide quite arbitrarily what kind of jury I want for the films and in most cases the decision does not turn out to be a good one. Fact orientated eyes do not like experiments and vice versa, as if science and experimentation can ever do away with each other' (Minh-ha, 1992: 218). Yet festivals offer many advantages: an opportunity to see what others are doing internationally, publicity, promotion, reviews, discussions, sales and filmmaker contacts.

William Raban: *Thames Film*

After almost three years in the planning and making, *Thames Film* was screened at the London Film Festival in 1986. The event proved to be pivotal. Afterwards Raban was invited to a champagne breakfast at the National Film Theatre. There he met Alan Fountain, then commissioning editor for independent production at Channel 4, who hadn't seen the film. After Raban launched a brief but effective verbal sales campaign, Fountain asked the filmmaker to book a preview theatre, exclusively for him to see it. He loved it and decided there and then to purchase it, despite the odd length of 55 minutes, which didn't seem to bother him. Raban could now afford to pay wages and make rights clearances. Previously he had only cleared single territory theatric rights. C4 paid him £20,000; the UK television rights clearance for two transmissions cost £5,000, thus enabling him to pay the Port of London Authority £2,000 as a buy-out for archive and to clear his debts. As he says, 'you don't get rich with what I do' (author interview, 2005).

The next surprise was the fan mail that he received when the film was transmitted. One viewer, in a letter requesting a video, wrote: 'I have lived the past thirty years in London and have loved the river – your film, in vision and sound, evoked it so remarkably for me.' Another viewer described the documentary as a 'hypnotically beautiful film. The sound/vision mix was superb.' Viewer comments such as these inevitably helped Raban to gain a commission later for another project. The assistant editor for independent film and video at Channel 4 wrote: 'I thought it was a beautifully achieved piece of work and what we should have more of!'

It wasn't until late 2004 that the British Film Institute brought out a DVD of Raban's collected works, again to enthusiastic reviews. 'Thames Film (1986) is a fantastic voyage across the river that uses a 1787 travelogue, T.S. Eliot's Four Quartets and obscure port footage to build up a rapturous portrait of a waterway that by the 1980s was full of the ghosts of industry.' Thames Film and the other films on the DVD 'also show valuable histories bleeding away and induce in us a certain sadness' (Sandhu, 2004). Another review commented on the importance of the filmmaker's timing: 'Seen from 20 years later, it's clear Raban caught the Thames and London at the end of its era of imperial commercialism' (Morriss, 2004).

When it comes to public screenings, Raban demonstrates that selection of an appropriate venue and special interest group is important. I recently attended his screening at London's Docklands Museum to a local history group, who clearly appreciated the film. The venue is the former West India Warehouse in West India Dock, opened for trade in 1802 as the first ever enclosed dock in the world. At the time the warehouse was the world's biggest brick building. The company had a monopoly on trade to the West Indies for over 30 years, and the dock was one of the last to close in the 1980s when Raban was making Thames Film. The film and the venue have the same roots:

> It has also been a river of trade, and a river of power. Its docks and wharves and factories were once part of the great machine of empire – the machine of oppression. That is why it is known as a dark river. It has been touched by sweat, and labour, and poverty, and tears. Yet it still calls to the forlorn and the neglected, with some siren-song of darkness. It is the great vortex of suicide. (Ackroyd, 2004)

At the screening, Raban's use of the Bruegel painting in Thames Film prompted a debate about the metaphor of death that reviewers have focused on. The river 'becomes a living organism with its own laws of growth and change. We get the sense that London is not controlling it. It is controlling London. It is London' (ibid.).

Rights clearance

A film can only be sold if the distribution rights have already been cleared, which costs money. Producers who want to hedge their bets usually opt to pay less by only clearing the rights for their own country. This can be shortsighted. One filmmaker that I interviewed had made a documentary entitled *Charles et Camilla* for French television.

> The film was only cleared for two French TV transmissions, and had been made prior to the royal marriage. When the couple's engagement was announced, there was a sudden demand for films, and this one could have been sold world-wide, netting considerable profits. But the archive film hadn't been cleared for screenings elsewhere, and could only now be cleared further at huge costs – over

a barrel springs to mind. If a story is likely to have any kind of 'legs', clear for 'worldwide unlimited' for 3–5 years. (Author interview, 2005)

Audience responses

Documentary makers often travel with their films to attend screenings and to participate in discussions afterwards. 'While our close involvement in the processes of fundraising and distribution often proves to be frustrating, we also realize that this mutual challenge between the work and the film public, or between the creative gesture and the cinematic apparatus, is precisely what keeps independent filmmaking alive' (Trinh T. Minh-ha, in Kaplan, 2000: 335).

Trinh T. Minh-ha: *Surname Viet, Given Name Nam*

'The truth is, a first encounter with Trinh's films is often unsettling for the viewer, because it decentres his/her positioning as a subject. Instead of centring the subject/viewer with the comfortable notion that a quantum of "knowledge" about something was provided by the film, it sends him/her back to his/her own essential displacement' (Berenice Reynaud, in Minh-ha, 1999: 51). The viewer has been duped, according to Reynaud, who confronted Minh-ha in a discussion after a screening:

> Even when you talk about yourself in the large sense, meaning your own culture, meaning Vietnamese women, you still generate controversy because in your film *Surname Viet, Given Name Nam* you commit the absolute crime. You make a movie of Vietnamese women in English. Second, you make a 'documentary' in which you treat the spectator shamelessly. It is only halfway through the film that the spectator starts scratching the head and says, 'Wait a minute, this is staged. I have been had!' To create in the spectator the distance from buying in the raw as if it were a documentary. (ibid.: 55)

Minh-ha admits:

> The recognition that the early interviews in the film are re-enactments comes at different places and stages for different viewers. This is deliberately planned . . . some viewers were furious because they expected to be told about it at the outset of the film (as the norms dictate). But other viewers felt that to reveal the re-enactment from the start would be to give away the 'plot' of the film. (1992: 146)

'For me, interacting with the viewers of our films is part of independent filmmaking. The more acutely we feel the changes in our audiences, the more it demands from us as filmmakers. (Kaplan, 2000: 335).

Therefore, the significance of distribution from the documentary maker's point of view is that it represents a process of exposure, through the end product, to the public, and as such it is a time when other people's perceptions can be compared to one's own. When other people see a film in a different light than the maker imagined they would, it fuels a useful discourse about gaps between aim and end result. Audiences should experience viewing actively, not passively. Reactions to aspects of production can confirm or reject the filmmaker approach. As Dai Vaughan says, 'We cannot boast of leaving our films open ended and at the same time complain if people draw from them conclusions we dislike' (Nichols, 1985: 713).

Connie Field: *The Life and Times of Rosie the Riveter*

Field took the film to union and community group meetings throughout the Midwest. At an all male union meeting, one member of the audience did not realize that actresses were used in the archive newsreel, and that therefore the images were constructed rather than authentic: 'One man . . . complained, "What's wrong with you women today? *She* had the right attitude, that one they interviewed"' (Williamson, 1981: 45).

> One thing that I found when I toured round with *Rosie* is that it leaves a lot of space for people to relate to it personally. People who had lived through the period always wanted to stand up and give testimony about their own experiences. And many viewers talked about their fear that the government is going to get us into another war. (Johnston, 1981: 21)

She believes that the film has a relevance to audiences because it is about an economic phenomenon 'endemic to our system and not just an event . . . Some of the issues that affected working women in the 1940s affect us today – like the need for childcare and equal pay for comparable work' (Tammer, 1981: 358).

Support literature and Internet usage

Connie Field received government funding for a study guide to fill in background information to go with *Rosie the Riveter* (see case study). She felt that it helped distribution a lot (Tammer, 1981: 411). But there are occasions when filmmakers would prefer to leave their audience undirected so that different viewers will take away varying messages and memories of their viewing experience. Most of Chapman Clarke Films' educational series have been accompanied by a range of material, varying from workbooks, teacher's guides, compilation 'best of' videos to CD-ROMs. As the producer of our 10-part educational series for Britain's Channel 4, entitled *Maths Everywhere*, I was expected to have a very clear approach concerning what content was suitable for the television programmes as opposed to the follow-up books and CD ROM.

These days, the Internet offers possibilities for exploitation of a project. There are also documentaries where the primary platform is a website. The non-linear, interactive features of the web can be used in combinations of written text by makers and users, photographs, speech and film sequences. However, a traditional interaction between audience and topic through a screening will maximize the message by focusing the audience, whereas interactive web features with elements of choice can deflect. The fragmentation of the material reduces the overall impact.

Markets and television sales

Distributors, production companies and other media players do much of their business in buying, selling and setting up deals at annual trade markets for television such as MIP in Cannes. Documentary has its own events such as MIP

DOC, Sunny Side of the Doc in Marseilles, and Docs for Sale at the International Documentary Film Festival Amsterdam (IDFA). However, filmmakers who are seeking a distributor can usually find one simply by checking media directories and the Internet: it is not necessary to visit such events for this purpose.

Although nature films, travelogues and cookery always seem to sell, other documentaries are not always broadcast in the form that they were made. For instance, the news may be interested in purchasing a short section – no more than 10 minutes, for a background piece. At the other end of the spectrum, the documentary, *Manufacturing Consent: Noam Chomsky and the Media* (1992) was several hours long originally. Subsequently five different versions were made, each to fit a different broadcaster time slot (Kilborn and Izod, 1997: 244). This ensured that the film received the attention that it deserved internationally. It is advisable to study the numbers involved in distribution carefully. Reversioning can be costly, and distributors always deduct a percentage. The amount varies and can be negotiable – 25 per cent plus transfer and duplication costs is not unusual; in specialist educational fields it can be much higher.

The amount that an individual television 'licence' will pay varies tremendously both between countries and within countries, between channels. At the time of writing, in Japan, amounts range from about $5,000 to $15,000, in the UK, from $25,000 to $50,000, in Eastern Europe from $1,000 to $8,000, and in the Middle East, from $2,000 to $5,000. So, if the producer is seeking to recoup some of the production costs by television and other sales later, it is worth noting that sales prices for the finished product do not match up in any way to production costs, even low budget ones.

In addition, individual screenings are likely to happen over a protracted period of time, so it could take up to five years or more, and maybe 20 or so different sales, to recoup even part of the most modest production costs. Over that time, there may be interest rates and loan costs to take into consideration. In the case of our first ever series, *Feeling for France*, inflation and interest charges plus distribution costs weakened our chances of even breaking even on original costs. As distributors point out, it can take some time – up to two years – to create a specific market for individual documentaries, and some acquisitions departments will need to wait a year before funds become available to them in their budgets; fairly long time scales are involved and decisions sometimes only occur at certain times in the annual calendar.

With *Feeling for France*, sometimes broadcaster buyer reactions were rather simplistic: we would receive responses such as 'France had been "done"' by their channel recently, as if an entire country could be disposed of with just one competitor television programme! Nevertheless, our distributor obtained a PBS contract and a variety of cable and satellite sales worldwide, also some less obvious sales outlets such as the American forces overseas network. Over a 10-year sales period, there were also high points, such as the occasion when the episode on Normandy was screened by British commercial television on the fortieth anniversary of the Second World War D-Day landings. As well as revisiting this important piece of history, it also gave viewers an opportunity to reflect on the province as it is today: such approaches to a mixture of travel and history are popular.

Franny Armstrong: *Drowned Out*

Drowned Out was nominated for a BIFA in 2004, and also received other nominations. Spanner Films have now paid back the three or four 'rich' individuals who loaned money for the production: 'if we make money now, it goes to them', says Armstrong (author interview, 2005). The production company is therefore no longer in debt for the film and their first action was to hire a generator and take it to the village for the participants and people to see the completed film – a 'moral' imperative, according to the filmmaker.

She describes the introduction to PBS as 'serendipitous': it happened due to a conference on Flaherty that she talked at. 'Somebody saw *Drowned Out*, and mentioned it to somebody else.' Word of mouth at festivals can clearly be efficacious. *Drowned Out* fitted well into the PBS strand of *Wide Angle*. The series provides 'American audiences with an insight into the economic, cultural and political factors shaping the world today. Each program focuses on a single subject, with character-driven narratives revealing the humanity behind the headlines of international events and issues' (see <http://www.pbs.org/wnet/wideangle/about/index.html>). The series producers renarrate films and use voice-over where there is foreign dialogue. The film was renamed *The Damned*. *Drowned Out* is now on DVD and has a limited theatric release via Cinema Libre in the US.

Anand Patwardhan with Simantini Dhuru: *A Narmada Diary*

The themes of discrimination against the Adivasis that motivated the production of *A Narmada Diary* and against religious minorities featured in *In the Name of God* has prompted one editor in chief to refer to the filmmaker as a 'professional dissenter whom we must value greatly' (Tarun Tejpal in *The Hindu*, 28 May 2004). The Narmada anti-big dam struggle continues, reinforcing the continuing relevance of these words: 'the strength of people's resistance to the dams in the Narmada Valley is echoed by others in different places and at different times, although perhaps not always with the same fortitude and life or death struggle. They protest against gross injustice to millions of people perpetrated in the name of development' (*A Narmada Diary*, First Run/Icarus Films, 1997).

The film went on to win an award from the Indian central government, which, in those days, guaranteed screening on public broadcaster Doordarshan. However, not only did the state refuse to issue a censorship certificate, despite this official accolade, but it declined to show it on national television. Patwardhan had to resort to the courts to enforce his rights. Meanwhile the filmmaker argues that:

> The Indian government continues to finance its folly. The only lesson our politicians and project builders have learnt is that large projects mean large kickbacks. So now the great new game in India is a multi-billion dollar, thoroughly improbable project to inter-link our rivers. How could all this happen? My view is that it has to do with the near absolute ideological control that is exercised over the global media. The images the world needs to see, the facts it needs to hear, are often doctored or suppressed. (Patwardhan, 2004)

Media responses

Craig Gilbert: *An American Family*

The broadcaster (WNET) publicity campaign set the media pace. What Gilbert expected the critics to focus on and what actually happened were very different.

> Except for the length of time spent with the subjects and the creation of a series rather than a single program, we had done nothing new. Since *An American Family* had not been directed, at least not in the usual sense, direction was an aspect of the series which the critics could not evaluate . . . For all these reasons I felt, naively, that the critics would have no choice but to deal with the material that was up there on the screen, and that in doing so they could not avoid dealing with their own lives . . . I couldn't have been more wrong. (Rosenthal, 1988: 296)

Participant Bill Loud was less philosophical: 'We let Gilbert and his crew into our house to do a documentary, and they produced a second-rate soap opera' (Ruoff, 2002: 122). Gilbert was defensive: 'We had all been keenly aware that we had a responsibility not to play fast and loose with the trust the family had placed in us. The fact that the family had approved of each and every episode was proof enough for us that we had lived up to their trust' (ibid.: 295).

The media were sensationalist. Gilbert had wanted viewers to watch the series as if the cameras were not there, but they refused to do so. There were many articles, and an entire episode of one television series – the *Dick Cavett Show* – was devoted to the making of the series. During the show, Gilbert admitted a truism: producers cannot control the reception of their work. Many people saw the series as symptomatic of the moral decline of the US family, but a 'vocal minority' focused on what is more relevant here: 'troubled by the premise of observational cinema, many concluded that a documentary could not be made of real life' (ibid.: 129).

Meanwhile, Pat Loud wrote an autobiography (with the help of a co-writer), and spoke out to the media, raising issues about how the family were treated. She was used as an example to discuss issues related to the women's movement at the time. Most of the public debate centred on the effect of the camera, despite Pat claiming that, due to the filming, she had stayed with Bill *longer* than she would have otherwise, and Lance protesting that he had been gay both before and after the shooting event.

In fact, it was American television as an institution that came out of the closet on the gay issue. The camera became the catalyst. The series 'may be best remembered as a non fiction program *haunted by the presence of the camera*, an unwittingly reflexive work.' Interestingly, in most of the media debate, the series was not compared to other documentary examples but to other fiction, despite the fact that this was the first time that the observational style had reached large mass audiences (ibid.: 109, 117, original italics).

Cinema

Emile de Antonio: *In the Year of the Pig*

'Going to movies is too passive. I want the audience to strain. I don't want it to be easy for them' (Rosenthal, 1978: 9). 'The film seems to touch lots of people, simply at the informational level, of showing them on a screen . . . the reaction of right wing students has been revealing. At Dartmouth [university] a young man got up, his temples throbbing and said to me, "I was a sergeant in the Green Berets. Are you insinuating that the Americans tortured prisoners?"' (Eisenschitz & Narboni, 1969: 48, author's translation).

'I would have liked police and working class, blue collar guys who were for the war to have seen it. I would have liked them to have seen that the Vietnamese were fighting for their country, even though they might have hated the film' (Rosenthal & Corner, 2005: 109). Cinemas showing the film faced a direct action form of censorship. At the cinema in Los Angeles, where the film was due to start its cinema release, 'someone broke into the theatre in the middle of the night and painted on the screen a hammer and sickle and the words "Communist traitor". News of this spread to other theatres, and that was the end of the film theatrically' (Emile de Antonio in ibid.: 102). Bill Nichols remembers: 'The Los Angeles screen I saw was painted "PIG"; our own screen in Kingston, at the National Film Theatre branch here, was severely slashed (in 1977!)' (Kellner & Streible, 2000: 225). The filmmaker was naturally disappointed: 'My films are didactic . . . but this film on Vietnam is more complicated, has more levels of symbolism, so that there are no slogans or purely didactic messages' (Ciment & Cohn, 1970: 28, author's translation).

Rightly, he hoped that his films would live on. 'My bet's with history. I'm an American who believes in history. I think that people will be looking at *Pig* and *Point of Order* long after I'm dead . . . Those images that you have to struggle to find and to make effective will endure, because history endures. That's an optimistic view of the human race' (Rosenthal & Corner, 2005: 108). De Antonio's technique of contrasting archive footage with actuality interviews influenced many other filmmakers, including Connie Field's technique in *Rosie the Riveter*.

The potential for theatric distribution merits discussion. Documentaries are now seen as films, not as documentaries. The public seem more prepared to pay for a ticket to see a documentary that would normally only be seen on television. Reasons for the wider acceptance of documentary in the cinema are various: some people argue that reality television has created a realization that ordinary people can be as interesting to watch as Hollywood stars. Others say that in the United States the trauma of 9/11 had the effect of making many people realize how little they understood, or knew about, the world outside their televisions. In Britain, as choice of television channels has increased, terrestrial television's range of documentary content has narrowed. Similarly, in the United States, it may well be that television has familiarized the audience with watching reality, 'whilst frustrating them that the reality they were watching was too limited and controlled' (Search & McCarthy, 2005: 16).

All of this means that there is potential for the theatric documentary and for exploitation of the festival and art-house circuits. The success of the French film *March of the Penguins* demonstrates documentary's ability to continuously produce a new rabbit from the hat. In the US it helps to have a cinema launch in New York, with reviews and critical response which can help to generate public enthusiasm via word of mouth – another crucial factor amongst theatric audiences.

Although distributors are always keen to pick up *all* the rights to a film, it is advisable to hold them at bay, and to separate out theatric from non-theatric. For the former, a specialist may know the cinema market better than a television distributor, who deals primarily with the latter. Of course, distributors sell on rights, or sub-contract them, amongst themselves, but this internal way of working may not benefit the producer financially. Similarly, college and educational rights have specialist distributors.

Michael Moore: *Roger and Me*

The wider promotion of the film was substantially aided by the fact that it was eventually distributed by the Hollywood major Warner. This obviously made it accessible to much larger audiences than most documentaries; indeed, a feature length documentary on a social issue does not normally obtain general release.

Critics have debated the cost of the film's popular approach. Does the film's personalization, with all its self-display, actually distract from the ostensible purpose, which is the enquiry into General Motors' responsibility for the demise of the town of Flint? 'Moore has shown himself to be acutely aware of the difficulties of holding a popular audience without a strong narrative device, and such a firm placing of himself in the frame is central to his idea of maintaining a comic, indeed black-farcical, impetus to the story of Flint' (Corner, 1996: 159).

Moore has been referred to as a 'Gonzo demagogue' by one critic who accuses him of compressing the events of years and 'fiddling with the time sequence' and, in doing so, he 'chases gags and improvises his own version of history' (Pauline Kael, *New Yorker*, 8 January 1990). Pauline Kael's damning review in the *New Yorker* sparked a critical debate about Moore's production ethics, which is said to have been responsible for the fact that the film was not nominated for an Academy Award. Meanwhile, General Motors managed to get the film withdrawn from the leadoff position in the Detroit Institute of Arts' film series – an act of backyard censorship.

Moore goes for laughs that also bring a propaganda value, but at the expense of 'the sort of contextual information or analysis of issues that any good documentary provides' (Cohan & Crowdus, 1990: 28). The investigative journalism is sacrificed for humour, often cheaply obtained at the expense not just of a multinational corporation, but also of ordinary working people.

Legal problems, censorship

Factual reporting and documentary making have always involved an element of risk-taking if the material is important or contentious within the public sphere, so the maker must be prepared for legal problems. The production of committed films requires courage, motivation and perseverance. The provocative nature of documentary can arise from lack of certain visuals as well as from the way that they are arranged and selected. For *Fahrenheit 9/11*, Michael Moore had a bevy of libel lawyers standing by to sue anybody who defamed the film.

In the case of American law, and the protection of the First Amendment, there is still a danger that a news organization or filmmaker could be held guilty of libel if they knowingly use information about a public figure that is false and/or malicious (Hickey, 2001: 57). Therefore, documentary makers with controversial projects need to be informed about libel laws in their own country.

In the United Kingdom, defamed public figures are more likely to sue than in the United States, where the existence of the First Amendment has the effect of actively discouraging legal redress against the media. However, when Nobel Peace Prize winner and Northern Irish protestant politician David Trimble threatened to sue publishers and journalists for libel over a book accusing him of complicity in the government-sanctioned murder of innocent people, legal experts made the point that such litigation could have the positive side-effect of uncovering some truths about the sensational allegations (McMenamin, 1999: 40). This proved to be true, for the author of the book in question then followed up with a 1991 Channel 4 documentary called *The Committee*.

Documentaries have sometimes had the effect of increasing transparency within the public sphere. The $120 million milestone libel case in the US, brought by General Westmoreland in 1982 against CBS and the producers of a documentary entitled *The Uncounted Enemy: a Vietnam Deception*, springs to mind. The film claimed that military leaders encouraged the public impression of a successful conflict by deliberately understating the numbers of North Vietnamese and Vietcong troops in South Vietnam. Although Westmoreland withdrew his legal action, the case had the effect of bringing to light more than 500,000 pages of highly classified documents about the war. In the process, 'top officials of the Kennedy and Johnson administrations were grilled, shedding important new light on the Vietnam quagmire' (Hickey, 2001: 57).

Anand Patwardhan: *In the Name of God*

For more than 20 years Patwardhan's films have been smuggled out of the country, banned from being broadcast on national public television and made the subject of almost continuous court proceedings and legal action.

In the Name of God has turned out to be disturbingly prophetic. It was completed shortly before the destruction of the mosque in December 1992. Pujari Lal Das, the government-appointed Hindu priest at the Hindu *chabutra* on the contested site, who was interviewed by Patwardhan, stated on camera that he could not understand how he had managed to remain alive so long. In November 1993 he was murdered. This is the reason that, when referring in chapter 4 to the risks that he takes as cameraperson, Patwardhan states that these are nothing compared to the risks taken by some of the people that he films.

Patwardhan has faced almost continuous opposition from the censors. 'Of the many attempts made by fundamentalists to shut down our screenings, very few have succeeded. In Kerala . . . *In the Name of God* was banned by a district officer who gave in to threats by the Vishwa Hindu Parishad [fundamentalists]. But a month-long agitation that included street marches by secular Keralites forced the ban to be withdrawn' (Maclay, 2004). The film went on to win national and international awards such as the Filmfare award for the best documentary and the national award for the Best Investigative Documentary produced in 1992. It was not shown initially on national television, so Patwardhan found himself in the Bombay High Court, arguing yet again that the broadcaster had a duty to respect the public's right to information by screening it and that not showing the film on television was a denial of freedom of speech, both guaranteed in the Indian Constitution.

In the Name of God was only shown in Doordarshan in 1997. 'I feel my work is under-utilized. I don't feel despondent when the films are actually used, but I feel they should be used much more than they are . . . So if and when we win a case, and the film is shown on

Anand Patwardhan spends more time on court battles over the screening of his films than he does on production

television, that's a major breakthrough' (Kripalani, 1998: 164). India is one of the few democracies where censorship rules are being followed rigidly (*The Hindu*, 9 June 2005), which means that as a documentary producer, Patwardhan applies more effort to fighting legal battles than he has done to making films. He travels with his films, holding discussions in schools, film clubs, civil liberty groups, trade unions, women's groups, student unions, slum and Dalit [lower caste] areas and community groups, after the viewing of the film. By creating his own circuit, he can reach more people and receive feedback. 'If I didn't personally screen my films and talk to audiences I think I'd lose my motivation for making them' (Goldsmith, 2003: 11)

By his own admission, his films are 'polarized things', so they provoke heated discussions. Since the Bombay riots in 1993, he has not been able to screen outdoors, but in a closed room backed up by sufficient numbers of his supporters, there is still excitement. 'The films are in Hindi [and in the languages of the participants] . . . Because they are tied to movements for communal harmony they have a campaign value: people who are campaigning against fundamentalism have very little to use as material. It's the same in Britain, America, Canada as there are so many Indians there. They are shown in festivals, universities' (Akomfran, interview in *Pix*).

After *In the Name of God* was broadcast on Britain's Channel 4, hundreds of protest letters were sent in. The experience of the film in New York City demonstrates that censorship is still on the agenda, even in 'democratic' societies. In 2002 the Margaret Mead Festival in New York decided to screen *In the Name of God* and *We Are Not Your Monkeys* at the American Museum of Natural History to complement an exhibition. Faced with protests, the museum quickly cancelled the screenings, which were moved to New York University. At that venue, the campus police quintupled their security staff. As Patwardhan commented, 'The events in New York City also reveal the way Hindutva [Hindu fundamentalism] exploits liberal guilt and the rhetoric of multiculturalism, while showing no compunction about its own record' (Rajagopal, 2002: 279). Almost immediately an online petition in support of Patwardhan collected nearly 500 signatures.

Since *In the Name of God*, Patwardhan has returned to the themes of fundamentalism and communal violence in a way that has made him 'an emblem of a growing gap between India's secular, liberal elite and Hindu nationalists' (Waldman, *New York Times*, 24 December 2004). Now he is active within the Indian filmmaking community in campaigning that censor certificates should no longer be required for national awards and films (see <http://www.freedomfilmsindia.org>).

Conclusions

For the first-time documentary maker, a completed film is a showcase for work, and an incentive to take on another project. By McElwee's own admission, *Sherman's March* opened a lot of doors, enabling him to raise money more easily in the future (Rhu, 2004: 11). However, it is the journey that provides the revelations. As screenwriter Trevor Griffiths said to me in an interview for a Chapman Clarke Films' BBC 2 series about filmmaking, entitled *Showreel*: 'If I had known at the beginning what I eventually knew at the end, I would never have made the journey.'

What about the forgotten films? So many are made, yet so few are remembered. How far a documentary is promoted and exhibited is a function of its rights ownership, decided through the funding arrangements and subsequent contracts. Some very good films have been made as local television programmes and never been fully exploited – presumably due to the assumption that the content is too regional for today's global world and therefore has insufficient commercial value. In fact many of these films raise wider themes that have stood the test of time; their existence as an archive source for the future is threatened by broadcaster closure of film libraries and cutbacks on cataloguing expenditure.

Yet I am confident about the continuing popularity of the genre. Hopefully, in the future, even more documentaries will be made. Work is likely to continue to be innovative in choice of aesthetics and portrayal, as long as makers continue to display a social conscience and take risks.

Summary

Documentaries should have as much exposure as possible, and the filmmaker has an obligation to ensure this happens. Audience discussion and feedback provide learning points for the future, whilst festivals provide opportunities for promotion and for interaction with the wider documentary-making community. Distributors can help to enhance the life of a film, which is probably more important than any money that it makes.

References

Ackroyd, Peter (2004) *William Raban* (British Film Institute DVD), essay with cover.

Akomfrah, John, 'Interview in *Pix*'. 'Interview with Anand Patwardhan' <www.Patwardhan. com/interviews/index.htm> (accessed February 2005), reproduced from John Akomfrah (1997), 'Storming the Reality Asylum', *Pix* 2: 75–6.

Alper, Susan (2003) Review of the 8th Annual Montreal Jewish Film Festival.

Armstrong, Franny (2002) '*Drowned Out*: The Truth Will Out', *Guardian*, 26 August.

Barbash, Ilisa and Lucien Taylor (1997) *Cross Cultural Filmmaking: A Handbook for Making Documentary and Ethnographic Films and Videos* (Berkeley: University of California Press).

Barnouw, Eric (1974) *Documentary: A History of Non-Fiction Film* (New York: Oxford University Press).

Buckell, Gareth (2005) 'William Raban' (review of DVD release), *Filmwaves* 26: 50.

Chanan, Michael (1993) 'Coping with Co-production', *DOX* 0 (Winter): 37–42.

—— (2000) 'The Documentary Chronotype', *Jump Cut* 43.

Chapman, Jane (2005) *Comparative Media History* (Cambridge: Polity).

Chatterjee, Vidyarthy (1997) 'Nation's Conscience Keeper', *Deep Focus*, 30: 29–33.

Ciment, Michel & Bernard Cohn (1970) 'Entretien avec Emile de Antonio', *Positif* 113 (February): 28–39.

Cohan, C. & G. Crowdus (1990) 'Reflections on *Roger and Me*, Michael Moore and his critics', *Cinéaste* 17(4): 25–30.

Corner, John (1996) *The Art of Record: A Critical Introduction to Documentary* (Manchester: Manchester University Press).

——, Kay Richardson & Natalie Fenton (1990) *Nuclear Reactions: Form and Response in 'Public Issue' Television* [a.k.a. *A Study in Public Issue Television*], Acamedia Research Monograph 4 (London: John Libbey).

Curtis, David (ed.) (1994) *A Directory of British Film & Video Artists* (London: Arts Council of England; Luton: John Libbey Media /University of Luton).

Eisenschitz, Bernard & Jean Narboni (1969) 'Entretien avec Emile De Antonio', *Cahiers du Cinema* 214 (July): 43–56.

Ellis, Jack C. & Betsy A. McLane (2005) *A New History of Documentary Film* (New York: Continuum Books).

Emm, Adele (2002) *Researching for Television and Radio* (London: Routledge).

Gangar, Amrit & Sudhir Yardi (1993) 'The Documentary Aesthetic: A Discussion on the Documentary Medium with Anand Patwardhan', *Cinema in India* 4(2): 18–25.

Geduld, Harry M. (ed.) (1967) *Film Makers on Film Making* (Harmondsworth: Penguin Books Ltd).

Georgakas, Dan, Uayan Gupta & Judi Janda (1978) 'Politics of Visual Anthropology, an Interview with Jean Rouch', *Cinéaste* 8(4): 22.

Goldsmith, David A. (2003) *The Documentary Makers: Interviews with 15 of the Best in the Business* (Mies, Switzerland and Hove, Sussex: RotoVision), chapter 10: 6–15.

Grant, Barry Keith & Jeannette Sloniowski (eds) (1998) *Documenting the Documentary: Close Readings of Documentary Film and Video* (Detroit, MI: Wayne State University Press).

Hampe, Barry (1997) *Making Documentary Films and Reality Videos* (New York: Henry Holt and Co.).

Hardy, Forsyth (ed.) (1979) *Grierson on Documentary* (London: Faber and Faber).

Hickey, Neil (2001) 'Libel? You'll Have to Prove It', *Columbia Journalism Review* 40(4) (November/December): 57.

Jackson, Bruce (2004) *Conversations with Emile de Antonio* <http://www.sensesofcinema.com/contents> (accessed 1 March 2006), also published as *Emile de Antonio in Buffalo* (Buffalo, NY: Center Working Papers, 2003).

Jacobs, Lewis (1979) *The Documentary Tradition*, 2nd edn (New York: W.W. Norton & Co. Inc.).

Jacobson, Harlan (1989) 'Michael and Me: Interview', *Film Comment* 25(6): 16–26.

Johnston, Sheila (1981) 'War of the Sexes', *Time Out* 587 (November): 21.

Kael, Pauline (1990) *New Yorker*, 8 January.

Kaplan, E. Ann (ed.) (2000) *Feminism & Film* (Oxford: Oxford University Press).

Kellner, Douglas & Dan Streible (eds) (2000) *Emile de Antonio: A Reader* (Minneapolis: University of Minnesota Press).

Kilborn, Richard & John Izod (1997) *An Introduction to Television Documentary: Confronting Reality* (Manchester: Manchester University Press).

Kochberg, Searle (ed.) (2002) *Introduction to Documentary Production: A Guide for Media Students* (London: Wallflower Press).

Kopple, Barbara & Hart Perry (1980) 'Harlan County, USA', in Alan Rosenthal (ed.), *The Documentary Conscience: A Casebook in Film Making* (Berkeley: University of California Press).

Kripalani, Gulan (1998) ' "My method of Filmmaking is a Diary Approach" – A Conversation with Anand Patwardhan', *West Coast Line* 32(2–3): 164–76.

Levin, G. Roy (1971) *Documentary Explorations: 15 Interviews with Film-Makers.* (New York: Doubleday & Co.).

Lewis, Randolph (2000) *Emile de Antonio: Radical Filmmaker in Cold War America* (Madison: University of Wisconsin Press).

Lucia, Cynthia (1993) 'When the Personal Becomes the Political: An Interview with Ross McElwee', *Cinéaste* 20(2): 32–8.

Luxonline (2005) <http://www.luxonline.org.uk/articles/essays/williamraban/detail1.html>.

MacDonald, Scott (1988) 'Southern Exposure: An Interview with Ross McElwee', *Film Quarterly* 41: 12–23.

—— (1992) *A Critical Cinema: Interviews with Independent Filmmakers* (Berkeley: University of California Press).

Maclay, Kathleen (2004) *Anand Patwardhan, the Michael Moore of India, brings his Hard Hitting Films to Campus.* Interview with Michael Moore at University of California, Berkeley on 13 October, <http://www.patwardhan.com/interviews/index.htm> (accessed February 2005).

McMenamin, Michael (1999) 'Truth, Terror and David Trimble', *Reason* 31(5) (October): 40–6.

Mayne, Judith (1990) 'From a Hybrid Place: An interview with Trinh T. Minh-ha', *Afterimage* 18: 6–9.

Michelson, Annette (ed.) (1984) *Kino-Eye: The Writings of Dziga Vertov*, trans. Kevin O'Brien (Berkeley: University of California Press).

Minh-ha, Trinh T. (1992) *Framer Framed* (New York: Routledge).

—— (1999) *Cinema Interval* (New York: Routledge).

Morriss, Steve (2004) 'William Raban – BFI, E', *Evening Standard Metro Life*, 28 October.

Movie (1963) Interview on Rouch's working methods within a feature on the Cinema Vérité movement, *Movie* 8 (April): 21–3.

Nichols, Bill (ed.) (1985) *Movies and Methods: An Anthology*, 2 vols (Berkeley: University of California Press): vol. 2.

—— (1991) *Representing Reality: Issues and Concepts in Documentary* (Bloomington: Indiana University Press).

—— (2001) *Introduction to Documentary* (Bloomington and Indianapolis: Indiana University Press).

Obiter Dicta (1993) 'Sued for Satire', *ABA Journal* (January).

O'Sullivan, T., J. Hartley, D. Saunders, M. Montgomery & J. Fiske (1994) *Key Concepts in Communication and Cultural Studies* (London: Routledge).

Parmar, Pratibha (1990) 'Woman, Native and Other: Pratibha Parmar interviews Trinh T. Minh-ha', *Feminist Review* 36 (Autumn).

Patwardhan, Arnand (2004) Keynote address to the International Documentary Conference, Silverdocs Documentary Film Festival (16 June), <www.centreforsocialmedia.org>.

Raban, William (1984) Memo to Marion, 2 January, unpublished.

—— (1984) 'The Thames: Seaward Route to the City', proposal to the Arts Council England, unpublished.

—— Progress Report on *Thames Film*, unpublished.

—— (1998) 'Lifting Traces', *Filmwaves* 4 (Spring): 14–16.

Rabiger, Michael (2004) *Directing the Documentary*, 4th edn (Burlington, MA: Focal Press).

Rajagopal, Avind (2002) 'Reflections on a Controversy', *Critical Asian Studies* 34(2): 279–83.

Rhu, Lawrence F. (2004) 'Home Movies and Personal Documentaries', *Cinéaste* (Summer): 6–12.

Richman, Paula (1994) Film and video reviews, *The Journal of Asian Studies* (August) 53(3): 1033–5.

Rosenthal, Alan (1971) *The New Documentary in Action: A Casebook in Filmmaking* (Berkeley: University of California Press).

—— (1978) 'Emile de Antonio: An Interview', *Film Quarterly* 32(1): 4–17.

—— (ed.) (1988) *New Challenges for Documentary* (Berkeley: University of California Press).

—— (1990) *Writing, Directing, and Producing Documentary Films* (Carbondale & Edwardsville: Southern Illinois University Press).

—— (1996) *Writing, Directing, and Producing Documentary Films and Videos*, rev. edn (Carbondale & Edwardsville: Southern Illinois University Press).

—— & John Corner (eds) (2005) *New Challenges for Documentary*, 2nd edn (Manchester & New York: Manchester University Press).

Rudolph, Eric (1999) 'Points East: Documentary's One-Man Band', *American Cinematographer* 80(1): 107–8.

Ruoff, Jeffrey (2002) *An American Family: A Televised Life* (Minneapolis: University of Minnesota Press).

Sandhu, Sukhdev (2004) 'William Raban' (DVD review) *Telegraph*, 30 October.

Search, Jess & Melissa McCarthy (2005) *Get Your Documentary Funded and Distributed* (London: Shooting People).

Sharma, Miriam (2002) 'Anand Patwardhan: Social Activist and Dedicated Filmmaker', *Critical Asian Studies* 34(2): 279–94.

Tammer, Monique (1981) Interview with C. Field on the making of *The Life and Times of Rosie the Riveter*, *Cinema Papers* 43 (September): 358–9, 409, 411.

Tejpal, Tarun (2004) 'In Battle for Freedom of Expression', *The Hindu*, 28 May.

Vaughan, Dai (1976) *Television Documentary Usage*, British Film Institute Television Monographs 6 (London: British Film Institute).

Viljoen, Dorothy (1997) *Art of the Deal* (London: Pact).

Waldman, Amy (2004) 'A Brahmin Filmmaker's Battle to Tell India's Story in India', *New York Times*, 24 December, 'Arts Abroad': 1.

Watts, Harris (2004) *Instant on Camera: The Fast Track to Programme-Making* (London: AAVO).

Weiss, Marc N. (1974) 'Emile de Antonio: An Interview', *Film Library Quarterly* 7(2): 29–35.

Williamson, Judith (1981) 'When the Boys Came Home', *City Limits*, 20(8) (November): 45.

Zimmermann, Patricia R. (2000) *States of Emergency: Documentaries, Wars, Democracies*, Visible Evidence 7 (Minneapolis: University of Minnesota Press).

Zuilhof, G. (2001) *Essay for Film Retrospective* (Catalogue, Rotterdam Film Festival, 907561506 X).

Index

NOTE: Page numbers in italics indicate an illustration.